DATE DUE

JAN 24 '85			

SOUTHERN ANGLICANISM

Contributions to the Study of Religion
Series Editor: Henry W. Bowden

SOUTHERN ANGLICANISM

The Church of England in Colonial South Carolina

S. Charles Bolton

CONTRIBUTIONS TO THE STUDY OF RELIGION, NUMBER 5

Greenwood Press
WESTPORT, CONNECTICUT · LONDON, ENGLAND

Library of Congress Cataloging in Publication Data

Bolton, S. Charles.
  Southern Anglicanism.

  (Contributions to the study of religion, ISSN 0196-
7053 ; no. 5)
  Bibliography: p.
  Includes index.
  1. Church of England—South Carolina. 2. Church of
England—Southern States. 3. South Carolina—Church
history. 4. Southern States—Church history. I. Title.
II. Series.
BX5881.B64   283'.757   81-6669
ISBN 0-313-23090-0 (lib. bdg.)   AACR2

Library of Congress Catalog Card Number: 81-6669
ISBN: 0-313-23090-0
ISSN: 0196-7053

First published in 1982

Greenwood Press
A division of Congressional Information Service, Inc.
88 Post Road West, Westport, Connecticut 06881

Printed in the United States of America

10 9 8 7 6 5 4 3 2 1

For Jan

CONTENTS

TABLES

SERIES FOREWORD

Conventional wisdom about colonial Anglicanism is usually confined to the Virginia establishment, and most references to it imply its generally negative effect on cultural life. This book serves as a corrective in two ways. It expands our awareness of early churches to include those in South Carolina, the richest of southern colonies and one more socially significant than its northern neighbors. It also looks carefully at the clergymen who spent their careers on this side of the Atlantic and concludes that the majority of them were sober and capable ministers.

Not content with reconstructing the origin and development of Carolinian Anglicanism, Charles Bolton pushes beyond that to investigate how the established church functioned in an increasingly complex society that made Anglicans a minority. He finds that certain indigenous qualities in these churches facilitated good relations with dissenting groups and cooperation with civic programs. Bolton follows the convolutions of local politics and shows that Anglican clergymen usually sided with colonial interests rather than with British imperial interests—the reverse of what is usually charged. He employs a readable, nononsense style to demonstrate how South Carolina did not harbor the popular stereotype of an overbearing clerical elite who denounced non-Anglicans and whose loyalties lay primarily with the Crown. When the Revolution occurred, three-fourths of the ministers supported the American cause. On balance then, the church made considerable contributions to politics, social life, and religion between 1704 and 1778.

Perhaps more importantly, Bolton provides the results of his thorough inquiry into the Anglican church from its beginning to disestablishment. He offers a substantial corrective to caricatures that portray ministers as profligate and undisciplined. With solid historical documentation he assesses *all* Anglican priests, not just the few exceptions who scandalized the profession, although he includes their foibles with refreshing candor. But the majority of clergymen were individuals of sound moral and religious character. Their natural inclinations made them leaders in colonial education, letters, religious toleration, and social stability. They were also amenable to lay control. In the absence of episcopal discipline, local parishioners exerted great influence in monitoring clerical habits. Bolton observes that this circumstance had beneficial consequences in South Carolina where there emerged a comfortable alliance with the popular authority that supervised ministerial activities and held clergymen to high standards. Clerical cooperation with lay control shows that South Carolinian Anglicanism did not antagonize the populace nor make itself a target for revenge in revolutionary times.

Still this moderate, lay-controlled church aligned itself with the financial and social aristocracy; it did little to incorporate dissenters, lower-class whites, blacks, or Indians within its structure. Although it differed from Anglican examples in other colonies, it too was stripped of its power in republican times. Bolton explains how and why this came about, and also examines the strands that survived as the Protestant Episcopal church after the Revolution. Because of his penetrating analysis of colonial experiences, we can also see how the church served to buttress some of the ideals that shaped antebellum southern culture.

Henry W. Bowden

PREFACE

This study deals with a neglected and significant aspect of the history of South Carolina and of the South in general. The last book dealing with Anglicanism in South Carolina was Frederick Dalcho's *The Protestant Episcopal Church in South Carolina*, done in 1820. Maryland and Virginia, where the church was no more important, are the subjects of modern monographs. Scholarly interest in South Carolina has been hindered by a preoccupation with New England and the Chesapeake, and Anglicanism itself has been neglected as historians have pursued a passion for Puritanism.

Chapter 1 is a discussion of Southern Anglicanism in general, based on recent research dealing with Virginia, Maryland, North Carolina, and Georgia. The emphasis here is on the indigenous quality of the southern churches, the fact that they were an expression of colonial interest and identity rather than of English imperialism. The next three chapters deal with the history of the state church in South Carolina; among the topics are the politics of establishment and disestablishment, the support of the Society for the Propagation of the Gospel in Foreign Parts, the leadership of the commissaries, and the problems of the clergy. Chapters 5 through 8 deal with the relationship between the church and the society in which it operated. "The Character of the Clergy" examines the behavior of the ministers and the degree to which it changed over time and in relationship to the control exercised by the laity. "Red, Black, and Anglican" discusses the involvement of the established church in the conversion of Indians and slaves. "The Aspirations of the Laity" deals with the difficult question of why people were

Anglicans, and "The Authority of the Laity" discusses the role of the vestry and the degree to which it allowed the Anglican gentry to control their church and also govern local society. The meaning of all of this is summarized in a concluding chapter.

A number of individuals and institutions have made my work on this project more enjoyable and more fruitful than otherwise would have been the case. Stanley N. Katz, who was my advisor at the University of Wisconsin, has provided advice and encouragement since I first became interested in South Carolina Anglicanism. David S. Lovejoy read the resulting dissertation and provided valuable criticism. A Summer Stipend in 1975 from the National Endowment for the Humanities allowed me to begin writing the book manuscript. The staffs of the South Carolina Department of Archives and History, the South Carolina Historical Society, and the South Caroliniana Library have been unfailingly gracious and helpful. The University of Arkansas at Little Rock has provided travel funds for research, and the Department of History has been a congenial and stimulating environment for scholarship. One of my colleagues, Tony Freyer, read an early version of this manuscript and convinced me that it would be a book. Conevery Bolton, Jesse Bolton, and Bill Dillard III, unknowingly and each in special ways, have encouraged and inspired me.

SOUTHERN ANGLICANISM

1
SOUTHERN ANGLICANISM

The Anglican church of colonial South Carolina was a unique institution functioning within an environment of its own, yet it was also part of a regional phenomenon that may be called Southern Anglicanism. The Anglican established churches of the colonial South shared qualities that set them apart from the national church of the mother country and also from the Church of England in the American North. Anglican laymen in the South fashioned the established churches to suit their own needs and remained in control of them. Most of the Anglican clergy came to accept this situation, and they used traditional doctrines to support social and political authority within the colonies rather than on behalf of the English government. At the same time they disseminated spiritual and intellectual values that helped to shape the emerging culture of the South.

Some historians have emphasized negative aspects of Southern Anglicanism: the Church of England in the colonies sometimes operated as an arm of British imperialism, the structure of the established churches was weakened by the absence of a bishop and the presence of numerous dissenters, and the moral and intellectual quality of the clergy was sometimes too low.[1] These are valid claims, but they conceal larger truths. The absence of a resident bishop hampered the operation of the American church, but it also allowed the laity a larger role than in England. In the southern colonies where Anglicanism was the state church, lay control meant that the religious establishment expressed the interests of the colony and the colonial gentry rather than those of the mother country and its ruling class. Except for a small minority, Anglican clergymen were capable men whose efforts made Southern Anglicanism a vital religious institution.

The power of its laity was a distinguishing characteristic of colonial Anglicanism. There never was an Anglican bishop in the colonies, and the absence of episcopal authority allowed laymen to play an important role in church government. Colonial Anglicanism seemed incomplete to some American churchmen; an episcopal church without a bishop, after all, is a contradiction in terms. Moreover, the trip to England by American candidates for ordination was a severe hardship, and parishes often found it hard to get clergymen. Yet the absence of a bishop also gave the American church a new and stronger character. Throughout the American colonies Anglican vestries involved themselves in the appointment and dismissal of their ministers, something unheard of in England where wealthy patrons, bishops, and ecclesiastical courts handled those matters. A principal opponent of lay power was the Society for the Propagation of the Gospel in Foreign Parts (SPG), the London-based philanthropic organization that sent missionaries to the colonies and provided them with salaries. The benevolence of the Society gave it a great deal of leverage, yet Anglican parishes in the North and South asserted their authority to accept or reject the missionaries sent to them and to select clergymen of their own.[2]

The English government gave its governors the right to make clerical appointments in the southern royal colonies, but the colonists fought against this executive prerogative and here, as elsewhere, they were successful. Maryland was an exception to the rule, because the charter gave clerical patronage to the proprietor and the lords Baltimore maintained their right. Elsewhere in the South the laity exercised the power to hire and often to fire their ministers by the middle of the eighteenth century. Because the induction, or formal installation, of a minister gave him a freehold right to the parish and made his removal almost impossible, Virginia vestries adopted the practice of having their clergymen serve on a year to year basis. The church in Virginia, as Daniel Boorstin wrote, "was a group of independent parishes, governed in temporal matters by the House of Burgesses and in doctrinal matters by no central authority at all."[3]

Within the colonies the political status of the Church of England was sharply differentiated by geographic region. In New England the Church of England was a dissenting institution, operating in a cultural environment still shaped by the weakening influences of Puritanism and restricted by the political privileges of the Congregational state church. In the Middle Colonies the church was largely on its own, functioning in a religious free market that foreshadowed the denominationalism that would characterize American religion after the Revolution. In the South the Church of England was the established church of every colony by the time of the American Revolution. Northern Anglicans were more free than their fellow churchmen in the South, since the colonial legislature had almost no authority over their affairs, yet they also had little opportunity to influence society as a whole. In the South, where Anglicanism was everywhere allied with the state, the Church of England played a larger role.

The Church of England was the national church and its character was shaped by that experience. Like the Lutheran church in Germany and Scandinavia and the Presbyterian church of Scotland, in the words of H. Richard Niebuhr, it "consciously or unconsciously adopted the principles of nationalism and identified itself with a particular culture." These Protestant churches accepted the Roman idea that church and state were linked and they tied themselves to the emerging nation-states of post-Reformation Europe. Having dispensed with papal authority, they looked to the national monarch and later the national legislature for leadership and support. National churches shared a number of characteristics: they were strongly institutional in nature and highly structured in organization, their doctrines and liturgy created a standardized form of worship, the acceptance of which was the basic test of membership; they preferred a calm and predictable religious style to a highly emotional one; and they accepted the authority of the state and the actions that flowed from that authority, restricting "the application of Christian ethics to the more individual phases of human conduct or to social conduct within the bounds of the family." The archetypical state church of early modern Europe was an impressive institution. It was, as Richard Hofstadter has written, "the inherited, the normal church...; its local churches stand at the center of community life, and in the rhythms of daily existence it supplies the beat and tolls the bells. It is the core of the whole system of values, spiritual, intellectual and political, and provides them with their distinctive texture."[4]

Standing at the center of social and cultural life, the state church was in a strong position to influence public opinion. Christianity had less ideological competition in the early modern world than it does today and it played a more important role in the world view of most people. Moreover, the ministers who served the church were educated men at a time when few people were well equipped to understand the changing world around them. Clergymen played a number of influential roles. Lawrence Cremin describes the English country priest of the seventeenth century as a "religious leader, moral overseer, civic administrator, legal counselor, medical advisor and purveyor of news" and "a fount of cultural, political and technical information." As a result of the catechism they taught, the sermons they delivered, and the schools they operated, the Anglican clergy were the most significant educational institution outside of the home in early modern England. Because of its ability to create and disseminate moral values and influence public opinion generally, the church was an ideal propaganda vehicle for the state. The relationship between the two institutions was reciprocal: the state used its coercive power to see that people gave money and respect to the established church, and the church used its moral authority and its communication system to create an ideological environment that favored obedience to authority and peaceful behavior. James I of England testified to the political significance of the church in his famous dictum, "no bishop, no king"; so also did the eighteenth century squire who claimed that the way to defeat Jacobitism in his parish was "to get an honest parson in."[5]

In the American colonies the Church of England retained its character as a national church, but the established churches of the South shifted their allegiance from the mother country to the individual colonies. In one sense the colonial church was a dependency of the Church of England and it came under the administrative supervision of the bishop of London. The sending of missionaries by the SPG emphasized this subordinate status. Colonial clergymen found themselves dependent on the colonial gentry for financial aid and political support, however, and they became divided in their loyalty. In the South the state churches came under direct legislative control and English involvement was minimal. Moreover, the relationship between church and state required that the political establishment and the religious establishment support one another. The change took place gradually and without either design or recognition, but eventually most Southern Anglican clergymen came to think of themselves as members of a colonial church rather than an imperial one. The controversy that developed in the years before the Revolution over an American episcopate illustrated the change that had taken place. Northern clergymen wanted an American bishop in order to strengthen the church within what they saw as a hostile environment. A resident bishop, however, would have reduced the power of the vestries and asserted the dependent status of the southern establishments. Anglican laymen in the North were cool to the idea and in the South they were strongly opposed. Under the circumstances the southern clergy for the most part refused to join their northern brethren in this project. In Maryland a group of ministers did petition for a bishop, but they represented less than twenty percent of the clergymen in the colony. In Virginia something less than ten percent of the ministry went on record as being in favor of an American episcopate, and there was no petition. In North Carolina, South Carolina, and Georgia there was no positive response at all. The Reverend Thomas Gwatkin explained the inaction of most Virginia ministers in a way that applied to the South as a whole: "In Virginia the clergy connected themselves with the Civil Powers, placed the Church under their protection, and consequently have given up all Right (if such they ever had) of making Alterations without their express approbation and consent...."[6]

The relationship between church and state in Virginia that Gwatkin described as if it were a social contract between clergy and government was actually the product of an evolutionary process. Early in the seventeeth century the Church of England began to accommodate itself to the social and political environment of Virginia, making alterations, Niebuhr suggests, that "the position of a privileged church made inevitable."[7] Thus it was that the Anglican church of Virginia came under the substantial control of the laity, acting in the legislature and in the vestry. Furthermore, the doctrines and forms of the church assumed a latitudinarian quality that the laity found preferable to the High Church style. In the twenty-five years prior to the American Revolution there were growing signs of discontent within the established church of Virginia, but few Anglicans questioned the value of a state church itself. Patrick Henry vilified the clergy for failing to do their job, but he did not question that the job should be done. The clergy for their part were not disaffected from the Virginia church. Something less than one-third of

them supported the Parsons' Cause and less than one-sixth sided with
the mother country after 1776.[8]

The established church of Virginia was a model for the South as a
whole, although in other colonies the Church of England did not reach
its full potential as a national church. In Maryland the proprietor held
the right to appoint clergymen to the Anglican parishes, and successive
lords Baltimore used their patronage with little regard for the parishioners. The vestries in Maryland were weaker than those in other colonies
and incumbent ministers were exempt from discipline of any kind. By
the time of the Stamp Act, however, the laity were restless. All Saints
Parish physically ejected the notorious Reverend Bennett Allen, and
Conventry Parish stubbornly refused to accept clergymen of whom it
did not approve. In 1770 the salaries of the clergy became involved in a
legislative controversy over the fees collected by proprietary officers,
and the popular leaders of the lower house eventually took the position
that the state church was without legal foundation because the establishment law of 1702 had been passed in an unconstitutional manner.
Despite their anticlericalism and their hostility to proprietary prerogative, the laity of Maryland were at least as positive toward the established church as were those of Virginia. After asserting that the
establishment was void, the lower house in 1771 proposed a measure
that would have created a new state church and provided ministers with
a salary of £200 sterling.[9]

The established churches of North Carolina and Georgia were weaker
than those of the Chesapeake, but they shared similar characteristics.
The presence of numerous dissenters and the absence of substantial
wealth hampered the growth of the state church in North Carolina.
Vestries operated from early in the century, but complete establishment
was not achieved until 1765. The early clergymen in the colony were
missionaries supported by the SPG and they were few in number. The
passage of a Vestry Act and an Orthodox Clergy Act provided a basis
for growth, however, and with the support of Governor William Tryon
the number of ministers increased so that in 1771 fully one-half the
parishes had incumbent clergymen. Problems still remained: the Anglican laity were unhappy because the governor now had the right to
present clergymen, and the dissenters disliked the fact that they were
prohibited from running schools and restricted in the performance of
marriages. In Georgia the Church of England became established in

1758, but it was never a powerful force. There were few Anglican clergymen and many of them were erratic or disreputable. Here as in North Carolina, the majority of clergymen came as missionaries of the SPG. The religious situation in Georgia seems to have been conditioned by the youth of the colony. Successful established churches took time to grow and they depended on a stable gentry class that also developed slowly.[10]

We know more about the development of the established churches in the South than we do about their function. What was it that Anglican colonists expected to gain when they gave the Church of England privileged status? Mary Quinlivan's analysis of the ideological controversy over disestablishment in Virginia suggests that it was the civil utility of religion that seemed most important to Anglican supporters of the state church. The doctrine of civil utility, associated in the eighteenth century with William Warburton, Bishop of Glouchester, held that church and state were separate but mutually supporting institutions. The function of the church, according to Warburton, was to make men understand that there is a God, that He is concerned with the affairs of men, and that their souls depend on choosing good actions over evil ones. The bishop asserted that these doctrines were a necessary moral foundation for an orderly society. Because a stable and peaceful environment worked to the advantage of the state, it was in the interest of the government to protect and support the church. The doctrine of civil utility appears to have been a fundamental principle for those who supported the link between church and state in Virginia, and one suspects it underlay the broad support for an established church throughout the South.[11]

Politics and social structure were closely related in colonial America, and the Church of England played an important role by helping to define and maintain the class structure of the South. The natural quality of social hierarchy and the importance of submitting to one's betters were major Anglican doctrines, enshrined in *The Whole Duty of Man*, a manual of piety and godly behavior, espoused in the published sermons of leading eighteenth-century English clergymen, and echoed in the homilies of American parish priests. This must have been a comfortable message to the American gentleman, often newly arrived in his station and lacking clear emblems of his rank. In any case, it is clear that while members of all classes attended Anglican services, the Church of England clergy maintained a special relationship with the Anglican gentry. Wealthy planters and merchants acted as the patrons of the church, serving on the vestry, protecting its interests in the legislature, and contributing to philanthropic efforts. On the eve of the Revolution, about one-half of the members of the House of Burgesses in Virginia were vestrymen of the Church of England.[12]

The relationship between the Church of England clergy and the Anglican gentry is insufficiently studied, but the nature and significance of the connection have been suggested by Rhys Isaac. Isaac studied the social and religious tension present in prerevolutionary Virginia and believes its source was the Great Awakening. Until evangelicalism began to make inroads in Virginia, the established church was peaceful and the clergy and laity lived in mutual harmony. Beginning in the 1740s, a series of acrimonious developments spoiled the calm. Vestry-man Landon Carter attempted to oust the Reverend William Kay after the clergyman preached a sermon against pride; there were the Two Penny Acts and the Parsons' Cause; a group of clergymen defended the rights of a patently immoral minister named Brunskill; and the lay visitors of William and Mary College quarreled with the clerical professors. These difficulties, according to Isaac, resulted from the fact that despite the best efforts of Anglican laymen and clergymen more and more Virginians were joining the Presbyterian and Baptist churches. Feeling threatened by this development, the laity of the established church blamed their own clergy and attempted to bring them under closer control; for their part the clergy claimed that they could not be effective unless they were given independence and an adequate income.[13]

The evangelicals were not simply challenging the doctrines and forms of the Church of England, they were also an implicit threat to the gentry style, the manner of living and behaving that set the upper class apart from their social inferiors. Pride was a major aspect of the gentry style, an exaggerated sense of one's self that encouraged lordly bearing, placed a great deal of emphasis on horseback riding, and showed itself in the dancing of a jig. Wealth was the basis of membership in the gentry and it was conspicuously displayed. Gentlemen wore fine clothes and lived in elegant homes; they gambled at cards, cocks, and horses; and they partied a great deal. All of this produced awe and envy in the lower classes until the Great Awakening. Evangelical preachers and their followers, however, affected a sober and modest demeanor, contented themselves with limited material goods, and proscribed liquor, gambling, and dancing. The class solidarity of the gentry was paralleled by the fellowship of the evangelical religious community. The Virginia gentry feared that their social leadership would be rejected and after that their political leadership. In fact the evangelicals were something less than victorious, yet their rapid growth did lead to religious denominationalism and to a cultural pluralism in which evangelical preachers became the hortatory models for aspiring politicians.[14]

Rhys Isaac's articles demonstrate the reciprocal relationship between the established clergy of Virginia and the upper class. Sunday worship was an important social event in colonial Virginia, and the gentry used it as a vehicle for asserting their position: the dress of the great men distinguished them from others, so also did the position of their pews, and, if emphasis were needed, they were accustomed to enter the service at one time. In the same way that the priest encouraged respect for government, he also was expected to encourage respect for the class of people who were in power. He might do this in his sermons; he undoubtedly did so in the social interaction that followed. The reliance of the gentry on the established church is indicated by the fact that even as they blamed the clergy for the growth of dissent, they used laws supporting conformity as a means of suppressing evangelicalism.

The established church also played a role in the administration of local government in the South. Each of the southern colonies was divided into parishes and each parish had an elected vestry to administer its affairs. The basic responsibility of the vestry was to maintain the buildings and grounds of the church and, outside of Maryland, it also exercised control over the selection and maintenance of a clergyman. The vestry also functioned as an agent of local government, in particular by using public funds to relieve the parish poor. Sometimes dissenters served on Anglican vestries, but not normally. The role of the Anglican vestry as a governmental institution in the South emphasized the national character of the Church of England.[15]

Aside from its political roles, the Church of England influenced southern society in a number of ways. One of these was education. The schooling of young men and women in the eighteenth century South was largely in the hands of Anglican clergymen. In Virginia and Maryland there were few nondenominational schoolmasters, and it was usually the Anglican priest who opened a parish school. In North Carolina and Georgia the SPG made an important contribution by sending missionary schoolmasters who augmented the efforts of parish clergymen. The children learned reading, writing, and arithmetic and occasionally classical languages. At the same time, however, they received the moral, social, and political message that was part of colonial Anglicanism. These schools were open to dissenters as well as members of the Church of England, and through them the influence of the established church spread well beyond its communion.[16]

Anglican clergymen also made efforts to educate southern slaves and bring them into the Christian faith, but the enormity of the task and the indifference of the owners were difficult to overcome. The missionary effort was strongly supported by Bishop Gibson in London and by Commissary James Blair in Virginia as well. A number of Virginia missionaries did succeed in baptizing blacks and one of them, the Reverend John Garzia, baptized 695 slaves in eight years. Dr. Bray's Associates, an English philanthropic organization, also founded a school for slaves in Williamsburg. Down to the American Revolution it appears that the Anglican effort in this regard was at least as substantial as the better known activities of evangelicals. On the other hand, as a whole the slaves remained heathens.[17]

The quality of Southern Anglican clergymen is too often judged by the behavior of the worst of them. Scandalous activity did occur, but recent studies suggest that less than 10 percent of the ministry was involved. Notoriety on the part of every tenth clergyman does reflect badly on the church, but it should not overshadow the activity of the other nine men. At the other extreme, it is clear that some clergymen are notable for their intellectual and literary merit. Richard Beale Davis's recent survey of southern literature documents the existence of a plain style sermon in the South that was very similar to pulpit oratory in New England. Among the most skilled practitioners of this mode are Anglican luminaries such as the Commissaries Bray and Blair, lesser lights such as Thomas Cradock and Thomas Bacon, and comparatively unknown clergymen such as Robert Paxton. The majority of the Anglican clergymen were neither immoral nor intellectual, but well-meaning and well-educated by the standards of the time, and generally effective in their role.[18]

Southern Anglican clergy have been disparaged, and so has been the religious commitment of the laity. One author calls Southern Anglicanism "predominantly formal, practical, and decorous" and notes that while William Byrd II attended church, said prayers, and read sermons, he was also sexually promiscuous, gambled, and enjoyed other worldly pleasures. One senses that Anglicanism is being faulted for controlling the conscience less than Puritanism and the emotions less than evangelicalism. A useful antidote for such narrow-mindedness is George N. Clark's comment on seventeenth century Anglicanism: "The desire to find shelter and emotional stability in a dignified and well-regulated community, a church, is no less an authentic form of religion than the passion to be saved as an individual and to rescue fellow individuals."[19]

Henry F. May provides a realistic evaluation of the spiritual quality of Southern Anglicanism. The religious message was "rational piety, . . . a golden mean between Calvinism and Arminianism. God was sovereign, but could not violate his own goodness or forget his promises. . . . Always emphasizing repentance and hope, discouraging too much speculation about predestination and eternal punishment, the church sometimes seems to hint that everybody would eventually be saved." According to May, these doctrines appealed to "Americans who considered themselves modern, rational, moderate, enlightened—in a word English." He claims that the Church of England in the South was controlled by planters and that they were not interested in "theological disputation or mystical contemplation." Instead they wanted "a decent orderly religion which would remind everybody of his position, his duties, and his limitations."[20]

The role of the Church of England as the national church of the American South, in Niebuhr's sense of the term, came to an end with the American Revolution. The question naturally arises as to why, if the established churches were successful, they were so rapidly and uniformly struck down. Part of the answer is that the Revolution created an ideology that was opposed to religious privilege as well as political privilege. Probably more important is the fact that the religious complexion of the South had undergone a major change in the quarter of a century prior to 1776. During the eighteenth century southern colonial governments were interested in augmenting their white populations in order to provide a buffer against the Indians, offset the growing numbers of slaves, and increase the value of western lands. They offered a variety of incentives to attract settlers, the most important of which was fertile and inexpensive land. Scots-Irish and German settlers began to move from Pennsylvania into the Valley of Virginia in the 1730s; in ensuing decades they swelled in numbers and met other newcomers coming up from the coast. In the 1750s and 1760s a vast throng of settlers moved into the backcountry of North and South Carolina and across the river into Georgia. The migration into the southern backcountry was heterogeneous in national origin and in religion, but it contained few Anglicans. Moreover the Presbyterians and Baptists who were dominant in numbers were also self-conscious about their evangelicalism and hostile to restraints on their religious liberty.[21]

The social and political power of the Anglican gentry allowed the Church of England to retain its hegemony during the colonial period, but the Declaration of Independence created a new situation. Anglicans were outnumbered two to one in Maryland and Virginia, and more so further south. Most of the dissenters lived in western areas, and it soon became clear that eastern politicians had to placate the backcountry in order to present a united front against Great Britain. In western Maryland the settlers were anxious for revolutionary change, while in the piedmont of North Carolina they were loyal to Great Britain.[22] In the process of manufacturing unity, Maryland, North Carolina, and Georgia disestablished the Church of England in 1776, and Virginia relieved the dissenters from the obligation of paying religious taxes. Not until 1785 did Virginia create a situation of religious freedom based on Jefferson's famous bill; only narrowly defeated was a measure that would have allowed a tax assessment for the support of religion in general. The idea of a general assessment or a Protestant establishment also had support in Maryland, a testament to lingering support for a state church based on the civil utility of religion.[23]

Southern Anglicanism served as the national church of the colonial South. In doctrine and liturgy it was similar to the Church of England with a decidedly low church flavor. It supported not only the government of England but also the government of the colony in which it existed. Eventually loyalty to the latter government became stronger. It also supported the interests of the southern gentry and helped to shape their sense of public responsiblity. The tie between the established church and the upper class was strengthened by the fact that the American laity exercised far more power within the church than did their counterparts in England. The end of the church came about not because the laity disliked their church but because they became a minority within their own societies. For a fuller exposition of these themes we now look to the established church of South Carolina, its history, and some of its more important characteristics.

CHAPTER 2

ESTABLISHMENT AND SETTLEMENT

A state church was inherently political, and the act of establishment was always controversial in a colony with plural religious allegiance. Virginia escaped the consequences of these truths because the Church of England held a privileged position from the beginning and the colony was dominated by Anglicans during its formative years. Maryland established the Church of England only after the Glorious Revolution, and any opposition by Catholics or dissenters was stifled by the determination of the Crown to give Anglicanism a preeminent position.[1] In South Carolina internal conflict was extreme. Anglicans and dissenters were evenly matched, and the churchmen were successful only because of proprietary aid. The Anglicans immediately put the state church to political use by disfranchising their religious enemies. Factionalism eventually declined, however, and the church remained. Its permanent features were similar to those of Virginia in the sense that religious forms were only an approximation of those in England and the laity exercised large powers. Imperial authorities and resident clergymen fought this unorthodoxy, but the people of South Carolina eventually molded their church to fit their disposition.

The charter in which Charles II granted the area that included South Carolina to eight "right trusty and right well-beloved Cousins and Counsellors" in 1663 described the proprietors as "excited with a laudable and pious zeal for the propagation of the Christian Faith and the enlargement of our Empire." There is every reason to believe that the latter motive, with its promise of economic and political gain, was the dominant one. Nonetheless, in addition to the ownership of the land and the right to govern it, the charter gave the proprietors the "patronage and advowsons" of the Anglican churches that would be built and the right to grant as much toleration as they wished to non-Anglicans, providing the recipients were peaceful and loyal to the Crown.[2] The proprietors laid out their program for the government of Carolina in a document known as the Fundamental Constitutions, drawn up in 1669 by Anthony Ashley Cooper, then Lord Ashley, later the Earl of Shaftesbury, assisted by John Locke. Ashley hoped to create a feudal society in the colony, with political rights linked to land ownership and size of estate, but his elaborate plans did not exercise a great deal of influence on the development of the colony. The religious provisions of the Fundamental Constitutions, however, envisioned a model structure of religious toleration that helped to attract dissenters to South Carolina.

Ashley's basic policy was to discourage atheism and encourage free religious worship within a context of social order. No person could be a freeman of Carolina or own land or a house there who did not acknowledge the existence of God and the need for public and solemn worship. Each colonist over the age of seventeen had to be a member of some church in order to have any benefit of the laws. Any seven persons, however, could form their own church. Ashley felt this liberal policy would allow Indians as well as Europeans of differing religious persuasions to live together in harmony. He also believed that "heathens, Jews, and other dissenters from the purity of Christian religion . . . should not be Scared and kept at a distance from it," but rather converted by familiarity.

Other religious provisions demanded that "the terms of admittance and communion with any church" be written out and include tenets acknowledging the existence of God, the duty of public worship, and the necessity of members bearing witness to the truth when asked by the government. The swearing of oaths, anathema to Quakers, was not required. No member of any church was to "disturb or molest" any rival religious assembly, verbally reproach or abuse a member of another church, or "disturb, molest, or prosecute another for his speculative opinions in Religion or his way of worship." No irreverent or seditious things were to be spoken against the government in any church. Ashley made it clear that religious assemblies disobeying these rules would be considered "unlawful meetings, and be punished as other riots." Slaves were permitted to join churches, but membership would have no effect on their servile status.

Ashley hoped that religion would be politically neutral. Other proprietors, however, wanted the government to maintain a special relationship with the Church of England. They revised the Fundamental Constitutions in 1670 and inserted the following provision:

> As the Country comes to be sufficiently Planted and Distributed into fit Divisions, it shall belong to the Parliament to take care for the building of Churches and the public Maintenance of Divines, to be employed in the Exercise of Religion according to the Church of England, which, being the only true and Orthodox, and the National Religion of all the King's Dominions, is so also of Carolina, and therefore, it alone shall be allowed to receive public Maintenance by Grant of Parliament.

Two more versions of the Fundamental Constitutions appeared in 1682. The leading proprietors at that time were the Earl of Craven, a member of the Church of England, and John Archdale, a Quaker: both men favored religious toleration and wanted to make Carolina attractive to prospective settlers. In January 1682, they deleted the reference to the Church of England as "the only true and Orthodox, and the National Religion of all the King's Dominions" and called it simply "the Religion of the Government of England." In August of the same year they provided that members of confessions other than the Church of England would not be taxed for its support and allowed them to be assessed for the benefit of their own churches. At the same time they forbade any minister to sit in the legislature or hold public office. These liberal revisions were designed to make Carolina attractive to nonconforming settlers, and they were effective.[3]

Sugar planters in Barbados, pressed by the shortage of land on the island, had shown an early interest in South Carolina, and immigrants from there formed the dominant element in the new colony. Their cultural baggage included experience in the management of plantations and slaves and a preference for the Church of England. In the 1680s, as a result of the promotional efforts of Craven and Archdale, an influx of dissenters came from England and, to a lesser extent, New England and Scotland. French Huguenots, fleeing the intolerance of Louis XIV, also found South Carolina a welcome haven.[4] White colonists numbered about 4,000 in 1700. There were about 500 French Calvinists and the remaining settlers were divided into about 1,700 Anglicans, 1,300 Presbyterians, 400 Baptists, and 100 Quakers.[5]

Despite the variety of their faiths and a significant amount of political disputation, the early settlers maintained religious harmony. Saint Philip's, an Anglican church, was built in Charles Town, probably in the early 1680s. Atkin Williamson, a disreputable Anglican minister, probably officiated there for a time.[6] Elizabeth Blake, a Puritan and the granddaughter of an executed regicide, contributed to the furnishings of Saint Philip's. Her husband, Joseph Blake (the nephew of Cromwell's admiral) donated the Charles Town land on which a Presbyterian church was built. In 1696 Blake became governor of the colony and two years later, despite his dissenting views, signed the first law providing public funds for the Church of England in the colony.[7]

While peaceful coexistence characterized denominational interaction in South Carolina, Anglicans in England were experiencing a revival of power. The Restoration returned the Church of England to mastery over Protestant dissenters, and the Glorious Revolution removed the fear that James II would impose Roman Catholicism. A sense of triumph and security infused the church. This Anglican confidence was heightened by the optimism that came to Englishmen as a result of the remarkable progress rational thought was making against ignorance and superstititon. Newton had demonstrated that the universe operated in an orderly and comprehensible manner, and Locke convinced many that the human mind could come to a knowledge of God without the assistance of divine revelation.[8] Possessing a new political security, a new trust in the physical world, and a renewed confidence in themselves, the churchmen of England were ready for new projects.

The form this activity took owed much to a surfeit with the theological controversy that had taken so much mental and physical energy during the previous century and a half. Dominant elements within the Church of England now favored a simple piety demonstrated by good works. Norman Sykes has called this "the theology of Divine Benevolence,"

> the simple faith in God the Father, maker of heaven and earth, whose creation is universal proof of His beneficience toward Man, and the corollary of Man's duty to be thankful to God and to imitate the divine benevolence in his dealings with his fellows.[9]

Latitudinarians, as the leading exponents of these ideas were known, accepted Locke's confident, rational, and sober view of God. They scorned both the pettiness of elaborate theology and the uncertainty and ecstasy of experiential religion and advocated "the religion of common sense." They emphasized a practical morality that concentrated religious energy on the improvement of social conditions at home and the promotion of religion in the colonies.[10]

The Reverend Thomas Bray was a key figure in mobilizing the resources of practical piety. He combined a partisan love for the Church of England with a lucid intellect and superb promotional and organizational abilities. When he published a volume of catechism lectures in 1698, Bray came to the attention of Bishop of London, Henry Compton, whose office involved maintaining a supervisory capacity over the Church of England in America. That same year Compton made Bray ecclesiastical commissary for Maryland, and Bray turned his attention immediately to colonial Anglicanism. The needs as he saw them were twofold: competent clergymen for the colonies and the books necessary for their work. In 1699 four prominent laymen joined him in forming the Society for Promoting Christian Knowledge, which soon grew into a large philanthropic organization dedicated to the idea that "the growth of vice and immorality is greatly owing to gross ignorance of the principles of the Christian religion." With respect to America, its intent was "to assist Dr. Bray in raising of Libraries for the Clergy, and in distributing practical Books among the laity."[11]

A second organization founded through Bray's initiative was to have an even greater impact on the colonies. After spending six months in Maryland, Bray returned to England in March 1700. Immediately he published *A Memorial representing the Present State of Religion on the Continent of North-America*. It characterized South Carolina as "a very thriving Colony, and so large, as to want at least Three Missionaries, besides one lately sent there." Bray persuaded Compton and Archbishop of Canterbury, Thomas Tenison, that the need for colonial clergy would be met only by organizing a new society dedicated solely to that purpose. In June 1701, William III granted a charter incorporating ninety-four lay and ecclesiastical notables as "The Society for the Propagation of the Gospell in Forreigne Parts" and impowered it to receive funds and maintain orthodox ministers in the "Plantations, Colonies, and Factories beyond the Seas, belonging to Our Kingdome of England."[12]

This Anglican resurgence occurred at the same time that the Church was beset with severe factional divisions. A schism had occurred in 1689 when eight bishops and some four hundred clergymen refused to swear allegiance to William and Mary, holding that the doctrine of nonresistance to temporal power bound them to James despite his policies. The Glorious Revolution also deepened the division between High Churchmen, who followed the late Archbishop William Laud in demanding a rigid adherence to Anglican doctrine and ceremony, and Low Churchmen, who were latitudinarian in their commitment to the essence of Christianity rather than its particular forms and were willing to make accommodations in order to comprehend dissenters or at least to live peaceably with them. From 1688 to 1716 these differences complicated and embittered the religious and political life of England. In general the Whigs were the party of the Low Church and the Tories fought the High Church battle against toleration.[13]

John Grenville, Earl of Bath, who became a Carolina proprietor in 1694, played an important role in transmitting English religious disputes to South Carolina. Bath became the fourth Palatine of Carolina, or chief proprietor, in April 1697 at the death of the Earl of Craven. He had been a strong supporter of the Stuarts and had pledged allegiance to William III only with hesitation.[14] In 1698 Bath approved a final set of revisions in the Fundamental Constitutions that deleted the religious provisions favoring dissenters and restored the provision that called for establishing the Church of England. Before his death in 1701, the earl sent two Anglican ministers to South Carolina. Bath was succeeded in January 1702 by his second son, Sir John Granville, a staunch, almost fanatical, Tory. In 1701 he was said to be the only member of the House of Commons to oppose openly the settlement of the royal succession in the Hanoverian line; he became Lord Granville in 1703 when Queen Anne needed Tory strength in the House of Lords.[15] From 1702 until his death in 1707, Granville was the leading force on the Carolina proprietary. His influence was immediately and consistently exerted in favor of the Anglican party in South Carolina politics.

The first fruits of the Anglican revival in England reached South Carolina in 1698, in the person of the Reverend Samuel Marshall, who came with a commission "to take Accompt of and Register all marriages Births Christenings and Burialls" and with the proprietors' instructions that he be given "such a Settlement as may make him easy." Thomas

Bray had recruited the minister and Bishop Compton recommended him to the proprietors. With Marshall, Bray sent books to form the basis for a provincial library.[16]

Marshall was well received in South Carolina. "An Act to settle a maintenance on a Minister of the Church of England in Charles Town" passed without undue opposition. The preamble noted that by the charter only the Church of England could be supported with public funds. Besides an annual salary of £150 sterling, the Act provided Marshall and his successors with land, a house and outbuildings, livestock, and a Negro man and woman. It named commissioners to administer the law. Funds were to come from the general treasury, but if that source failed, the commissioners could levy an assessment that the constables would collect. In the latter case the law provided for distraint of goods in the event of default.[17] A member of the assembly later wrote that the provision for the use of general funds rather than an immediate assessment saved much ill will by making it unlikely that a dissenter's property would be taken for the sake of the Church of England.[18] Governor Blake sent letters to Bray and Compton thanking them for their efforts. The Commons House also voted public thanks to Afra Cuming, a woman who donated seventeen acres of land next to Charles Town for the use of Marshall and his successors at Saint Philip's.[19] Marshall died of a fever in January 1700. Blake and his council wrote to Compton praising the minister and asking for another. Their comments suggest dissenters as well as churchmen heard his services: "By his easy, and as it were natural use of the ceremonies of our Church, he took away all occasions of scandal at them."[20]

At the beginning of the eighteenth century political controversy arose in South Carolina, shattering the religious harmony that had characterized the earlier years and leading directly to the establishment of the Church of England. The political factions were new, but they represented old divisions within the colony. During the 1680s the Barbadian element, known as the Goose Creek men because of their heavy settlement along that Berkeley County stream, had quarreled with the proprietors over debts, land policies, and the Indian trade; the newly arrived dissenters, lacking vested interests in the colony and grateful for religious toleration, tended to support the proprietary; and, for reasons that are unclear, the Huguenots joined the Anglican, Goose Creek faction.

These political differences were resolved in the mid-1690s, and a few years of peace ensued; new resentments developed in 1700 following the death of Governor Joseph Blake. The Council chose Joseph Morton, a dissenter, to succeed Blake, but the election was contested by two Anglicans, James Moore and Robert Daniel. Eventually Moore became the new governor, but Anglicans and dissenters were now in separate camps.

Governor Moore's administration began peacefully enough, but disagreement developed over regulating the lucrative Indian trade. The governor had extensive personal interests in the trade, and dissenters in the Commons House accused him of thwarting regulation in order to continue his profits. External threats to the colony escalated the internal party conflict. South Carolina traders had been more than a match for their Spanish rivals in Florida, but more formidable opposition appeared after 1699 when the French established themselves at the mouths of the Mississippi and Alabama rivers. As England prepared to enter the War of the Spanish Succession, Carolina faced a strong threat to her commercial interests and to her very existence.

Political struggle became intense early in 1702 when Governor Moore asked for funds to attack the Spaniards at Saint Augustine. Dissenters controlled the Commons House and their leader, John Ash, a Puritan from New England, believed Moore was more interested in glory and booty than in the welfare of the colony. The House refused to vote the money, and Moore retaliated by dissolving the assembly. At hotly contested spring elections, the Anglicans gained seats although the dissenters continued in power. Ash and his allies began an investigation of the election and refused to do anything about defense; in August, however, a declaration of war reached the colony and the Commons House funded the Florida expedition. The governor himself led the Carolinians, who devastated the town of Saint Augustine but failed to take the Spanish fort; they finally burned their ships and returned over land. The expedition cost £4,000 sterling more than had been appropriated; leading the dissenters to charge that the whole thing had been mismanaged. When Moore asked for bills of credit to cover the expenditures, Ash attempted to bargain for legislation that would reform the Indian trade, regulate elections, and revise the naturalization law to the disadvantage of the Huguenots. Moore refused to trade, and the dissenters walked out of the assembly. Shortly thereafter leading dissenters were assaulted during a week of riots incited, they said, by the governor's friends.

Believing there was no local recourse, Ash went to England to protest the governor's policies and tactics.[21]

Meanwhile Sir John Granville had come to power on the South Carolina proprietary, and in June 1702 he packed the colonial government with staunch Anglicans. The new governor, Sir Nathaniel Johnson, was a Jacobite who had resigned the governorship of the Leeward Islands rather than swear loyalty to William and Mary and who took the oath of allegiance only in January 1702, after the death of James Stuart.[22] Moore was moved to the post of receiver general and Job Howe, an Anglican leader in the Commons, became surveyor general. Johnson's son-in-law, Thomas Broughton, also joined the council, and Nicholas Trott became chief justice of the court of common pleas. Trott was a man of many talents who later published several important legal compilations. He corresponded with the SPG and vigorously pressed the interests of the Church of England in the colony.[23]

With Ash gone, leadership of the dissenting party fell to Thomas Smith, one of the colony's leading landholders. Other important dissenters were Joseph Morton, Edmund Bellinger, the Stanyarne and Elliot families from Barbados, and Lady Blake, the widow of the governor. The new political factions had a sectional as well as a religious basis. Most of the dissenters lived in Colleton County, southwest of Charles Town, the area most vulnerable to attack by Indians, Frenchmen, and Spaniards. A number of Anglicans living or owning land there supported the dissenters, probably because of a common interest in regulating the Indian trade. Among these dissident Anglicans were Stephen Bull, John Barnwell, and Hugh Hext. Their leader was Thomas Nairne, the chief advocate of a more enlightened Indian policy. Robert Stevens, a staunch Anglican from Goose Creek, also sided with Nairne and the dissenters against his neighbors in the church party.

Sir Nathaniel Johnson led the Anglican offensive that resulted in the creation of a state church. He took over the governorship in March 1703 and immediately called for new elections to the assembly. The Anglicans swept Berkeley County, probably because of a general dissatisfaction with the dissenters' opposition to defense spending. Johnson concentrated on military matters for a year, and then in the spring of 1704 he struck at the dissenters in a manner that would have pleased James II. The governor called an emergency session of the assembly, and Colonel James Risbee quickly introduced a bill in the Commons

House to exclude non-Anglicans from House membership. Seven members still had not arrived when the measure passed by one vote. At the fall session of the assembly, the Anglicans solidified their position. Johnson began by handing over to the Commons House several letters written by Thomas Smith to John Ash in the summer of 1703, which the governor said "villified and abus'd this Government." The House took Smith into custody on October 9 and the next day began proceedings against the Reverend Edward Marston, rector of Saint Philip's.[24]

Marston was a nonjuring Anglican clergymen sent by the proprietors in 1699 to replace Samuel Marshall. He was a staunch defender of the church constitution, and he feared that the Anglican legislators were about to set up a Low Church establishment. He claimed that Johnson had warned him in the spring "that some of the Members of the Assembly were endeavouring to wrest the Ecclesiastical Jurisdiction of the Province out of the Hands of the...Bishop of London, and out of the Hands of the...Governour...as Ordinary." When the fall session of the assembly opened, Marston began to attack the legislature in his Sunday sermons. Accused by the Commons House of demeaning its proceedings, he refused to turn over his sermon notes on the grounds that the House was not a judge of ecclesiastical matters. An indictment by the legislators accused him of setting his spiritual authority above their temporal power. "You did assert that you was no ways obliged to the Government for the bountiful Revenues they have allowed you, for that the same was due to you of Divine Right, and that you did not think yourself inferior to us, or obliged to give an account of your actions to the Government, for though they gave you a Maintenance, yet you was there Superior, Your Authority being from Christ." The legislators deprived Marston of his salary as rector of Saint Philip's, but allowed him to keep the office, being unwilling to "meddle with...his Function."[25]

Having dealt with its critics, the Anglican government proceeded to set up a state church. The Establishment Act declared that places of worship using the liturgy of the Church of England were "Settled and Established Churches" and provided for their administration and support. Charles Town became the parish of Saint Philip's, but it continued to be governed by the Act of 1698. The new law divided Berkeley County into five other parishes and provided for the building of six churches, including one in Colleton County. It granted ministers a corporate capacity as parish rectors and made provisions for each of them to have a parsonage, farm lands (or glebe as it was called), and yearly incomes of £50 in South Carolina currency. Money from an export and import tax passed at the same time was to be used to pay the salaries of the ministers; £2,000 from the same source was allotted for the six new churches. Vestries were also allowed to raise up to £100 per year by assessing the real and personal estates of all inhabitants, Anglicans and dissenters alike.

As Marston feared, the government of the church was entirely in the hands of the laity. Church of England parishioners who were freeholders or taxpayers were to select the rector of the parish; they would also elect vestrymen who would then appoint a parish register, a clerk, and a sexton. A closed corporation of commissioners named in the act would exercise supervisory power over the church as a whole. "In case of any immoral or imprudent conduct" on the part of an incumbent minister, on the request of nine parishioners and a majority of the vestry, and after a hearing, the commissioners could remove the offender from his position. Sir Nathaniel Johnson apparently reached a modus vivendi with the members of his party who favored lay power. Citing "his great zeal and affection for the Church of England," the law empowered the governor to veto any removals made by the commission, but the power was granted to Johnson personally and would expire when his tenure ended.[26]

The establishment of the Church of England was closely tied to a political alliance between Anglicans and Huguenots. Johnson opened the fall legislative session by calling for an act to naturalize aliens; and after creating their state church the legislators passed a measure that gave the French full power to hold and transfer property and to carry on business. They could vote for members of the assembly but could not hold office themselves. One Huguenot was even put on the church commission.[27]

Outmaneuvered in the colony, the dissenters and the dissident Anglicans were more successful in England. John Ash died shortly after arriving in England, and Joseph Boone, a Charles Town merchant, replaced him as the agent of the dissenting party. Boone got nowhere with the proprietors who were controlled by Granville, but John Archdale, the Quaker proprietor, still supported toleration, and he and Boone took their case to the House of Lords and to the public. They were apparently responsible for two publications, *Party-Tyranny* and *Case of the Protes-*

tant Dissenters, probably written by Daniel Defoe, which stated the position of the South Carolina nonconformists. These pamphlets argued that the law disallowing dissenters from serving in the Commons House was not only unprecedented in the colonies but also contrary to the Carolina charter. With respect to the Establishment Act, they took the position that the lay commission posed a threat to the constitution of the Church of England, an effective argument if somewhat disingenuous for the dissenters. The pamphlets also contained letters from Edward Marston in which the minister, now deprived of his office by the church commissioners, asserted that the Establishment Act was being used to serve the political ends of its supporters. Throughout this lobbying effort, the dissenters stressed their importance to the economy of South Carolina.[28] Granville responded with *An Account of the Fair and Impartial Proceedings of the Lords Proprietors, Governor and Council of the Colony of South Carolina*, which pointed out that ecclesiastical machinery did not exist on the other side of the ocean and that lay power was an accepted custom in America.[29]

Whatever the effect of this debate on public opinion, the House of Lords was dominated by Whig nobles and bishops who took a tolerant view of religious differences in the interest of national unity and of Whig political power. After hearing from Boone, Archdale, and Granville, the Lords resolved that the Carolina measures were at odds with reason, the Carolina charter, and English law. They advised Queen Anne to disallow both acts, and in May 1705 the Board of Trade suggested that the Queen begin proceedings against the charter. The proprietors thereupon instructed Johnson to repeal both pieces of legislation.[30]

Meanwhile in South Carolina there was a reaction against the partisanship of 1704. Early in 1705 the Commons House proposed a repeal of the exclusion law, but the measure was vetoed by the council. Another conciliatory bill did become law. The Establishment Act had neglected to provide for the election of church wardens; when the legislature acted to correct this oversight, it also included a statement, avowedly designed to remedy "difficulties and disputes," that the power given to Church of England ministers to christen, marry, and bury their parishioners was not to infringe on the rights of the dissenting clergy and their congregations. Despite the Exclusion Act, dissenters were elected to the House later in 1705; when they failed to take the prescribed Anglican oath, Johnson dissolved the assembly.[31]

In the fall of 1706 South Carolina learned that the Crown opposed both the Exclusion Act and the Establishment Act. On Johnson's advice, the assembly repealed the offending measures and passed a new Establishment Act that took away the church commission's power to discipline an incumbent clergyman. Parishioners still elected their ministers, however, and the commissioners administered the elections and had other supervisory powers over the establishment. Under this law Saint Philip's was governed in the same way as the other parishes except that the town minister received a higher salary than his rural colleagues. The measure provided for a total of ten parishes, including one for the French settlers on the Santee River in Craven County and another for those in Orange District in Berkeley County. Until a majority voted to use English, services were held in French in those areas.

While there remained a French Calvinist church in Charles Town and another small one in western Berkeley County, most of the former Huguenots were now nominally affiliated with the Church of England. French refugees in Virginia were doing the same thing about this time. Francophobia, in England and in the colonies, doubtless impelled the Huguenots to insure their own security by affiliating with the national church of their adopted home. They also had reason to be grateful to the Church of England. Wealthy Anglican laymen and important ecclesiastics, Bishop Henry Compton in particular, had aided the French Protestants in England and helped them to find new homes in the colonies. Moreover a French Calvinist could join the colonial church more easily than the mother institution, since there was little episcopal authority in America and church government approximated the Presbyterian model. The lay power that Edward Marston found so obnoxious must have appealed to the Huguenots. In South Carolina the Anglicans welcomed their political allies into the church. One Frenchman was made a church commissioner in 1704, and in 1706 the commission included four former Huguenots.[33]

In the ten years that followed its establishment in 1706 the Church of England gradually became a functioning reality in South Carolina. The colonists built churches, some of them fine stone structures, and they provided accommodations for the ministers who arrived. In 1702 the Society for the Propagation of the Gospel in Foreign Parts had sent the Reverend Samuel Thomas as a missionary to the Yamasee Indians in

South Carolina; Thomas, however, settled among the colonists, and in 1705 he returned to England and convinced the SPG to support the nascent state church. The society sent ten missionaries between 1706 and 1716, providing each with a salary of £50 sterling; another six clergymen came to the colony through the efforts of Bishop Compton; three arrived on their own; and one local Presbyterian went to England and returned in Anglican orders. The colony benefited less from this influx than might have been expected since one missionary accepted a living in Bermuda on his way to South Carolina, another left the colony after a year, and four clergymen, including Samuel Thomas, died within a year of their arrival. Nonetheless, during these early years the parish posts were generally filled, and the ministers took turns serving the vacant ones.[34]

In 1708 Bishop Compton sent Commissary Gideon Johnston to South Carolina as his personal representative. The bishop of London had a traditional but undefined jurisdiction over the American colonies, and in the seventeenth century Compton had gained the right to pass on the doctrinal soundness of candidates for colonial cures and to exercise a supervisory capacity over the Church of England in America.[35] The function of a commissary was to supervise the clergy and the affairs of the church in a particular part of the diocese, and Johnston was a staunch defender of episcopal authority, clerical privilege, and church doctrine and forms. Unhappily for him, during eight years in the colony he found much with which to be displeased.

Johnston's arrival was inauspicious. He was marooned without food or water for several days on an island off the coast near Charles Town. After being rescued, he found that the parish of Saint Philip's, to which he had been sent by Compton, was occupied by the Reverend Richard Marsden, who had recently come to South Carolina from Maryland. Marsden was very popular with the parishioners, but Governor Johnson prevailed on him to resign and accept another parish. Still the disgruntled parishioners complained, "What has the Bp of London to do with us?" Only 7 of 200 eligible voters elected the commissary to his new office.[36]

Despite this shaky beginning, Johnston gradually began to exercise his authority within the church. In 1710 he improved an unpleasant situation between a minister and his parish. John Maitland was well-liked in 1708 when he was elected rector of Saint Paul's Parish in

Colleton County, "particularly," wrote Johnston, "by the Presbyterians, who were wonderfully taken with his way of preaching which was Extempore and in all points conformable to the usual Method of the Dissenters." Maitland had a passionate temper, however, and was eager to reform the ways of his parishioners. By the beginning of 1710 the congregation that had formerly filled the church was down to three people. Johnston first visited the parish and secured a temporary truce between the rector and his parishioners. When this broke down, he issued a "preemptory Citacon" that brought Maitland before the commissary to explain his conduct. Finally Johnston prevailed upon the parishioners to pay Maitland £70 to resign and leave the Parish. They wanted the commissary to use "Ecclesiastical Censures," but Johnston's powers were limited. He could "suspend him from his Office," presumably by revoking the license issued by Compton, "but not from his Benefice or Salary thro' a defect in the Church Act."[37] The removal power taken from the lay commission in the Act of 1706 was not delegated to any ecclesiastical authority. Once inducted into a parish by the process of election, a minister could not be removed for his behavior.

Johnston was also concerned with enforcing conformity to Anglican liturgy and procedures. South Carolina Anglicans, accustomed to makeshift spiritual arrangements and influenced by their dissenting neighbors, were apt to resent practices that seemed to them senseless or unsuited to local conditions. Johnston found, for instance, that many who partook of the Eucharist in Saint Philip's would not give their names for the parochial records despite his repeated urgings. Moreover some Carolina Anglicans possessed only modest denominational loyalty and were willing to attend dissenter services if the Church of England did not accommodate their scruples.[38]

To some Anglican ministers it seemed logical to humor the prejudices of the people rather than risk alienating them by demanding a rigorous adherence to form. Johnston blamed the late Samuel Thomas, who he said "baptized with or without the sign of the Cross, Godfathers and Godmothers, and would administer the Communion kneeling, sitting or standing as People would have him." By thus "playing fast and loose with the Canons and Rubrick," the commissary believed Thomas achieved a popularity with the Carolinians that set a bad example for later ministers.[39] Johnston complained that some ministers did not use the *Book of Common Prayer* during services in private homes but followed their own form "after the Dissenting manner." Another minister reported that some of his colleagues married people who had not been baptized.[40]

At a meeting of the clergy, probably in 1711, Johnston gave a sermon enjoining strict adherence to Anglican form and ceremony. He admitted that the colonial environment made some allowances necessary, but asserted that no minister could "legally pretend to any latitude or indifference in things which are legally established and are an Essential part of...the Church of England constitution." The commissary tried to steel his colleagues against criticism from the laity: "Certainly a Minister may be a peaceable, moderate, and good natur'd man, without being either asham'd or afraid of doing his duty." Firmness, Johnston believed, would promote an easier acceptance.

Johnston had particular difficulties with three clergymen who were former Huguenots now in Anglican orders. Their parishioners encouraged these men to use Calvinist forms, and all too often the ministers accommodated them. Johnston was particularly upset with John La Pierre, the rector of Saint Dennis Parish. The commissary warned him that since the Establishment Act specified Church of England ministers, an unorthodox clergyman could be denied his salary. Bishop Compton supported Johnston, and the clergy as a whole formally resolved to act correctly in the future.[41]

Gideon Johnston also expended a good deal of effort attempting to have, as he put it, "the old Brittanick Episcopal way of Institution &c settled here as it is at home."[42] His concern was that local law and practice be brought into closer conformity to that in England. The problem was essentially a political one, however; Johnston found that the dissenters had more power than he and that the Anglicans disliked episcopacy as much as dissent.

Political controversy continued in South Carolina after the passage of the Establishment Act in 1706. With the dissenters restored to full political participation, Governor Johnson's enemies were able to push through the House a measure to regulate the Indian trade. Johnson vetoed the bill and dissolved the assembly, but this obstructionism alienated some of his supporters, and the dissenters triumphed at new elections in May 1707. The new House put a great deal of pressure on the governor, questioning the credentials of his ally, Chief Justice Nicholas Trott, and even passing a measure that would have compensated Edward Marston for the salary he had lost from 1704 until his removal from Saint Philip's in 1705. Johnson vetoed that bill indignantly, but eventually he agreed to regulation of the Indian trade and to other measures advocated by his political enemies.[43]

The Anglicans were now worried that Joseph Boone, who was still in London lobbying against the establishment of the Church of England, might be successful. The SPG had disliked the Establishment Act of 1704 because of the lay commission and had planned to withdraw their missionaries from the colony unless it was repealed. In September 1707, Trott asked the SPG to approve the new measure so that the proprietors would confirm it, explaining that "the Faction here endeavor all they can to destroy the Act." Several days later Governor Johnson and several of his councilors wrote to the same purpose. They also described opposition to a recent assessment made to pay the parochial expenses of Saint Philip's Parish. At Joseph Boone's house the collectors were met by Thomas Smith and his brother George in addition to Mrs. Boone. Thomas claimed that the new act had probably been nullified in England, George asserted that "it was only fit to wipe his A——se with," and Mrs. Boone added "that it was a great pitty that Mr. Trott had not been hanged seven Years past." The Anglicans returned to power in 1708, and in the fall they passed a much needed law to define parish boundaries.[44]

Political tranquility in South Carolina became possible after the death of Palatine John Granville in 1707. The proprietors commissioned Edward Tynte as governor in place of Sir Nathaniel Johnson and sent him to reduce the friction between Anglicans and dissenters. Tynte arrived in the colony in November 1709 and died seven months later, but his brief administration saw the beginning of a resolution of the religious disputes. An amendment to the Establishment Act, passed in April 1710, declared that parish levies were "inconvenient, dilatory and troublesome" and provided that vestries could draw up to £40 yearly from the public receiver to cover their parochial expenses. Thus in no case would a dissenter be assessed specifically for the expenses of the Church of England.[45] Factionalism rekindled after Tynte's death, but finally came to an end with the arrival of Governor Charles Craven in March 1712. In his first speech to the legislature, Craven declared his love for the Church of England, but also his intention "to show the greatest tenderness to those who are under the misfortune of dissenting from her, and to do nothing that may seem to endanger them that liberty." In words that Ashley would have approved, he suggested that despite their religious differences the colonists agree "to live amicably together, consult the common good, the tranquility of our province and the increase of its trade."[46]

While the dissenters struggled against the Establishment Act, the Carolina clergy tried to reduce the amount of control exercised over them by the laity. In May 1707 the SPG had decided not to send a clergyman for any parish that would not agree in advance to elect the minister that it provided. Commissary Johnston tried to implement this policy, but there was much opposition, and Nicholas Trott warned in 1711 that Carolina parishes were very jealous of their right of election.[47] Indeed they wanted more power than they had. Francis Le Jau, respected rector of Saint James, Goose Creek, reported popular agitation for a law that would "empower Lay persons joined in Commission with some of the Clergy...to Cite, suspend, and turn out Ministers." Johnston and the Reverend Robert Maule of Saint John's, Berkeley County, were put on the church commission early in 1711, perhaps in the hope of winning their support for a more powerful commission. Despite this climate of opinion, Commissary Johnston was cautiously optimistic about improving the establishment until a new measure passed in 1712 dashed his hopes.[48]

The most important provisions in "An Additional Act to the several Acts relating to the establishment of Religious Worship" were those that strengthened the church commission. Under the law of 1706 the commissioners issued writs for the election of ministers, but their authority over clergymen ended there. The new law gave them the power to arbitrate disputes dealing with the qualifications of electors and the outcome of elections. It also enlarged their administrative power over church property, so that the commissioners could oversee the maintenance of parsonages and glebes during periods when a parish had no minister. To insure that the commission would meet, its semiannual sessions were scheduled at the same time as those of the provincial courts.

Several provisions in the new law benefited the clergy. Henceforth if a minister was sent to South Carolina by the SPG or the bishop of London and elected to a parish, the province would pay his salary retroactive to the date of his arrival in the colony. It would also pay any such minister a bonus of £25 on his arrival, provided that he agreed to return the money if he refused election to a parish or left the colony within two years. Most important among the remaining provisions was one that created Saint Helena's Parish out of Granville County, the area around Port Royal.[49]

The Church of England clergy disliked the new law and they turned to the mother country for aid. Gideon Johnston returned to England in the spring of 1713 to improve his health and to lobby for an improvement in the establishment. The clergy raised £200 on their own bond to pay his debts and asked the SPG to "give Credit" to his account of the "Particular necessities" under which they operated. The clergy hoped that the SPG would encourage the government of South Carolina to consult with them before making any new laws affecting the establishment. Their major complaint was that the power given to the Carolina laity by the establishment acts weakened the authority of the bishop of London and was contrary to the "Constitutions and Practice of the Church of England." "Ye manner of Instituting and Inducting Ministers" through parish elections was the major sore point. Moreover the ministers claimed that the new authority given to the ecclesiastical commission meant that a minister's election could be disputed for capricious reasons. Johnston believed it was merely a device for putting removal power into the hands of the laity. Similarly obnoxious was the fact that South Carolina vestries rather than the ministers selected parish clerks and sextons; furthermore, vestrymen refused to give a veto power over their proceedings to the parish rector and even carried on business without him. In explaining that "the Episcopal Authority and Jurisdiction is Extremely deprest if not almost quite sunk," Johnston noted that the bishop of London had been called "a Pope, nay worse than the Pope." Some of the people who spoke in this manner were those who attributed the establishment of the church to their own efforts. For Johnston it was "plain by the new Schemes of Church Government Erected in the Transmarine parts that our Constitution at home is, in the Opinion of our Foreign Legislators, all wrong."[50]

Johnston offered the SPG an opportunity to assert its authority against that of the Carolina laity. Gilbert Jones, sent by Bishop Compton to Saint Bartholomew's Parish in Colleton County, had instead been hired by Christ Church Parish, located just across the harbor from Charles Town. Christ Church had petitioned the SPG for a missionary, however, and at Johnston's insistence the church commission waited eight months before issuing a writ for Jones' election. Several months after Jones had been elected, Nathaniel Osborne arrived, sent by the SPG to serve Christ Church in the position filled by Jones. Osborne served Saint Bartholomew's while Johnston carried the news to England and suggested that the case provided "a good handle for the Society to insist upon their Right." He wanted the SPG to give Osborne the choice of either parish in order to rebuke the laity. The SPG apparently did not share the commissary's interest in a show of strength since it allowed the ministers to stay where they were and even gave Jones a missionary's allowance.[51]

Johnston was similarily unsuccessful in another attempt to strengthen the church using English authority. While in England he learned that Philipe De Richebourg, a former Huguenot clergyman now in Anglican orders, was continuing to use Calvinist forms despite several warnings. Johnston recommended that the licenses of both Richebourg and John La Pierre be withdrawn. La Pierre had behaved since his first warning, but Johnston believed that his heart was "not with us, but at Geneva or Elsewhere" and that "the Love of Loaves oblige them to dissemble."[52] Johnston's suggestion went to John Robinson, the new bishop of London (Henry Compton having died in July 1713). Robinson was much less interested in American affairs than his predecessor had been: his reaction to this proposal is unknown, but the two ministers kept their licenses.

The pleas for spiritual authority that came from South Carolina and other colonies were not ignored by religious leaders in England. For some time plans had been underway to settle a bishop in the American colonies. Henry Compton had believed a suffragan bishop would be best. Suffragan bishops had no political power and so were deemed less offensive to vested colonial interests, but they could confirm laymen, ordain ministers, and consecrate churches. At first the SPG favored this idea, but by 1713 it had evolved a program calling for four American bishops with full authority, two to be stationed in the West Indies, one in New Jersey, and another in Virginia. Queen Anne apparently approved this idea, and a bill was being prepared at her death in August 1714. The SPG petitioned George I along the same lines, but the new Whig government was not interested.[53]

Political events also made it unlikely that the SPG would take the interventionist approach to colonial affairs that Johnston advocated. An era of High Church ascendancy ended with the death of Anne. In 1715 the Society for Promoting Christian Knowledge (SPCK) came under attack by the Whigs for its Jacobite sympathies. The SPCK and SPG memberships overlapped to a great extent, and moderate or timid members of both organizations resigned rather than face political persecution. The setback was only temporary, but in 1716 the SPG had to reduce its expenditures owing to a falling off of contributions.[54]

Gideon Johnston remained in England for two years, improving his health and gaining some financial aid for himself from the proprietors. He returned to South Carolina in the summer of 1715 while the colony was in the midst of the Yamasee Indian War.[55] The clergy performed creditably during the conflict, but their old problems remained when it was over. In December 1715, Johnston urged the SPG to consult with the proprietors about a reformation of "the senseless and ridiculous Church Government" of South Carolina. In April 1716, a parishioner warned him of the consequences that would follow a strict enforcement of Anglican procedure: "In case I cannot have Mr. Whitehead [Johnston's assistant] to Cresend my Children at my hows I can have them Cresend by a dissenter Minister which I don't Dout but they will git as sone to Heaven that way as the other. . . ." Johnston's involvement with these issues came to an end on April 23 when he drowned in Charles Town harbor following a boating accident.[56]

The establishment of the Church of England was effected in 1704, but its "settlement," to use Commissary Johnston's term, took much longer. Part of the process involved a compromise between Anglicans and dissenters in which the former retained their state church and the latter won a broad toleration. Another aspect involved the constitution of the church. In 1706 the Anglicans weakened their lay commission under pressure from England, but they had no intention of placing the church as a whole under ecclesiastical control. In the ensuing years Anglican parishioners chose their own ministers, and the government carefully preserved the rights of the laity in all legislation affecting the church. Lay power was a settled policy by 1716, a fact recognized even by the clergy, who nonetheless refused to accept it.

CHAPTER 3

THE CHURCH OF ALEXANDER GARDEN

Despite the manifest determination of the provincial laity to control the establishment themselves, the Anglican clergymen in South Carolina continued to identify with authorities in England. This was particularly evident in 1719 when the colonists overthrew proprietary government and the ministers continued to support a defunct regime, earning for themselves a great deal of local ill will. Fortunately for the church, Anglo-American politics did pay off when Sir Francis Nicholson became the first royal governor and used his position to strengthen the establishment. Commissary Alexander Garden laid a more solid foundation for the church by disciplining ill-behaved clergymen and humoring the prejudices of the laity; under him the establishment became a more integral part of the social and political structure of the colony. Garden's work was none too soon because in 1740 George Whitefield brought the Great Awakening to South Carolina and launched a powerful attack on Anglican religious hegemony. In the years after the Awakening the establishment changed again: the SPG and the bishop of London ceased to be important influences, and the state church finally began to operate on its own.

The Yamasee War, which began with a surprise attack by the Indians in 1715, inaugurated a difficult period for the clergy of the Church of England. All the ministers were temporarily dislocated by the hostilities and some, permanently. Two parishes, Saint Bartholomew's and Saint Helena's, were so devastated that they were not resettled for some time, and the SPG finally transferred one missionary out of the colony. Gideon Johnston's death was another blow, and it was followed in December 1715 by the death of Francis Le Jau and in 1716 by that of Robert Maule, both of whom had served in the colony since 1707 and were liked and respected by clergy and parishioners alike.[1] The clergy also suffered along with the colonists as the result of a severe inflation following the Indian war. Robert Johnson, the son of Sir Nathaniel, became governor in 1717, and he helped to secure an increase in salary for the ministers.[2] Finally there was bad publicity resulting from the activities of the Reverend William Wye, a dishonest and disreputable Anglican clergyman, who caused a scandal in the colony before fleeing to Virginia in 1720 to avoid paying his debts.[3]

The clergy suffered less from William Wye, however, than they did from their own refusal to support the colonists in their struggle against the proprietors. In December 1719, the Commons House turned itself into a governing convention of the people and petitioned the Crown to accept South Carolina as a royal colony. The proprietors had taken very little interest in the welfare of the province, and when they did involve themselves they were apt to listen to the wrong people, particularly Nicholas Trott. Against the wishes of Governor Johnson, they vetoed a number of important measures that might have controlled inflation. Nor were they any help in matters of defense; just as they fended for themselves during the Indian war, the Carolinians had to deal with a pirate menace in 1719 without aid from their lordships. Rumors of an impending Spanish invasion provided the final impetus for the revolt. Governor Johnson remained loyal to the proprietors who had appointed him, and the convention replaced him with James Moore, Jr.[4]

William Tredwell Bull, rector of Saint Paul's Parish and Gideon Johnston's successor as commissary, articulated the position of the church on the revolt. Bull advised the SPG that he would not acknowledge the new government until it was confirmed in England: he was happy that none of the clergy had supported the rebels since "the people can never be Supposed to be ye proper Judges in such a case."[5] A conservative political philosophy was probably not the only factor motivating Bull. Despite their recent support for toleration, the proprietors had given the church a good deal of aid, and Trott and William Rhett, another proprietary favorite, were closely attached to the SPG. Probably Bull felt the interest of the church would be better protected by the proprietors than by the people or the Crown.

Events rapidly forced the clergy to take sides. Governor Moore ordered the ministers to marry no one without a license from him, and Johnson, now a pretender to the executive office, declared that he alone was commissioned to issue marriage licenses. In a quandary, the Anglican clergy attempted to have people merely post banns rather than use licenses. When this failed they resolved to obey Johnson and found themselves "but coldly loo ed upon by yt prest Governmt here" and insulted, first "by some of the inferior sort," and later "by many & by some that Are none of the meanest of the people." Nor did the colonists stop with insults: parishioners in Saint George's Parish refused to elect Peter Tustion, an SPG missionary who had arrived early in 1720.[6] William Guy, rector of Saint Andrew's Parish, reported that "ye people in genl have Entertaind an Extraordinary prejudice againt ye Clergy. . . ." The assembly considered a motion to end the ministers' salaries and "to send ym out of ye Country to get a better Sett of Clergy as they were pleased to term it." Guy heard that the motion had failed only because someone pointed out that the measure might prejudice the colony's case in England.[7]

The clergy were "Comforted" at the end of 1720 by the news that Sir Francis Nicholson would be the new royal governor of South Carolina. Nicholson was one of England's most experienced and capable colonial administrators and also a strong proponent of the colonial Church of England. His disposition, military training, and political allegiances made him an advocate of the more authoritarian aspects of British government, and he seems to have viewed the church as a natural and necessary vehicle for promoting popular obedience. As lieutenant governor of Virginia he had pushed the interests of the Church of England, and in Maryland in the 1690s he was instrumental in molding the new Anglican establishment. He was a charter member of the SPG, and in the summer of 1720 he accepted a "Deputation" to look into SPG affairs in South Carolina.[8]

Nicholson arrived in the colony in May 1721 and immediately began. to improve the state of the establishment. In July he wrote the SPG asking for more missionaries, and on receipt of the letter it agreed to provide them.[9] In March 1722 the Carolina government created a new parish named Prince George in the rapidly developing Winyaw section in the northern part of the colony, and in June it passed "An Act for the advancing the Salaries of the Clergy." The Anglican clergy believed

that the quick and unanimous approval of the latter measure was owing
to Nicholson's "earnest and pathetick Speech to both houses of assembly." Each clergyman would now receive about £75 sterling each year
from the government, "a very generous Settemt," they called it, "as
much as we cou'd reasonable expect or desire."

Describing the "Flourishing State of ye Church," the clergy also
noted that Nicholson's example and encouragement were chiefly responsible for the fact that the new Saint Philip's Church would soon be
finished. Moreover, on the governor's recommendation the assembly
voted funds to improve churches in the parishes of Saint Paul's, Saint
Andrew's, and Saint George's, and to rebuild the parsonage of Saint
James, Goose Creek, that had recently burned.[10] The magnitude of the
change in attitude that had taken place is indicated by the comments of
Arthur Middleton, president of the council, and James Moore, speaker
of the Commons House, in a letter to the SPG: "We have this peculiar
happiness that our Clergy not only by their preaching but by their lives
and example show forth the Doctrine they profess...."[11] The animosi-
ties of 1720 seem to have been forgotten; once more the state church
had the backing of the government.

There was a limit, however, to the support that the representatives of
the people would give to the Church of England, as Nicholson found
when he attempted to curtail the privileges of the South Carolina dissenters. The first in a series of conflicts had to do with marriage licenses, which were issued by bishops in England but by governors in
the colonies. In 1713 the Anglican clergy had complained that the
privilege of marrying people was extended to dissenting ministers, particularly to two "Anabaptist Teachers,...Mechanicks...one being a
Ship Carpenter and the other a Tallow Chandler." In 1721 and again in
1722 they renewed their complaints, arguing that dissenters in the colony enjoyed a greater latitude than they did in England, which was
probably not true.[12] In any case, Nicholson did for a time stop issuing
licenses to dissenting clergymen. Archibald Stobo, a Presbyterian minister, responded by drawing up a petition to the Commons House asking
for the joint establishment of Presbyterianism in the colony, based on
the recognition of the Presbyterian church in the Act of Union between
England and Scotland. Nicholson appears to have backed down: Stobo
did not present his petition, and no more complaints about marriage
licenses came from either side.[13]

In 1721, when his influence in the colony was fresh, Nicholson did succeed in forcing the Commons to accept a qualifying oath for new members that had to be sworn on the Bible. This was obnoxious to some legislators, probably Quakers, and in 1724 the Commons sought to have the provision removed. "Protestant Dissenters," it claimed, were a "great part of ye Body of this Province," they had supported and defended the colonial government, and their "truly Scrupulous Consciences" deserved indulgence. Nicholson replied by questioning the size, the motives, and the loyalty of the dissenting population and by pointing out that the oath was required by his instructions. The lower house dropped the matter, but its moderate religious views worried the governor. He warned the SPG that if the Salary Act of 1722 were not confirmed in England it might be repealed in the Colony.[14]

Nicholson was also bothered by an influx of dissenting ministers. In July 1724, Nathan Basset, a recent graduate of Harvard College, arrived in Charles Town to fill a vacancy at the Presbyterian church. The congregation had written to Boston for a minister, and Basset was ordained and recommended by three eminent divines of that city, Cotton Mathcr, Benjamin Colman, and William Cooper. Nicholson interviewed Basset and flew into a rage, asserting that the Boston clergy had no right to send Basset to a particular church since the preference to clerical livings was the governor's prerogative. Basset remained nonetheless, and a month later two more Presbyterian ministers arrived from Scotland. Nicholson warned the bishop of London that these undesirables "Infuse Ante Monarchical Principles into the People and are Setting up for an Independt Government both in Church and State...."[15]

Sir Francis Nicholson left South Carolina in 1725 and never returned to the colony. The Church of England was much stronger than he had found it, but several basic problems remained. Some difference still existed between the Anglican clergy and the provincial laity with regard to the government of the church and the position of the dissenters. In addition the difficult problem of internal control within the establishment persisted. Several years after William Wye left the colony in disgrace, the Reverend Francis Merry was discharged by Saint James, Goose Creek Parish, for excessive drinking, and there were other problem clergymen as well. William Tredwell Bull returned to England in 1723 and resigned his post as commissary.[16] His successor, the Reverend Alexander Garden, was not appointed until 1728, but he served for nearly twenty years and did a remarkable job of dealing with the problems of the church.

Garden held a master's degree from the University of Aberdeen and had been a curate at the prestigious Barking Church in London before coming to South Carolina in 1720. He began to serve Saint Philip's Church immediately, but was not elected rector until 1725 because of the popular resentment toward the clergy that followed the Revolution of 1719. As pastor of Saint Philip's, Garden received a higher salary than did the country clergy and served in a church that the clergy described as "a Work of. . . Magnitude Regularity Beauty & Solidity. . . , the greatest ornamt of this City & an Honor to the whole province being not. . . paralleled in his Majestys Domminions in America."[17] Garden's position made him something of a natural leader for the clergy, and his strong personality fitted the role. In fact he acted to discipline unruly ministers even before he received his appointment as commissary.

In the spring of 1725 Garden became annoyed when John La Pierre, a former Huguenot and the rector of Saint Dennis Parish, baptized a child at the home of the parents in Saint Philip's Parish without Garden's permission. Garden could find no extenuating circumstances and said that the action fitted "a thief and a robber" better than "ye Shepherd." He complained to the bishop of London that he had brought his parish to a "tolerable good Order and Conformity," particularly in regard to baptizing children in church, and that his good work was now threatened by La Pierre's action. Unless steps were taken to prevent the intervention of one clergyman in the affairs of another, "one disorderly Brother will be able easily to break down whatever the rest shall be able to build up."[18]

Garden took stronger action in the fall of 1728 with regard to the Reverend John Winteley of Christ Church Parish. Winteley's penchant for women and liquor had postponed his election as rector; finally the vestry gave up hope for his reform and dismissed him. The members were concerned that the SPG would be upset, but they felt more than justified since Winteley's behavior was driving local Anglicans to the Presbyterian church. Meanwhile Winteley wrote to the SPG, claiming that he was the target of a politically motivated attack, and asked to be transferred to another parish. Despite the dismissal he attempted to continue serving in Christ Church and was successful for one Sunday.

Subsequently, his opponents locked the church and then the vestry house, and Winteley was reduced to reading prayers in the churchyard. When Winteley next came to church, the parishioners forcibly restrained him from entering until Alexander Garden had settled himself in the pulpit. Garden gave a full service, retired for dinner with the vestry, and later informed Winteley that he intended to officiate in Christ Church whenever possible. He also attempted to prosecute the deposed minister for disturbing the peace during his first service. Winteley left Christ Church, and the SPG later fired him from his missionary position.[19]

Garden's behavior was significant. By openly siding with the vestry and serving in the parish, he made it clear that he approved of the existing government of the church. Heretofore Church of England ministers had tolerated the election process and the attendant power it gave to the vestry and the people as a necessary evil, since the practice was utterly foreign to Anglicanism in its native land; now the rector of Charles Town gave positive sanction to the discipline of a clergyman by his vestry. His action supported and reinforced the idea that lay power should be used in the absence of ecclesiastical authority and that ancient custom should give way to present necessity.

While Garden was occupied with Winteley, events were taking place in England that would greatly strengthen the South Carolina church. Edmund Gibson succeeded to the See of London in 1723 and began to place his overseas authority on a more permanent basis. In April 1728, Gibson received "A Royal Commission for exercising an Ecclesiastical Jurisdiction in the American Plantations," which empowered him to appoint commissaries and provide for the discipline of Anglican clergymen. Not long after that, he made Alexander Garden Commissary for North and South Carolina and the Island of Providence.

Garden's commission gave license to his activist disposition. Gibson instructed his commissaries to hold yearly visitations for the purpose of imparting information to the clergy and conferring with them on church affairs. They were also to check into the credentials of each minister, to keep abreast of the state of church buildings and lands, and to inform the bishop on all matters relative to the Church of England. Detailed instructions explained the proper method for dealing with clergymen who were irregular either in their duties or their personal conduct. The commissary was to admonish privately, then publicly if necessary, and finally institute judicial proceedings against recalcitrants. The instructions encouraged temporary suspensions from office and benefice rather than permanent deprivations.[20]

Garden held his first visitation in the fall of 1729. He communicated his commission and Gibson's instructions to the clergymen and urged them "to behave in every Instance of their Duty, as the ministry May in Nothing be blamed," lest he suffer "the Pain of reducing any of them to the same by the Force of the Ecclesiastical Laws."[21] Whether owing to Gaden's influence or not, there were no serious disciplinary problems in the first four years following his appointment.

Garden created the first ecclesiastical court in the history of South Carolina in 1734 to deal with the Reverend John Fulton, who had replaced John Winteley in Christ Church Parish. Fulton was serving unelected, but the vestrymen were unwilling to remove him lest the bishop and the SPG take them for a "humoursome & Captious [capricious] people." They were happy that an ecclesiastical remedy existed, and Garden was willing, even anxious, to use his judicial power.[22]

The court was held at Christ Church in late April in conjunction with the annual visitation of the clergy. A "Promoter," a Charles Town attorney hired by Garden, brought the charge of habitual drunkenness. Fulton's parishioners gave evidence against him, and the judgment was made by Garden in the role of "Judge" and the Reverend William Guy and Thomas Hasel, who assisted him as "Assessors." Fulton received a two-year suspension, but this effectively deprived him of his parish since Christ Church did not intend to take him back. Bishop Gibson later faulted Garden for not admonishing Fulton in a "judicial" (presumably public) manner before proceeding to a court action. He also felt that the court costs were too high. Garden pled ignorance to the first charge and claimed the costs were as low as possible. Local lawyers were opposed to the use of ecclesiastical courts and therefore charged fees equal to those in civil cases: Garden's "promoter" would take nothing less than a guinea a day for each of his two trips to Christ Church Parish.[23]

So ended the first attempt at formal ecclesiastical discipline. The method was successful, but it was also troublesome, and Gibson's commission did not cover all circumstances. Garden lamented once that there was no legal way for him to bring to trial a loose-living chaplain of a garrison at Port Royal. Most of the evidence, however, indicates that Garden exercised effective control over the clergy. His visitations usually found the ministers functioning regularly. He allowed one wandering clergyman to officiate in long-suffering Christ Church Parish; the man turned out badly, but Bishop Gibson provided evidence against the culprit, who was quickly arrested. Perhaps the best example of effective discipline came in 1736 when the mere commencement of legal action by Garden induced a clergyman to give up his claim to a parish that did not want him.[24]

Moral behavior on the part of ministers was part of Garden's value system as a clergyman and as commissary, but clerical discipline arose from an interest in public relations as well as internal reform. It stemmed from an abiding concern for better relations with the laity. This was particularly clear in his handling of a series of difficulties between the Reverend Andrew Leslie and the parish of Saint Paul in Colleton County. Leslie arrived in the parish in the fall of 1729 and began to create animosity immediately. At the visitation in October 1730, Garden discussed with the clergy a letter from a churchwarden in Saint Paul's that claimed Leslie had refused to baptize children unless two communicants of the church stood as sureties or the child was near death. Leslie's brethren warned him that such rigid demands were not the usual practice in South Carolina and urged "not an absolute insisting on this Canon . . . , but a prudential only." Garden explained to Bishop Gibson that there were few communicants in the province relative to the number of children, and since sickness was frequent and often quickly fatal Leslie's policy could easily result in children dying without the sacrament. There was also the risk of the children's "Parents carrying them to Dissenting Teachers for the Administra'n of that sacred Ordinance." Leslie maintained his position for a time before heeding the advice. In 1731 Garden praised his general behavior, but noted there was a deep prejudice against him that would require time and effort to remove. In the spring of 1734, anxious to return to England for medical reasons, Leslie forced the issue of his popularity by obtaining a precept for his election from the church commissioners. The election was held and Leslie was rejected by a majority (forty-seven to sixteen). In justification the vestry claimed that the minister had obtained the precept without its consent and that the parish was unhappy with his overall behavior.[25]

Actually the situation was even more confused. As "some inhabitants" of the parish wrote to Garden shortly after the election, the main issue was simply whether any minister at all should be elected. It rained on the day of the election and few of the regular parishioners voted. Instead, a host of "mean & unknown" people from the coastal portion of the parish packed the election. They were motivated by the idea "that the Business of all ministers when Elected is to bear a tyrannicall Sway over their Parishioners...," from which followed the proposition "that it was better for the Parish to govern one man than for one man to govern the whole parish." Much of this was consistent with the sentiments in a letter signed "Liberty" that was circulated before the election. The author argued, on the one hand, that the office of minister was too important to entrust to any man, and, on the other, that Leslie was a particularly bad man. Garden's correspondents said "Liberty" was a man well known to the commissary and he had a long grudge against Leslie. They went on to say that the parish was soon to be divided and that not six of those who voted against Leslie lived in the main part. The division did take place, and it improved Leslie's position. About six weeks after his electoral defeat, the minister returned to England with the promise of future support from the new churchwardens and vestrymen of Saint Paul's. They claimed that Leslie's enemies were now in the new parish of Saint John's, Colleton County, which included the islands of Saint John's and Edisto. Only one of the old church officers remained. As for themselves, they expressed affection and respect for Leslie, promised him good treatment on his return, and were certain he could win a future election.[26]

The possibility of Leslie returning to Saint Paul's worried Alexander Garden. He explained the situation to the SPG, echoing the charge of the first vestry that Leslie had obtained an election precept without its consent. Although he believed the minister was "very acceptable to a considerable Majority of his Parish," Garden noted that there were "Still Some leading Men pretty Sanguine against him" and suggested that it would not be wise to "risque a new Sceen [*sic*] of Contention." To the bishop of London he added that Leslie's behavior was "Stiff & assuming towd his Parishioners, more like that of a young conceited Collegian, than of a prudent Clergyman." There were still some in the parish who would "make his Life uneasy...and create me trouble in hearing Complaints...." More about Garden's attitude was revealed when the SPG asked him whether an order from the vestry was necessary before an election precept could be issued by the church commissioners. The law, he replied, did not require a vestry order, but it was "expedient" in order to prevent an issuance to no purpose. Moreover the commissary went on to admit that the vestry had given a verbal order to the churchwardens to secure a precept, but they had not done it because Garden and Dr. Nicholas Trott had suggested waiting until a written order was issued. At this point Leslie had stepped in and requested the precept. Summing up, Garden was "rather inclin'd to think" it would be best for both the parish and the minister if Leslie did not return.[27]

Garden almost had his wish. Leslie vacationed in Ireland while recovering his health. In February 1735 he was still too infirm to journey to London and sail to America. He asked about the possibility of an Irish cure, and the SPG, taking his illness into account along with Garden's warning, resolved to dismiss him with a year's salary. Leslie pulled himself together, however, and was ready to sail in May. His return in September was triumphant: "Most of the Principall of the Gentlemen" met him at the parish boundary "with great marks of Sincere Joy and affection." The following year he was elected rector of Saint Paul's.[28]

The salient aspect of Garden's role in the Leslie affair was the consistency with which the commissary supported the parish against his own minister. In the baptism issue Garden seems to have taken a reasonable position although he acted after hearing from only one churchwarden in what must have been a private letter. His response to Leslie's rejection was much more peculiar. He dismissed without objection the anticlerical principles manifested by the voters. When an Anglican cleric was rejected by his parishioners on such grounds, one would think his superior would be provoked to a militant defense of ministerial prerogative; but Garden was content to avoid further difficulty regardless of the discomfort to Leslie. Nor was his attitude simply a due regard for public opinion: after the parish division, he admitted Leslie could be elected. The commissary was simply concerned about a small group (the vestry said one person) of the more important people. His attitude toward Leslie's return seems to have been dictated by the feeling that Leslie would offend a few people while a new minister would be acceptable to all. This was considerate of the parish but callous toward Leslie.

Besides favoring the laity, or some members of it, against his own ministers, Garden also displayed a tolerant attitude toward the feelings of the province as a whole. In the fall of 1732 he was upset because the new incumbent at the Huguenot church in Charles Town claimed to be an ordained Anglican clergyman while at the same time he officiated in the Calvinist manner. The Reverend Francis Guichard used whichever liturgy the people wanted and felt the matter of no importance. Garden did not know how to discipline the minister since Guichard's living was not within the church. Moreover, as he wrote Gibson, the French were on good terms with the Anglican church and many had been converted to it, but they were easily aroused, and if he were to take action against Guichard they "wou'd...be apt to make much ado about it, take up Much Prejudice agt the Chh upon it, & run it into a Party Quarrel." Gibson apparently felt this was sound counsel for no more came of the matter.[29]

Seven years later Garden showed similar restraint in a situation where he might have tried to gain a march on the dissenters. A Presbyterian minister named Moir left his congregation in the parish of Saint John's, Colleton County, and journeyed to England to seek ordination as an Anglican priest. After Moir's departure, dissenters in Saint John's publicized their view that his conversion to the church was motivated by monetary considerations and convinced local Anglicans that Garden had recommended Moir to be the Church of England rector of the parish. The Anglican laity informed Garden that it would not accept the turncoat. In fact, Garden had given Moir a character reference, but it said nothing about a future position. Now he suggested to Bishop Gibson that, if ordained, Moir be sent somewhere other than South Carolina. In a similar situation Gideon Johnston, Garden's predecessor, had attempted to use the conversion to a partisan advantage; Garden valued peace more than controversy.[30]

While Garden worked to make the church more acceptable within the province, he took steps also to make it more independent of English influences. He wanted it to be more of a church and less of a mission post, but there was some question whether the colony wanted the status and responsibility that he had in mind. Garden informed the bishop that South Carolina was capable of paying the full salaries of the ministers in its state church, but that there was no indication that the government would offer to do so. He suggested that the SPG take public note that the province was out of its "lower circumstances" and now "more Opulent & flourishing" and urge the assembly to undertake the full maintenance of the clergy, at least in the richer parishes. If the government did not act, Garden added, new missionaries would still have an adequate income if the SPG reduced their salaries from £50 to £40 sterling. The commissary made it clear that if Gibson were to make use of "these two Hints," Garden would like it done without the use of his name.[31]

Garden made his secret proposals at the end of 1733. The governor at that time was again Robert Johnson, the son of Sir Nathaniel and a staunch friend of the established church. In the spring of 1735 Johnson showed Garden a letter from the SPG stating that financial difficulty forced it to lower the stipends of new missionaries to £40 and noting its appreciation for the salaries offered by the South Carolina government. Johnson felt this last was a subtle hint that the province should make up the difference in the missionaries' salaries. Garden told the governor that despite the gentle wording the intended meaning was that the government should take over the entire burden, at least in some parishes. Johnson was not at all taken aback: "He made no question but the assembly wou'd make such Provision in 2 or 3 years time"; until then it was heavily committed to financial aid for new settlers. Garden seemed near his goal, but governor Johnson died on May 3 and the bright prospect darkened abruptly. These affairs required the active cooperation of the chief executive, and Garden could only hope that bishop Gibson would intercede with the new appointee in London.[32]

The clergy gathered in June 1736, feeling some concern about the state of the establishment. They agreed unanimously that missionaries who served in parishes for more than one year should insist on being elected or being informed in writing why they were not. They also sent a letter to the church commissioners asking that an adjustment be made in their salaries, since proclamation money had fallen in value relative to current bills, and the salary law provided for such periodic changes. Despite these brave ventures there was a note of pessimism in Garden's report. He reiterated that the "Zeal and Interest of a Settled Governr" would be necessary before the SPG was relieved of supporting South Carolina clergymen. Somewhat nervously he pointed out that if the SPG were to withdraw its aid before local provisions were made, all that the organization had successfully built up might be torn down.[33] Garden's hopes for the province seemed premature.

While the Anglican establishment in South Carolina was not everything its commissary would have liked, it was much stronger in 1740 than it had been twenty years earlier. That was fortunate because the Reverend George Whitefield visited the colony in January of that year; for the next twelve months his personal charisma and his evangelical message posed a massive threat to the state church.

The Great Awakening began in South Carolina on Sunday, January 5, 1740, when Whitefield preached in the dissenting meetinghouse in Charles Town. Garden was out of town, and his assistant had refused Whitefield access to the pulpit of Saint Philip's. The next day he preached once again at the meetinghouse and then later at the Huguenot church; both audiences were packed and visibly moved. He left the following day for Georgia, where he spent the next few months superintending the construction of the Bethesda orphanage and composing a series of letters that were printed in Philadelphia and widely read in the colonies.[34]

Whitefield's letters elaborated his attack on the Church of England, of which he was a nominal member. Archibishop Tillotson, beloved Anglican father and master of homiletics, "knew no more of Christianity than Mahomet," and Richard Allestree's *The Whole Duty of Man*, the standard Anglican handbook of popular piety, was "calculated to *civilize*, but...it never was a Means of *converting* one single soul." Whitefield based both criticisms on his firm belief in the doctrine of predestination in all its Calvinist rigor and his hostility to the Anglican position known as Arminianism.[35]

Of particular importance to Alexander Garden and the church was Whitefield's piece entitled *A Letter to the Inhabitants of Maryland, Virginia, North and South Carolina*, in which he argued that southern slaves should be brought into the Christian religion. The Church of England had long supported this position, but Whitefield argued for his own brand of conversion. Responding to the well-known argument of the planters that Christian blacks became worse slaves, he blamed their instruction: "They were baptized and taught to read and write, and this they may do, and much more, and yet be far from the Kingdom of God." He challenged anyone to produce a slave who had experienced the "New Birth" and who became a worse servant.

Having denounced their ministry, Whitefield went on to impugn the character of the clergy in the southern colonies. Heathen slaves were symptomatic of religious conditions: "A general Deadness as to Divine things, and not to say a general Prophaneness [*sic*], is discernible both in Pastors and People." Despite the large number of Anglican clergymen, Whitefield claimed that most southerners were without "any teaching Priests." He made an example of South Carolina by citing a series of disasters that had recently befallen the colony: a smallpox epidemic in 1738, a severe outbreak of yellow fever in 1739, and the Stono slave insurrection that same year. These events Whitefield saw as warnings to all the southern colonies: "God first generally corrects us with Whips; if that will not do, he must chastize us with Scorpions."[36]

Whitefield returned to South Carolina in the middle of March and visited Alexander Garden at Saint Philip's rectory. The commissary charged the young clergyman with an excess of pride and enthusiasm and demanded proof for his statements against the Anglican clergymen. Whitefield claimed they were proven by the fact that the ministers did not preach justification by faith alone; after further discussion he decided that Garden "was as ignorant as the rest" on that issue. The commissary then charged Whitefield with breaking his ordination vow and the canons of the Church of England and declared that if Whitefield spoke from any "public church" in the province, he would suspend him. The evangelist answered that he would treat that with the same respect as "a Pope's bull." Whitefield went on to attack the "assemblies and balls" that were held in Charles Town for the entertainment of the provincial upper class, and Garden responded that they were less a threat to religion than were the "Mobb-Preachings and the Assemblies" held by Whitefield where men, women, and children were encouraged to become conceited in their own righteousness and to attack the morality of others. The interview ended when Garden ordered Whitefield out of his house.[37]

Many people in Charles Town did not share the commissary's hostility toward Whitefield. The evangelist preached at the independent meetinghouse in the afternoon on Friday, March 14, the day of his confrontation with Garden, and then twice each day until he left the following Wednesday morning. On at least one occasion the meetinghouse could not hold the crowd, and Whitefield delivered his sermon in the churchyard. He was pleased with his reception and left South Carolina with the feeling "that God intended to visit some in Charleston with His salvation." *The South Carolina Gazette* praised his performance.[38]

Whitefield returned to South Carolina in July, and this time Garden followed through on his threat to use ecclesiastical censure. The commissary issued a proclamation enjoining all clergymen to inform Whitefield that his appearance was required in Saint Philip's Church on July 15 to answer charges against his behavior, in particular his failure to use the *Book of Common Prayer* during services. Whitefield appeared before his judges, Garden and several other clergymen, but immediately questioned the authority of the court. Garden produced his commission from Gibson, and after more wrangling he adjourned the court until the next day so Whitefield might assure himself the proceedings were justified in law. The commissary's understanding was that once the question of jurisdiction was established Whitefield would submit to a judicial ruling. Instead Whitefield responded with a plea of *recusatio judicis*, which claimed that Garden had shown himself to be unalterably prejudiced and asked that six arbitrators be appointed to rule on whether or not he was a fit judge in the case. Whitefield named three of the arbitrators, "two Independents and one french Calvinist and all of them his zealous Admirers," according to Garden. The commissary found these candidates to be defective through their own interest in the case and rejected the *recusatio* plea.

He later explained that if he had accepted the plea and appointed arbitrators of his own, the issue would almost certainly have been a tie. How to proceed in that event was a question for which Garden had no answer. Moreover, if the arbiters had found the commissary unfit, who then, he wondered, would be the judge, there being no other ecclesiastical official in the South. On the third morning of the trial Whitefield appealed Garden's rejection of the *recusatio judicis* to the High Court of Chancery in England. Garden accepted the appeal with the provision that Whitefield prosecute the case within one year.[39]

With the judicial proceedings in abeyance, Garden launched another attack on Whitefield. In August the *South Carolina Gazette* published *Six Letters from the Rev. Mr. Garden to the Rev. Mr. Whitfield* [sic], in which Garden attempted to refute Whitefield's major contentions. He claimed that the Church of England did teach that salvation came through faith, but the faith had to be "true and lively" and therefore it must produce "good Fruits or Works," which were a "necessary *Condition*" of justification but not a "*meritorious* Cause." Garden also accused Whitefield of taking much of his own material from Tillotson, plagiarizing the archbishop before damning him. To Whitefield's accusation that regeneration was not mentioned in *The Whole Duty of Man*, Garden answered that the term appeared only twice in the Bible, neither time in the sense Whitefield used it.[40]

Despite Garden's efforts, however, there is evidence that Whitefield had extensive support within the established church. He usually preached at the independent meetinghouse in Charles Town or in the dissenting churches outside the city, but the *Gazette* declared that the sermons met with "very general Acceptance," suggesting that Anglicans were present. Stronger evidence of Anglican support comes from the fact that Whitefield preached also at the Anglican churches in Christ Church Parish and Saint John's in Colleton County. At Christ Church the invitation came from the vestry and churchwardens, since the parish had no minister, and the circumstances were probably the same in Saint John's.[41]

There were also Anglican clergymen who did not share the commissary's harsh assessment of Whitefield. The Reverend Lewis Jones, rector of Saint Helena's Parish in Port Royal, had offered Whitefield hospitality there at least since January 1740. When the evangelist passed through Port Royal early in July, he and Jones had a pleasant discussion in which the rector took exception to Whitefield's views on justification and to his harsh treatment of Tillotson. Whitefield maintained his positions, but the two men shared a service in the evening, Jones reading prayers and Whitefield giving a sermon. On his way back to Georgia, Whitefield again preached at Port Royal. Garden was annoyed with Jones, but the clergyman claimed he would have alienated his congregation had he refused Whitefield use of the church. Whitefield's journal also mentioned a meeting with "Mr. T." at Pon Pon on July 22. This was probably the Reverend Thomas Thompson of Saint Bartholomew's Parish. Whitefield called the man "a church of England missionary who refused to preach or sit in judgement against me."[42]

Nonetheless the Church of England did articulate a strong position against Whitefield. Beginning in January 1740 an intellectual battle was waged in the pages of the *South Carolina Gazette* for the hearts and minds of the people of the province. The issues centered around George Whitefield and his religious style. The dissenters were anxious to show that Whitefield's success justified their own teachings, since the evangelist was a professed believer in the Calvinist doctrine of original sin. Anglicans responded to this with a more optimistic view of the human condition.[43] They also rallied behind the view that Whitefield's success owed more to human agency than to divine blessing. Whitefield's followers were taken in by his voice, "that enchanting *Sound*, the natural *and* alone *Cause*" of "all the Passion and Prejudice."[44] Moreover the

Awakening was as impractical as it was invalid. Whitefield was a comet, "a disorderly kind of a Star...that crosses and interferes with the Paths & Motions of...other Heavenly Bodies," but will soon "vanish like a Vapour."[45] In another metaphor, the evangelist was a will-o'-the wisp that "by a strolling kind of Light, seduces People out of the Way, misguides them into *Boggs* and *Fens*, and there bewildering leaves them—."[46]

For some time the Anglican arguments seem to have had little effect. Whitefield was in Charles Town from August 22 to September 1 and enjoyed a great success. His journal claimed that 4,000 people listened to his sermons.[47] Later in the fall the situation began to change. On November 24, Alexander Garden wrote a confident, almost brash, preface to a new publication, *Regeneration and the Testimony of the Spirit*, the tone reflecting his belief that time was weakening Whitefield's hold on the province. Immediate events may also have hastened the process unnaturally. Six days earlier Charles Town had experienced a catastrophe of massive proportions and the Church of England had dealt with the crisis in an effective manner while Whitefield was off in New England.

On November 18 a fire broke out in Charles Town and destroyed more than 300 homes and numerous mercantile establishments before being brought under control. The vestry of Saint Philip's Church assumed a major role in providing relief to the sufferers. The church officers met almost daily for two weeks after the disaster, receiving nearly £2000 in donations and dispensing immediate aid to victims of the flames. Collection at the church door on November 23, a fast day, totaled £683 12s. 6d. Other donations continued for another month and one-half. The assembly channeled £1,500 in aid through the vestry, the parish of Saint George gave nineteen barrels of rice, and £180 18s. collected at the Presbyterian meetinghouse was turned over to the Church of England for distribution. Poor families like Ester Brown and her nine children who received £10 for their "present necessities" and the numerous recipients whose names were followed by the designation "burnt out" were doubtless happy that the Anglican establishment was there to provide this mercy, however insufficient it may have been.[48]

If indeed there were those who saw the Church of England in a better light after the fire, there was at least one man who found in the same event confirmation of his distaste for the established church. This was

Hugh Bryan, a successful planter and a warm advocate of Whitefield. A letter from Bryan, dated two days after the fire, was published in the *South Carolina Gazette* for January 8, 1741. It interpreted the fire within the historical scheme Whitefield had set up in his piece on the need to convert Negroes. The fire now joined droughts, plagues, and military failures as the judgment of a righteous God against his wayward people. Bryan inveighed at length against priests who were too occupied with material interests to warn against present iniquity and future disaster. They were "Thieves and Robbers" who did not "follow the Foot-steps of our true Shepherd, but coveted the Fleece only." Bryan's letter got a ready response. On the day of its publication the author, the printer, and the Reverend George Whitefield were arrested for libeling the Church of England. Whitefield had been in Charles Town since January 4 and was accused of editing the letter for publication. He readily admitted the charge, but was able to obtain bail until the next quarterly court, by which time he was gone from the province.[49]

Garden was pleased at Whitefield's new legal difficulties; very likely he had instigated the action. Despite the fact that the charge was a public one, he reminded the bishop of London that funds would be necessary to see that prosecution was carried on in the most competent manner. Garden also appeared genuinely convinced that Whitefield's popularity had severely diminished by the time of his January leave-taking. The evangelist, wrote the commissary, had been "much elated at the Numbers that run to hear him; but now he has departed, greatly mortified on that Show's being over." Garden claimed that many former followers had left Whitefield. These statements have the ring of truth, although the *Gazette* declared that "great Companies of People" had visited Whitefield at his lodgings, and that "the congregations were numerous" at his twenty-two sermons.[50] In any event, the commissary had earned a little self congratulation: it had been quite a year.

George Whitefield did not return to South Carolina for a number of years after January 1741, and the excitement of 1740 gradually died down. On January 14, 1742, Commissary Alexander Garden officially suspended the evangelist from his office as a clergyman. Garden waited five months beyond the time when Whitefield should have prosecuted his appeal and acted only when Bishop Gibson informed him that no appeal was forthcoming. The suspension had no practical effect, but the commissary had done his duty and the case was closed.[51] The Great Awakening, nonetheless, remained a permanent influence. The *South Carolina Gazette* continued to carry debates about Whitefield, an Anglican school for Negroes came into existence, stimulated in part by the need to compete with Whitefield's good works, and evangelical ministers began to enter the province. These developments will be considered in some detail in later chapters. Here it is important to follow Garden's efforts to maintain order within the state church.

During the 1740s Garden found himself frustrated by the power exercised by the Society for the Propagation of the Gospel in the affairs of the South Carolina church. His attitude was tinged with pique: on one occasion he sharply reprimanded the SPG for using him as postmaster for a box headed to North Carolina.[52] For the most part, however, the commissary's ire was based on sound administrative principles. Conflict was inherent in the nature of divided authority, but it was exacerbated by the difference in perspective, by the slow and uncertain quality of communication between Charles Town and London, and by the fact that personal influence in England was often more important to a colonial clergyman's career than was his ability or the needs of the church.

An illustration of the general problem of divided authority occurred in 1740 when the SPG refused to discipline the Reverend Andrew Leslie. Leslie and another missionary made plans to leave South Carolina for the summer in order to preserve their health. Afraid these vacations would lead to others, Garden pressured the men to stay. The other minister was dissuaded, but Leslie resigned his post and left for good. Such precipitous leave-taking was unhandsome behavior toward the parish and the SPG, which expected its missionaries to remain until replaced, but the SPG ignored Garden's opinion and approved Leslie's conduct.[53]

King George's War offered new opportunities for Anglican clergymen, and the result was more conflict between the commissary and the SPG. The Reverend Stephen Roe, an Irish missionary and rector of Saint George's Parish, left South Carolina in 1742 when Bishop Gibson appointed him chaplain to the King's troops stationed in Boston. The following year a packet of letters in his handwriting fell into the hands of Joseph Blake, a vestryman and leading figure in Saint George's. As Commissary Garden explained to the SPG, the letters were directed to correspondents in Ireland and they concerned Roe's wife there, whom the minister was trying to divorce "on the cheapest Terms." What particularly aroused Garden's ire was the fact that Roe had always passed himself off as a bachelor and had wooed several ladies in South Carolina, including the daughter of Joseph Blake. The commissary wanted the SPG to encourage Bishop Gibson to discipline Roe.[54]

The SPG did not act with the force that Garden expected. Philip Bearcroft, secretary of the SPG, informed Roe of the charges and stated that the minister would have to prove his innocence. At the same time, however, Bearcroft declared that Garden had acted imprudently in making public the letters and notified Roe that the SPG had appointed him master of its school in Boston at a salary of £60 sterling. In Boston the Anglican commissary, Roger Price, wondered if Roe was fit to receive the sacrament, much less to dispense it. An answer came late in 1744 when after a long and steadfast denial Roe finally confessed to having fathered a child by his landlady's daughter. Learning of these developments, Commissary Garden indulged himself by criticizing the SPG for other aspects of Roe's mission: the minister had been overpaid and given duties that were too large for one man.[55]

Some of Garden's testiness was doubtless left over from his difficulties with the Reverend Thomas Thompson, whom the SPG had recently appointed to Saint George's parish. In the fall of 1742 the minister threatened to resign his original post in Saint Bartholomew's Parish because of its meager accommodations and the continued refusal of the vestry to agree to his election. The vestry believed that Thompson exaggerated the discomforts of the parish and that his recent appointment as chaplain to a man-of-war stationed in the area made him ineligible to be rector of the parish. Garden sided with the vestry, and, when Thompson did resign, the commissary forced the minister to leave the parish quickly so a replacement could be brought in. Thompson alleged that Garden also asked the vestrymen to add an accusation of wrongful behavior to their statement. In any case, the SPG had reappointed Thompson before it received the letter from his first parish.[56]

Thompson's case illustrates the complicated nature of Anglo-American church government. Garden claimed that the minister's behavior had declined from the time he became a naval chaplain. The commissary asked the SPG to prohibit missionaries from accepting such posts in the future since they always interfered with parochial duties. Further he asked the SPG not to determine cases "ex parte," but wait to hear the parish's side of the affair. Thompson defended his actions and asserted that Garden held a personal grudge against him. When the minister had returned to Charles Town in January 1742, after visiting England to improve his health, the commissary asked him to deliver a sermon in Saint Philip's. Thompson claimed he had prepared his discourse without knowing that Garden intended to read his final suspension of Whitefield during the service: the theme was "living peaceable [*sic*] with all men as far as 'tis possible," and it was looked upon by some as a rebuke to the commissary.[57] There is a plausible ring to Thompson's story, but Garden's complaints were also solidly grounded in fact. Moreover, while Thompson claimed to have suffered from his personal relationship with Garden, it seems likely that his success with the SPG was related to the goodwill of Philip Bearcroft, secretary of the SPG, to whose wife the missionary had brought a slave boy from South Carolina.[58] It is doubtful that Garden had moral scruples about the importance of personal influence in SPG affairs, but he undoubtedly felt frustration at the burden it put on his own administration.

Commissary Garden's efforts at keeping his church free from pluralism were also frustrated by Charles Boschi, whose English friend secured him an appointment as chaplain of the fort on Rattan, an island in the Gulf of Honduras. Boschi was a former Franciscan who had been an Anglican clergyman for some time before he arrived in South Carolina in the spring of 1745 to become the SPG missionary to Saint Bartholomew's Parish. Financial problems related to moving and settling plagued the minister, who had a wife and four children. The Rattan appointment, which they learned about in the spring of 1747, came as a windfall to the Boschi family: the salary was high, there were pension provisions, and Boschi's benefactor was working on an SPG appointment that would supplement the military position.[59]

At first there was nothing in this that bothered Alexander Garden. Boschi might be guilty of pluralism, but neither position was in South Carolina. Moreover Garden was probably happy to see Boschi leave: the missionary had preached in Saint Philip's once, and although Garden sat in the reading desk, he was unable to hear a sentence. When Boschi remained in South Carolina rather than taking ship for his new post, the commissary did become annoyed, thinking that the clergyman was trying to be rector of Saint Bartholomew's and chaplain of Rattan at the same time. Boschi claimed to be waiting for a man-of-war that would give him safe passage: as an apostate from the Church of Rome, he feared that enemy capture would mean being burned alive by the Inquisition. Garden hoped the war office would learn of this "pretence."[60] The situation was unchanged when the peace of Aix-la-Chapelle was proclaimed in South Carolina in June 1749, two years after Boschi might have left for his post. The minister was preparing to leave when news came that the Rattan garrison was reduced and the chaplaincy removed. Boschi had received the very considerable income from the Rattan position from the time of his appointment early in 1745, and he was financially secure by the end of the war; but his luck came to an end, and he died in October 1749. Sixteen months later Garden penned an uncharitable epitaph: the new missionary in Saint Bartholomew's made an excellent impression, particularly "after such a poor and unprofitable a Creature as Boschi."[61]

Boschi's reluctance to serve at his military post was not the fault of the SPG; in fact, the Society made an attempt to hurry him on his way. Still the SPG's ability to give lucrative appointments outside the province to favored missionaries weakened Garden's control over the establishment, and the commissary resented it. This animosity, however, should not be exaggerated. The conflict was real, but it existed within a general atmosphere of cooperation, and it seems apparent that the joint administration was successful. There were continual problems within the church, chiefly with regard to personnel, but they would have been much worse if the twin authorities had not been there to resolve them. The SPG rather consistently supported its missionaries, and Garden was usually found on the side of the parish. Garden wielded a degree of judicial authority while the SPG held the purse for part of a missionary's income. Out of these separate viewpoints and disparate powers a rough justice emerged that was generally accepted by parishioners and ministers alike. Although not the most logical and efficient form of administration, this one was generated by sheer circumstances, and it might have been much worse. Indeed that was the prospect.

By 1740 the SPG had begun a gradual process of disengagement from South Carolina. Saint John's Parish in Colleton County, created out of Saint Paul's in 1734, wrote to the SPG in 1739 asking for a missionary and received a negative reply. The SPG was not "in a Condition" to create a new mission. The policy was reaffirmed in 1741.[62] At the same time the SPG was stiffening its policies to force parishes to give their clergymen better treatment. As a result the SPG was as active in the 1740s as before, but the long term prospect was for gradual withdrawal. In 1740 Saint Philip's, Saint James, Santee, a predominantly French parish, and Saint John's, Colleton, were the only three lacking SPG missions. By 1750 two new parishes, Prince William's and Saint Peter's had joined the outsiders. Still there were missionaries in more than two-thirds of the parishes.

While the influence of the SPG suffered a gradual reduction, that of the bishop of London fell off precipitously in 1748 with the death of Bishop Gibson. Garden's commission lapsed immediately. Under normal circumstances the situation would have been a temporary one, but the next bishop of London, Thomas Sherlock, decided to push for an American episcopate rather than exercise his own jurisdiction. He refused to take out Gibson's patent for the colonies, and he would not use de facto authority as had earlier bishops. Sherlock does seem to have ordained and licensed clergymen for the colonies, but he exercised no other power. Government by commissary was no more. Garden declared in 1751 that the churches in America were "at 6s and 7s, without any Shadow of Authority amongst them"; he wished Sherlock would succeed or give up the program. That was not to be the case, however; the active involvement of the bishop of London in the religious affairs of South Carolina was at an end, and it was not to be replaced by an American bishop.[63]

With the passing of the old system of administration, new ways of operation were necessary if the church was to continue in existence. Beginning in 1749, the yearly visitations conducted by Alexander Garden came to an end. Instead the clergy convened for an annual meeting that became their only means of united action. The business of obtaining a clergyman gradually became a less formal procedcure. In 1748 Alexander Garden asked his friend James Crockatt, a London merchant, formerly of South Carolina, and member of the SPG, to find a minister who might be acceptable as the assistant rector of Saint Philip's. The vestrymen of Saint John's in Berkeley County also imposed on Crockatt to find a clergyman for them and to secure him an SPG salary.[64]

While he was no longer commissary, Alexander Garden continued to serve as the rector of Saint Philip's Church. Finally, beset with the illnesses that had plagued his adult life, he resigned his position in

October 1753, at age sixty-eight, after thirty-three years of service. His farewell sermon, delivered in April 1754, contained an element of the universal church:

> May all the Blessings of Heaven descend upon all the inhabitants of this *Province* in general;—those of *Charles Town* in particular. . . .

Moreover there was an element of worldliness that was appropriate:

> —May the ever blessed and glorious Trinity bless you in the *City*, and in the *Field*; in the fruit of your *Body*, the fruit of your *Cattle*, and the fruit of your Ground; Bless you in your *Basket* and in your *Store*, and in all that you set your Hand unto. . . .

But not excessive:

> Bless you with all the temporal blessings, of Health, Peace, and Prosperity; but above all, and as the Source of all, bless you with truly faithful and obedient hearts, and finally, conduct you safe to the Blessed Regions of Glory and Immortality.[65]

Alexander Garden's church was never exactly as he wanted it, but the outlines of the ideal are clear. The provincial laity would hire the ministers and define the nature of the church in a broad manner, while the bishop's commissary provided central ecclesiastical authority, in particular by disciplining errant clergy. The SPG was for Garden an extraneous institution that was no longer necessary for the province and that operated in ways that weakened local control of clerical behavior. Garden was unable to achieve his model, in part because the laity was unwilling to be as independent as he would have liked and in part because Sherlock did away with the office of commissary. Still he did accomplish enough to leave his impress on the middle years of the establishment: in particular the clergy and the laity came closer together, making the church something of an indigenous institution. Garden was also effective against his most powerful adversary, George White-field; here as in his other struggle the commissary did not win, but he did not lose either, and that was no mean feat.

Garden's career was far less grandiose than that of James Blair, Virginia's commissary from 1689-1743, but it bears comparison nonetheless. Garden left no tangible monument similar to William and Mary College, of which Blair was the founding father, nor did his published sermons equal Blair's five-volume *Our Saviour's Divine Sermon on the Mount*. Garden's political success was also less spectacular than Blair's unseating of three governors, but it was more productive for the Church of England. While Blair triumphed in what were essentially personal feuds, Garden's achievement was to create an effective working arrangement between the clergy of the established church and the political leaders of the colony. Blair sided with the Virginia vestries on the key issue of induction, but in the process he alienated royal governors and clergy alike and left the issue unresolved. Garden maintained a relative harmony among the clergy at the same time that he exercised a greater degree of discipline over wayward clerics than any other American commissary.[66] James Blair is a towering figure in the landscape of Southern Anglicanism, but it is doubtful that he strengthened the Church of England in Virginia more than did Alexander Garden the establishment committed to his care.

CHAPTER 4

THE CHURCH AND THE REVOLUTION

A significant number of new settlers began arriving in South Carolina in the 1730s, coming first from Europe and later from Virginia and Pennsylvania. Most of these people were not members of the Church of England, and they altered the religious balance of the colony at the same time that they extended its geographic frontier. By the era of the American Revolution the low country was the home of only a minority of the white citizens of the province, and the established church was the religious choice of an even smaller group. Still the establishment did not stagnate between 1750 and 1775. It continued to function effectively in the low country under the complete control of the laity, and in Charles Town it flourished. Three-fourths of the Anglican clergy sided with South Carolina in the Revolution; but the Church of England lost its privileged status in the constitution of 1778, and the state moved slowly toward complete religious freedom.

What has been aptly called the expansion of South Carolina began in 1730 when Governor Robert Johnson convinced the colony to sponsor the settlement of selected townships in the wilderness area lying in a broad arc to the west of Charles Town. Badly outnumbered by their slaves and fearful of attacks by Spain and France, the tidewater gentry offered substantial aid to foreign Protestants who would make their home in the pine forests and sandhills beyond the low country. Purrysburgh, founded on the Savannah River in 1732, was the first community resulting from the program; by the end of the 1730s there were six other towns. Many of the Swiss, German, French, and Dutch settlers followed the lead of the Huguenots by turning to the Church of England; others, particularly the Welsh and the Scots-Irish, had more experience with Anglicanism and were more resistant to its pull.[1]

Nor did the established church do as much as it might have to bring the new settlers into the fold; instead it tended to focus its attention on Charles Town and to prefer the settled parishes over the new ones. For example, in 1728 after he disgraced himself in Christ Church Parish, the Reverend John Winteley went on to serve in Saint Bartholomew's on the southwestern frontier. Garden explained to Bishop Gibson that Winteley would receive only the salary offered by the assembly, since the parish had little hope of becoming an SPG mission until it was "better settled & accomodated with a church etc." Obviously the commissary believed the frontier should accommodate itself to the church rather than the other way around.[2] There were, however, well-qualified Anglican clergymen who were willing to serve in places where the need was greater than the comfort, and their efforts for some time kept the Church of England a creditable force at the edges of expansion.

One of these hardy Anglican ministers was the Reverend Francis Varnod, a native of France, who began to serve Saint George's Parish in Colleton County, to the northwest of Saint Andrew's, in 1724. The parish was created only in 1717 and was on the edge of Indian country; it was also settled largely by dissenters and a Presbyterian meetinghouse predated the Anglican congregation.[3] None of these factors, however, was any great difficulty for Varnod. Almost immediately the new minister began to make the most of available opportunities. During his first summer in the province Varnod took a two-week trip among the Indians 150 miles from the English settlements. He baptized ten people among the Indian traders, including a married girl of fifteen years and her brother, both formerly Baptists, and preached at an outpost garrison where no minister had ever been and where two Creek chiefs were among the listeners. He was enthusiastic about outdoor living: "The Woods under the Noble Canopy of heaven was the place were I lay most nights." In June 1726 he journeyed three days through the wilderness to reach Fort Moore, a provincial garrison located some 100 miles up the Savannah River, where he converted a Canadian Catholic and baptized a Baptist woman and seven children. In 1729 he made the first appearance of any clergyman at Palachacolas Fort at the mouth of the Savannah. Varnod's unique talents proved of value to Jean Pierre Purry, the Swiss colonizer who took advantage of South Carolina's new policy of encouraging expansion. Varnod accompanied Purry on an expedition to the Savannah River to search for a township site, and the minister also preached in French to the Swiss settlers as they sojourned in his parish.[4]

Varnod did not neglect his parochial duties because of his occasional trips. In January 1733 he reported that twenty-nine of his parishioners, probably about one-half, had quickly pledged a total of £450 sterling for enlarging the church, proudly noting that the subscribers had "exerted themselves at least to the utmost of their ability." Dissenters seemed more friendly toward the Church of England, and every Sunday some of them attended his services. A few even told him they would subscribe for pews in the refurbished church, "Dicatur Sub Rosa." The parishioners also provided seventy-five acres of glebe and a new brick parsonage for their rector.[5]

Other ministers faced the same circumstances as Varnod. The Reverend Daniel Dwight, a New Englander stationed in Saint John's, Berkeley County, traveled to the "remote parts" of the colony in 1731 to visit some "poor Peoplc" living fifty to seventy miles beyond parish boundaries. Such concern apparently made a good impression, for he was elected rector by unanimous vote that same spring after being in the parish only a year. The Reverend Thomas Morritt represented the church less well. He settled Prince Frederick's Parish in 1727, when the Winyaw area was beginning to fill with settlers and when two Baptist preachers were the only available ministers. Eight years later he left under a cloud, having employed himself "in Merchandizeing and Planting to the Neglect of his Ministerial Duty." Morritt's successor was more dutiful, but there were difficult realities working against him. Writing home in 1739, the Reverend John Fordyce estimated there were 800 dissenters among the 1,200 inhabitants of Prince Frederick's, many of them recently arrived Scots-Irish Presbyterians.[6]

Prince Frederick's Parish encompassed the entire northern frontier beyond the Santee River and west of the coastal parish of Prince George's: Williamsburgh township as well as Great Cheraws on the Peedee River were in John Fordyce's jurisdiction, although the former was 30 miles and the latter nearly 150 miles from his church. He made a number of lengthy trips during the 1740s to visit his far-flung parishioners and reported large audiences and numerous baptisms. He was the first clergyman ever to visit the Cheraws area, and North Carolina families brought their children twenty and thirty miles to be baptized. In addition to Presbyterians, Fordyce encountered many Baptists who had emigrated from Pennsylvania. He claimed the Baptist preachers were ignorant, but he distributed Wall's *Abridgement*, a tract that argued for infant baptism, to Anglicans and dissenters alike. Still he grew increasingly fearful that the faith of his Anglican parishioners would not withstand the dissenting environment in which they lived. Fordyce encouraged the SPG to send an itinerant who would serve these frontier inhabitants on a regular basis. Such cries came from other clergymen as well.[7]

Despite the fact that Anglicans were in the minority even among the settlers living relatively close to his church, Fordyce seems to have carried on a peaceful and fruitful ministry. The vestry would rather not have elected him in 1742, but neither then nor later were there complaints about his personal or ecclesiastical behavior. At least two dissenters formally joined the Church of England, and the entire group often attended the Anglican service when a preacher of their own persuasion was not in the area. In 1748 the pastor boasted that his congregation was "as Regular and Orderly as any in the Province, & Staunch, & Earnest for the Interest of the Church of England." The vestry underscored his accomplishment in 1751 when they notified the SPG of Fordyce's death and requested a new missionary lest the majority of the congregation join the dissenters, of "Whom we are in the Midst."[8]

The Presbyterians and Baptists near the parish church of Prince Frederick's were advance elements of a folk migration that brought large numbers of western settlers from Pennsylvania and Virginia into the South Carolina piedmont in the years between 1750 and 1775. As a result of this influx, there were about 30,000 people living in the backcountry in 1770, making up some 60 percent of the white population of the colony. An enumeration of ministers taken at five-year intervals from the beginning of the eighteenth century suggests the religious dimensions of the change. From 1700 to 1710 there were more non-Anglican than Anglican ministers in the colony, reflecting the predominance of dissenters in the population. The five Anglican clerics in 1710 increased to twelve in 1715, however, as the benevolence of the SPG brought missionaries into the colony; meanwhile the eleven dissenters slipped to eight, probably because of hardships associated with the Yamasee War. From 1720 to 1730 the numbers were rather equal, about ten in each group.

During the 1730s the number of Anglican ministers gradually increased, but the number of non-Anglicans increased more rapidly: in 1750 there were fifteen of the former and twenty of the latter. The disparity increased over time so that in the last decade prior to independence the twenty or so clergymen of the established church competed with more than thirty ministers associated with dissenting denominations. A remarkable increase in Presbyterian churches in the period between 1750 and the Revolution indicates not only the magnitude of change but also its geographic nature. In 1730 there were eight of these, all in the low country; in 1750 there were thirteen, two of the new ones on the frontier; and in 1776 there were forty-four Presbyterian houses of worship, the bulk of them in the backcountry.[9]

The Reverend Charles Woodmason confronted this new frontier society in 1766 when he began service as an itinerant Anglican clergyman in Saint Mark's Parish, formed from the western part of Prince Frederick's Parish in 1757 and composed of an area fully as large as the entire low country. Woodmason came from England as a layman in 1752, when he was probably thirty-two years old, and for the next fourteen years he devoted himself to business and politics, functioning as a planter, merchant, and office holder in Prince Frederick's and then as a public official in Charles Town. He lost favor with the low country gentry after seeking the position of stamp distributor in 1765; shortly thereafter he applied for the itinerant post in Saint Mark's and returned to England to be ordained. Despite his secular background, Woodmason was devoted to the interests of the Church of England and he had a strong urge to serve the public. His complex psychology may have been influenced by the fact that he was sexually impotent, owing to the kick of a horse, and alienated from a wife and son in England.[10] Woodmason's clerical career was a way of fulfilling himself.

Woodmason exhibited the prejudices common to Anglican clergymen. He found it difficult to accept the rude standard of living and the unrefined manners of the majority of back-country settlers, whom he described in his journal as "a mix'd Medly from all Countries and the Off Scouring of America." He attributed their poverty to "extreme Indolence" and believed that they were content with "their present low, lazy, sluttish, heathenish, hellish Life. . . . Both Men and Women will do any thing to come at Liquor, Cloaths, furniture, &c &c rather than work for it—Hence their many Vices—their gross Licentiousness, Wantoness, Lasciviousness, Rudeness, Lewdness, and Profligacy. . . . "

Woodmason was particularly critical of dissenters; for example, he referred to Scots-Irish Presbyterians as "the Scum of the Earth and refuse of Mankind." Often, however, he exhibited a disgust that was nondenominational as, for example, in describing the behavior of a "vast Body of People" gathered at Flatt Creek in August 1768: "After service they went to Revelling Drinking Singing Dancing and Whoring—and most of the company were drunk before I quitted the spot." Woodmason was also caustic about his rivals, the Baptist and Presbyterian preachers of the piedmont. They were "a Sett of Rhapsodists—Enthusiasts—Bigots—Pedantic, illiterate, impudent Hypocrites—Straining at Gnats, and swallowing Camels, and making Religion a Cloak for Covetuousness Detraction, Guile, Impostures and their particular Fabric of Things."[11]

Woodmason's commentary is misleading for a number of reasons. He wrote his journal in part as unconscious therapy, relieving the frustrations that came from bitter experiences and exaggerating the events as he relived the emotion. His gift for colorful prose also made him choose words less for their descriptive accuracy than for their sound and force. Most important, however, is the fact that despite the contempt he expressed for the people committed to his charge, he pursued their interest with extreme vigor. The center of his activity was the little village of Pine Tree Hill that became Camden in 1768. He served there every two weeks and in between ranged wide to all of Saint Mark's, meeting groups of worshipers in twenty-four additional locations, some of them nearly 100 miles from Camden, and bringing the offices of the Church of England to a collective congregation which he estimated at 3,860 people. He also made at least one trip to Anson Courthouse in North Carolina and gave a sermon to 300 people.[12] The traveling was arduous. He often lost his way, sometimes spending the night in the woods and frequently in open cabins; several times he nearly drowned crossing flooded streams; and he carried his own food supplies to augment the primitive and uncertain provisions available from his parishioners. Thus he worked exceptionally hard to serve the people whose morals he condemned and whose mores he affected to despise.[13]

There was a similar inconsistency in Woodmason's attitude toward the dissenting clergy of the backcountry. He attacked their manners and their methods yet his own itinerant style was an unconscious imitation of theirs, and he even experimented with their preaching techniques in order to become more competitive. In a sermon given to an Anglican audience on the Congaree River he contrasted the "Solemn, Grave, and Serious Sett Forms" of the Church of England with the "Wild Extempore Jargon" of the dissenters, "nauseaus to any Chaste or refin'd Ear," and ridiculed an Anglican clergyman who had modified the practices of the church in a vain attempt to appeal to the Baptists and Presbyterians.[14] Woodmason's journal makes clear, however, that he himself succumbed to similar pressures. In April 1767, after he had been serving more than six months, friends told him that people avoided his services at Pine Tree Hill because they preferred the style used by the New Light Presbyterian and the Methodist preachers in the area. As Woodmason put it, the "lower Class chuse to resort to them rather than hear a Well connected Discourse." In response he memorized the Anglican liturgy, stopped using the *Book of Common Prayer*, and began each service with an extemporaneous prayer. At first he was unwilling to preach without notes: "Tho' certainly I could perform beyond any of these Poor Fools." By June, however, he had given extemporaneous sermons "to engage the Dissenters," but noted ruefully that "this disgusts the Church People, and made severals with draw." In August, near the North Carolina border, he had a happier experience when the Anglicans present asked him to give an impromptu service, "it having been a common Taunt by the Dissenters, that the Church Ministers could not preach or pray Extempore." According to Woodmason, his prayers and sermon lasted for an hour and fifteen minutes, and "the Dissenters were confounded and astonished and the Church people pleas'd and delighted."[15]

Woodmason was in Saint Mark's during the time of the Regulator Movement, an association of backcountry settlers who were unhappy with the lawless nature of their society and the failure of the provincial government to extend its institutions to newly settled areas. Woodmason's close relationship with the Regulators demonstrates that he won the confidence of the backcountry settlers despite his prejudices and the hostility of his religious enemies. He wrote the "Remonstrance" that articulated their discontent, and he preached to the assembled body of Regulators deputized to pursue the outlaw bands that terrorized the backcountry; when the Regulators considered sending a mission to England, they asked him to be one of the emissaries. Woodmason was certainly responsible for the fact that the "Remonstrance" emphasized the lack of church facilities in the backcountry. It called not only for more parishes, which were necessary for effective political representation, but also for "chapels, Churches, and Parsonages," and asked that more Church of England ministers be provided and that their salaries be increased. As an example of the evils present under the prevailing conditions, it cited "*Itinerant* and Stragling Preachers of various Denominations who poison the Minds of the People." One wonders if the Regulators read the handiwork of their spokesperson! One reason for Woodmason's influence was probably the fact, as Richard Maxwell Brown argued, that the Regulators came from among the more substantial element of backcountry citizens. Woodmason's sympathy with the plight of the backcountry settlers is evident throughout his writings dealing with the Regulator Movement, however, and this was surely an important factor in allowing him to play the role he did.[16]

Woodmason's ability to overcome his prejudices and win the confidence of the piedmont settlers suggests that the Church of England might have been more successful in that region if it had tried harder. What was needed was an energetic missionary program of the sort provided by the SPG for the low country during its formative period. Had the government set up parishes of reasonable size and sent ministers in sufficient numbers, the Church of England might have become an important cultural force in the backcountry. Instead the religious situation remained largely unchanged down to the Revolution. Two new backcountry parishes, Saint Matthew's and Saint David's, were created in 1768, but the latter never had an incumbent and the vestry at one point even offered the job to a dissenting clergyman on the condition he take orders.[17] Woodmason left South Carolina in 1772 and the Reverend Paul Turquand of Saint Matthew's appears to have been the only Church of England minister in the piedmont at the time of the Revolution.

While the Church of England failed to establish itself in a meaningful sense in the backcountry, it continued to function successfully in the low country during the quarter of a century that preceded the American Revolution, albeit in a somewhat different manner than it had during the time of Alexander Garden. The cessation of episcopal involvement and the gradual withdrawal of the SPG opened the way for a more active role on the part of parish vestries in the hiring and disciplining of ministers, and they were quick to take advantage of the opportunity. As the ecclesiastical ties with England loosened, the ministers became more dependent on the colonial laity but were also freer to bargain for their services with more than one parish, a situation enhanced by the general scarcity of clergymen. The effects of the Great Awakening and the increased number of dissenters in the province made things more difficult for the established church, but there is no evidence that it declined in overall effectiveness. Indeed in Charles Town the church seems to have gained strength from the increasing size and opulence of the city.

There was some tension between low country ministers and their vestries even in the 1740s, as illustrated by the case of the Reverend William Orr, who began service in Saint Paul's Parish in 1741. At that time the parsonage was run-down to the point of being uninhabitable, and a new one could not be built until the parishioners resolved a long-standing dispute about the location of their church. Saint John's Parish was carved from Saint Paul's in 1734, and the change left the parish church in the extreme southern part of Saint Paul's; northside parishioners, a majority, wanted their chapel to become the new church, but southside parishioners resisted. As a consequence, Orr found himself installed in a converted barn that lacked glass windows and whitewash and swayed in the wind. It was six miles from the church and twenty from the chapel. Orr also complained that the glebe lands were worn out and that the parishioners provided him with neither slaves nor livestock. After two years he warned the vestry that he would leave the parish unless it improved his situation and elected him rector. The SPG threatened to end their mission in Saint Paul's unless Orr's demands were met, but the vestry remained unmoved and things continued as they were. Orr claimed the vestrymen would rather have no minister than an elected one. Despite the ultimatum he continued to serve the parish until 1750 when he moved to the neighboring parish of Saint John's. The SPG refused to transfer the mission with him, 'but Orr apparently felt that local goodwill was more useful than distant benevolence.[18]

The Reverend Levi Durand, an SPG missionary in Christ Church parish, made a similar decision about the same time, although the circumstances were different. Durand was the elected rector of the parish, but the social composition and the religious attitudes of his parishioners caused him a great deal of trouble. Anglicans were a large majority in the parish, at least in 1741 when he arrived, but none of them were wealthy, and he welcomed the dissenters who attended his services much of the time and occasionally made sizable contributions to the church. This success with non-Anglicans led him to give a sermon attacking extemporaneous preaching, which proved a mistake since several of the leading dissenters were offended and ceased coming to the church. Others left when a Whitefieldian preacher, Joachaim Zubly, settled in the area. Durand's congregation further dwindled as Anglican colonists moved to newer areas where the soil was more fertile. He also complained of deism, infidelity, and religious indifference among those who remained.[19] Finally he decided to act. In 1751 Saint John's Parish in Berkeley County contacted Durand in response to his "publick Advertisements of. . . his intention to leave Christ Church Parish." A period of negotiation followed: Durand was unhappy with the list of subscriptions offered by the parishioners of Saint John's and warned them that he expected an offer from Saint James, Goose Creek. After further assurances by Saint John's a deal was struck. The new pastor took possession of the parish in November 1752 and became its rector following an election in March 1753.[20]

Durand's bargaining was particularly impressive because of the growing parish opposition to election of ministers because of the fact that the office of rector, which election conferred, gave the incumbent a freehold right to the parish and made his removal impossible. In 1742 the vestry of Prince Frederick refused at first to elect John Fordyce even though they were happy with his work. Commissary Garden suggested that Fordyce serve Prince George until the parish came round, and eventually it did. In the meantime the SPG warned that it would take action if missionaries were not elected according to the law of the province. This did not work for Orr, however, and it also failed with respect to the Reverend Charles Boschi in Saint Bartholomew's Parish. Opinion varied there on the merits of election. Boschi's friend, a Colonel Hyrne, believed that election was a clergyman's due; a Mr. Golightly, however, the richest man in the parish, suggested that it would be better to make up the thirty pounds sterling offered by the SPG than to elect a minister. A Dr. Skirven was explicit about his reasons for opposing election: "If a clergyman was Elected instead of coming to officiate at church perhaps he would stay at home drinking his bottle with his negro woman."[21]

The prevailing attitude of the South Carolina laity toward the tenure of their clergy is suggested by the proviso that Colonel John Gibbes attached to his will in 1770 when he left £1,000 to the parish of Saint John's in Colleton County for the support of a Church of England minister: "Sometimes it happens that a Minister proves disagreeable to the people of the Parish, and not to be worthy of the Interest, then it shall be in the discretion of my Two Sons. . . with the Church Wardens, & Vestry, not to pay the money, till he behaves to the satisfaction of the parish." A year later the vestry of Saint Michael's Church in Charles Town made it clear to its minister that he should not think himself entitled to the office of rector. Lieutenant Governor William Bull explained the situation as it stood in 1775: "When Clergymen are once inducted by an Election, there is no jurisdiction in this province which can remove them ab officio or a beneficio when they may give scandal either by their doctrine or manners, . . . for which reason the People now decline fixing in the Living by Election but. . . continue them dependent during the pleasure of the Vestry."[22]

Not everyone was happy about the new relationship between ministers and parishioners. In particular the Reverend Charles Martyn, who came to South Carolina in 1752 after taking a degree at Oxford and serving for four years as a curate in England, found much to criticize about the establishment, despite the fact that Saint Andrew's Parish elected him its rector and treated him well. Early in his tenure he noted that most of the parishes favored "keeping their ministers dependent" and claimed that the tendency of ministers to move from parish to parish occasioned a great deal of confusion within the church. He lamented that his predecessor in Saint Andrew's had often baptized children without sponsors and that this made it difficult for him to insist on that formality.[23] Martyn aspired to become commissary and during the early 1760s he wrote several reports to Bishop Osbaldeston designed to show both the need for a representative of episcopal authority and his own fitness to fill the position. In the absence of such an official, parishes acquired their ministers in irregular ways: "The Method used. . . is generally by an Application to some Merchant in Charles Town, who writes to his Correspondent in England and desires Him to export some Clergyman or other. . . ." He warned the bishop that Saint John's, Colleton County, "allways remarkable for its ill Treatment and Contempt of the clerical Function," had written for a minister but was resolved not to elect him. There was also a young man in deacon's orders in the province serving as a priest despite attempts by the clergy to dissuade him. Martyn's ambition motivated these reports, but they were accurate enough. In 1765 he pointed out that the Anglican vestries were behaving more and more like the lay governors of the dissenting churches. With the Stamp Act in mind and with reference to South Carolina, he claimed that "the Principles of most of the colonists in America are independent in Matters of religion, as well as Republican in those of Government." An American bishop of the Church of England, Martyn believed, would receive the same reception as a stamp distributor.[24]

The withdrawal of the SPG from South Carolina paralleled the demise of episcopal authority. In 1756 the colonial government added £30 to the salaries of clergymen not employed by the SPG to make them equal to those of the missionaries. Six years later Martyn resigned his mission in order to save the SPG money, winning the praise of the organization and the criticism of the remaining missionaries who pointed out that the dramatic gesture cost him nothing. In 1767 the SPG ceased to support its last low country missionary, the Reverend Alexander Garden, Jr. The parishes were now entirely on their own, eleven years before the fall of the state church.[25]

In its new independent capacity the establishment seems to have functioned in a stable and orderly manner. The minutes of Saint John's Parish in Berkeley County end abruptly in 1768, suggesting a lack of religious interest, but ministers served there after that; Prince William's Parish, erected in 1745, had a settled clergyman for only a brief period, but it built a handsome church and was often supplied by neighboring ministers. The remaining low country parishes had incumbent clergymen most of the time, and some of the ministers served for lengthy periods. Martyn was in Saint Andrew's from 1752 to 1772; the Reverend James Harrison served Saint James, Goose Creek, from 1750 to 1771; and the Reverend Samuel Fenner Warren was the minister of Saint James, Santee, from 1758 through the Revolution. Outstanding in this respect was the tenure of Alexander Garden, Jr., who served Saint Thomas Parish from 1744 until 1783.[26]

Charles Town was the metropolis of South Carolina, and in the years before the Revolution it was a lively and cosmopolitan place. The importance of the city for the established church is suggested by the fact that when the church commission was reorganized in 1745, fifteen of the new commissioners were from Saint Philip's Parish while the remaining eight were apportioned among the other parishes.[27] The clergy held their annual meetings in Charles Town, and they must have taken pride in the development of the Church of England as a major institution of the growing urban community.

Saint Philip's Church itself won recognition for Charles Town. In June 1753 *The Gentleman's Magazine* carried an octavo plate of the Anglican edifice, calling it "one of the most regular and complete structures of the kind in America." The church boasted a large and active congregation: in 1745 the vestry claimed that an average of 600 to 700 people listened to Sunday services. The size of the congregation convinced the assembly to provide an assistant for Garden, and over the years the post attracted some very capable men. Robert Betham, who was appointed to the position in 1746, had published a sermon in England before coming to America and was elegized in the *South Carolina Gazette* following his untimely death in 1747. The Reverend Samuel Quincy, who succeeded Betham, brought out an edition of twenty of his own Saint Philip's sermons, published by a Boston press in 1750. Meanwhile Saint Philip's and its clergymen found it increasingly difficult to serve the needs of the growing city. William Langhorne, an SPG missionary on his way to Saint Bartholomew's Parish, preached in Charles Town one Sunday in the fall of 1750 and was immediately offered a large sum to remain in the city and deliver a weekly sermon. Langhorne turned down the offer, fearing to offend Garden and his assistant as well as the SPG; in the following year the political leaders of South Carolina acted to provide more Anglican services on a permanent basis.[28]

An act passed in June 1751 divided Saint Philip's Parish, placed the southern part of Charles Town in a new parish known as Saint Michael's, and appointed commissioners to oversee the building of a new church and parsonage. Governor James Glen had vetoed the measure once, in part at least because he hoped to gain the right to appoint clergymen to South Carolina parishes. The legislators stood firm for the rights of parishioners, however, and Glen gave in.[29] On February 22, 1752, the governor laid the first stone for Saint Michael's Church and placed on it a donation for the building fund. Other gentlemen then laid stones, a large crowd applauded, and the principals retired to a tavern where the commissioners of Saint Michael's provided a dinner. Later a cannon was discharged at the Granville Bastion and a group assembled there drank a toast to the royal family. The *Gazette* concluded its account of these events with a bit of boosterism: "This Church... will exhibit a fine piece of Architecture when compleated; the Steeple, being designed much larger than that of St. Philip's will have a fine Set of Bells."[30]

Saint Michael's was completed in 1762. It cost above £50,000 in Carolina currency and was adorned not only with elaborate bells but also a clock, both items imported from England, the one costing nearly £600 sterling and the other nearly £200. The bells were something of a sensation: five years later the clerk of the church was still earning money by charging visitors to watch the ringers at their work. A new organ was added in 1768 for £568 sterling, most of the money coming from private subscriptions. It was played by Peter Valton, an excellent musician and a composer of some talent.[31] Saint Michael's and Saint Philip's thrived together. In 1764 the government created a position of assistant minister in the new church to match that in the old and provided the holder of each with an annual salary of £200 sterling. Pews in both churches were valuable pieces of property, often advertized for in local newspapers and reputedly worth between £1200 and £1950 in 1778.[32]

The Church of England did not hold a monopoly over religion in Charles Town any more than it did in the rural low country, but it does seem to have been preeminent. On the eve of the Revolution there were six meetinghouses in the city and small congregations of Quakers and Jews. The Presbyterians were well enough organized and sufficiently self-conscious by the 1760s to address the governor in a body on important occasions as the Anglican clergy had always done. Nonetheless the Church of England seems to have been socially as well as politically dominant. In 1755 when a delegation of English Masons arrived in Charles Town and organized a local lodge, Alexander Baron, rector of Saint Paul's Parish, preached a sermon for his assembled brother Masons, and other Anglican clergymen continued to provide the Masons with discourses on the anniversaries in the 1760s and 1770s. The "Fellowship Society," organized for charitable purposes in the 1770s, also heard annual sermons from Church of England divines. In 1759 a number of prominent Charles Town citizens took subscriptions for the English publication of two volumes of sermons by the Reverend Richard Clarke, who succeeded Alexander Garden as the rector of Saint Philip's. Four separate elegies in Charles Town newspapers commemorated the death in 1767 of Joseph Dacre Wilton, an assistant lecturer at Saint Philip's.[33]

The success of an organization called the Society for the Relief of the Widows and Orphans of the Clergy of the Church of England suggests that the established church was valued by its adherents. When first organized in 1762, it admitted only clerical members; in 1770, however, David Deas, a church warden at Saint Michael's, was allowed to join. The Society admitted a second layman in 1771 and changed its rules to allow laymen to become members for a fee of £10 annually. More and more laymen joined each year until by 1778 there were 178 members of the Anglican laity associated with this insurance program for the families of Church of England clergymen. The annual meeting in 1774 was reported in the press as follows: "A Sermon suitable to the occasion, was preached in St. Philip's Church, by the Rev. Robert Smith, and an Anthem, set to Music by Mr. Peter Valton, sung and played to universal Satisfaction. After Service, a handsome Collection was made for the Charity...."[34]

On Sunday, August 14, 1774, the Reverend John Bullman, assistant minister of Saint Michael's Church, preached a sermon entitled "The Christian Duty of Peaceableness" in which he attacked the tendency of "every idle Projector" and "every Silly Clown and illeterate Mechanic" to interest themselves in political affairs and criticize government officials. From this penchant, according to Bullman, "Misunderstandings, ...brooded by Discontent and diffused through great Multitudes, come at last to end in Schisms in the Church, and sedition and Rebellion in the State." The remedy was "for every Man to keep his own Rank, and to do his Duty in his own Station, without usurping an undue Authority over his Neighbour, or pretending to censure his superiors in Matter wherein he is not himself immediately concerned." The point was hardly abstract. In July a general meeting of South Carolinians had resolved to support the town of Boston by sending a delegation to the Continental Congress to formulate an American response to the Intolerable Acts. In the ensuing election white adult males had voted without reference to the usual property qualifications for suffrage.

The reaction to Bullman's sermon was so hostile that the vestry feared "a Desertation of, and Indignities to the Church." Bullman, however, remained adamant about his principles and about his right to express them from the pulpit. A meeting of parishioners then voted its disapproval of his conduct (forty-two to thirty-three), and the vestry dismissed the minister from his post. Bullman's supporters later claimed the meeting was not representative of the parish and appealed to the church commissioners for redress. The commissioners refused to intervene, however, and Bullman finally gave up hope of being reinstated and left the province in March 1775, carrying with him a monetary gift collected by his friends and a testimonial signed by eighty parishioners. The episode was sensational enough so that Henry Laurens sent his son John an abstract of the sermon six months after Bullman had delivered it in Saint Michael's.[35]

Bullman's case illustrates not only the movement toward Revolution in South Carolina, but also the evolution of the Church of England within the colony. The doctrines espoused by the young minister were conventional enough by Anglican standards, and similar sentiments had been expressed by earlier church of England clergymen in South Carolina. Clearly, however, they were out of character with the republican ideology that had developed in South Carolina as well as the other American colonies, stressing as it did the significance of the citizen in the political process and the tendency of public officials to be corrupted by unchecked authority. More important, his parishioners, offended by his remarks, were able to do something about their discontent. Republican ideas had altered the ecclesiastical constitution inherited from England even as it altered the political constitution. Bullman, who arrived in South Carolina from England only in 1770, either did not understand the nature of colonial institutions or chose not to accept them.

Other members of the Church of England clergy also remained faithful to English allegiances. Bullman's superior in Saint Michael's, the Reverend Robert Cooper, refused to honor a fast day proclaimed by the provincial congress for February 17, 1775. He remained in office, doubtless owing to divided political opinion in the parish, but was ejected in June 1776 when he offered public prayers for the King while British warships were attacking Sullivan's Island. Other loyalists were the Reverends James Stuart of Saint George's Parish, Robert Purcell, assistant rector of Saint Philip's Parish, and Edward Jenkins of Saint Bartholomew's Parish.[36]

For the most part the Church of England in South Carolina and its ministers identified with the colony and with the American Revolution. Although Cooper refused to observe the fast day in Saint Michael's, "the Assembly with their Speaker, preceeded by the Mace" and followed by "the General Committee . . . in Procession" marched to Saint Philip's where the Reverend Robert Smith delivered a sermon suited to the occasion. Smith was later banished by the British after they occupied Charles Town. Also banished was the Reverend John Lewis of Saint John's Parish in Colleton County, who became a patriotic counterpart to Bullman when he delivered a sermon that angered the occupation forces. The Reverend Paul Turquand of Saint Matthew's Parish served in the provincial congress; the Reverend Henry Purcell of Christ Church Parish was a chaplain in the Continental service and later a deputy judge-advocate general; and the Reverend William Percey preached to American troops and gave the first address celebrating the anniversary of independence. The Reverend Samuel Fenner Warren of Saint James Parish, Santee, was in England when the war broke out, but he sided with the Americans, refused a clerical living in the mother country, and eventually returned to South Carolina. All told fifteen of the twenty Anglican ministers in the colony on the eve of the Revolution stood with the Americans.[37]

The internal structure of the Church of England was not out of character with Carolina society, and the clergy were not disloyal in their politics, yet the constitution adopted by the state in 1778 disestablished the church and placed it on an equal footing with other Protestant denominations. On one hand the change reflected the developing consensus on the value of religious toleration and the separation of church and state that was part of the American Revolution; on the other, it was related to the particular nature of South Carolina society and to the internal political realities that accompanied independence.

The revolutionary movement in South Carolina was led by politicians long associated with the growth of political power on the part of the Commons House. These merchants, planters, and lawyers identified with the interests of South Carolina and shared a set of republican political assumptions based on the "country ideology" of England. They were supported, indeed pressured, by elements of Carolina society excluded from the aristocratic Commons House, in particular the mechanics of Charles Town, who found it possible to play an important role as political decision making became more informal. Despite loyalty to

Great Britain, the differing economic interests of merchants and planters, and those of rice planters and indigo planters, and the class differences between the gentry and the mechanics, there was an impressive effectiveness and an inexorable quality about revolutionary politics in the low country. Along with other colonies, South Carolina nullified the Stamp Act, organized economic opposition to the Townshend Acts, prevented the operation of the Tea Act, and sent delegates to the Continental Congress; on its own it purchased a marble statue of William Pitt and sent money to John Wilkes. In January 1775 it adopted the Continental Association and created a provincial congress to coordinate opposition to Great Britain. Meanwhile, it became clear that the sentiments that united the tidewater were not shared in the backcountry.[38]

Dissension in the western region was, of course, not a new phenomenon. The sectional divisions that had developed out of the settlement of the piedmont were evident in the Regulator Movement that flourished from the spring of 1767 until the summer of 1769. The Regulators were essentially vigilantes, intent on suppressing the outlaw gangs that infested the backcountry and disciplining the poorer elements of the region whom they believed to be lacking in industry and morality. The absence of government rather than oppressive government motivated them. Such absence occurred because the assembly had not created separate parishes that would have given the backcountry settlers adequate representation and because it had not set up a system of local courts where justice could be obtained without traveling to Charles Town. Neither the Commons House nor Governor Charles Montagu was indifferent to these grievances once they were made known, but the disallowance in England of the assembly's first circuit court act and divisions within the backcountry led the Regulators to defy the authority of the provincial government. They refused to allow colonial peace officials to perform their duties, and the resulting impasse very nearly degenerated into major violence. The Regulation came to an end eventually and the passage of a new circuit court act mollified the backcountry settlers, but they remained separated from the tidewater region politically and culturally as well as geographically.[39]

Following the outbreak of fighting at Lexington and Concord, low country patriot leaders became concerned about the political allegiance of the backcountry. A military struggle with Great Britain posed particular problems for South Carolina: Charles Town was a tempting target, and there were rumors an attack would come before the end of 1775. Fear of the British was compounded by the internal threat posed by the massive slave population and by the potential hostility of the Cherokees on the western border. To consolidate its strength the provincial congress approved a loyalty oath known as the association. This was administered in the low country without difficulty, but met resistance in the west. The Germans in Saxe-Gotha and Orangeburg quickly made it plain that they did not support the movement against Great Britain. The British governor, Sir William Campbell, quietly encouraged resistance in other parts of the backcountry, and militiamen in the Camden area signed a counter association declaring their loyalty to the mother country. British loyalists also seized a quantity of ammunition stored by the patriots at the piedmont community of Ninety-Six.

To counter these ominous developments the patriot council of safety sent a team of emissaries to tour the backcountry. The makeup of the commission reflected low country awareness of the religious composition of the piedmont. William Henry Drayton was an Anglican and a member of the tidewater gentry; William Tennent, however, was the pastor of the independent church in Charles Town, a fiery patriot as well as a member of the most prominent family of evangelical ministers in the colonies; and the third member was Oliver Hart, the minister of Charles Town's Baptist church. Arthur Middleton summed up the urgency and the goal of the mission: "We must have *peace* or rather *union* let it cost what it May." Throughout August and part of September the commissioners traversed the backcountry, making speeches on behalf of the patriot cause, warning that nonassociators would not be allowed to trade in Charles Town, and threatening their enemies with military force. They made headway, but the resistance was considerable. The effort ended in the middle of September when Drayton, supported by 1,100 militiamen, convinced a larger body of pro-British settlers to agree to the Treaty of Ninety-Six, by which they promised to remain neutral and the provincial congress promised to leave them alone. Trouble continued, however, and an uneasy peace was maintained only after a force of 4,000 militiamen returned to the area in the winter and captured a number of prominent loyalist leaders.[40]

The patriot leaders recognized the backcountry settlers would have to be integrated into the political life of the colony if the revolution were to succeed. When the extralegal general meeting, which had coordinated

opposition to Great Britain, moved in January 1775 into the more formal structure of a provincial congress, it took a major step in the
direction of backcountry representation: each parish was allowed six
representatives except Saint Mark's Parish, which was allowed ten representatives from each of three districts. Saint Mark's seems to have
actually sent 40 delegates, who were a substantial group among the 184
members. In March 1776 the provincial congress adopted a constitution
that again increased the political voice of the piedmont: 76 of 202
positions in the General Assembly were allotted to areas west of the
tidewater. This new government also established schools at three locations in the backcountry. Despite this recognition of the western settlers, the South Carolina constitution of 1776 was remarkable in its
conservatism. To sit in the General Assembly a person needed the same
property that had made him eligible for the old Commons House: 500
acres, 20 slaves, or personal property worth £1000. Suffrage require-
ments were also carried over from the colonial government, and the
voters elected only the General Assembly, which then elected an upper
house known as the Legislative Council from among its own members.
The two houses chose a chief executive who was given an absolute veto
over legislation. These provisions brought about a movement for reform
following the Declaration of Independence, and in that process the
status of the Church of England became an important issue.[41]

Backcountry discontent with respect to the established church was
first manifested in 1762 when the *South Carolina Gazette* published "A
Letter from some of the inhabitants of the Forks of Broad River and
Saludy," which complained that settlers in that area paid taxes to support Anglican churches and ministers in the low county while they had
none of either and were themselves mostly dissenters from the Church
of England. The "Remonstrance" of the Regulators complained about
the same situation and, probably because of Charles Woodmason, called
for parishes, churches, and ministers. With the Revolution, a different
solution was advanced. A meeting of dissenters called by the Baptists
was apparently held early in 1776 in the High Hills of the Santee River
to promote the idea of religious freedom. Later William Tennent drew
up a petition to the General Assembly that was signed by literally
thousands of backcountry inhabitants. In addition to praising the benefits of religious liberty, it made the point that a continuation of the
established church "lays a foundation for future discord and unhappi-

ness." In view of the uncertain quality of political allegiance in the dissenter-dominated backcountry, the phrase must have had an ominous ring to low country ears.[42]

On January 11, 1777, Tennant made a speech to the General Assembly on the subject of the petition that was even more explicit about the link between disestablishment and support for the Revolution: "Can you imagine that the numerous Dissenters who venture their all in support of American freedom would be fond of shedding their blood in this cause if they did not with confidence expect that they should have justice done them and that they should stand upon the same footing with their brethren? Can you imagine that a refusal of justice would not dampt their ardour, if not utterly disarm them?" Tennent also spoke of "the free and equal rights of mankind," gave a well-reasoned argument for religious liberty as an abstract principle, and neatly compared the dissenter's aversion to paying even a small tax for someone else's church with the unwillingness of the Americans to pay an insignificant but unjust levy on tea. The importance of sectional politics in South Carolina before, during, and after the Revolution and the reality of loyalism in the backcountry suggest that the compelling aspect of his presentation was the threat that without religious equality the low country could find itself alone against the British threat.[43]

The dissenting petition called for an end to the "establishment of any one Denomination or sect of Protestants by way of preference to another" and to the obligation of a "Protestant inhabitant... to pay towards the maintenance and support of a religious worship that he does not freely join in or has not voluntarily engaged to support" and for the creation of a situation in which "all Protestants demeaning themselves peaceably under the government established under the constitution shall enjoy free and equal privileges, both religious and civil." During the ensuing debate in the General Assembly the low country leadership was divided. Christopher Gadsden and Charles Cotesworth Pinckney argued strongly for the proposal; Rawlins Lowndes and Colonel Charles Pinckney fought against the measure in its entirety. Many other members were less adamant: they rallied behind the idea that the establishment be continued, but that dissenters be exempted from paying taxes for its support. This concept lost by a vote of seventy to sixty, whereupon a motion for disestablishment passed unanimously.[44]

In March 1778 the General Assembly adopted a new constitution that met many of the complaints against the one in force since 1776. It

lowered the suffrage qualification to a fifty-acre freehold or its equiva-
lent in other property, abolished the Legislative Council, replacing it
with a Senate elected by the people, and denied the governor the right to
veto legislative acts. It disestablished the Church of England, but not in
the uncomplicated manner advocated by the dissenting petition. The
new fundamental law required voters to believe in God and legislators
to be Protestants; ministers, however, could not serve in a legislative
capacity, an exclusion probably owing to resentment at the activities of
the Reverend William Tennent. Henceforth, "the Christian Protestant
religion" would be "the established religion" in South Carolina. The
Church of England retained its property and the corporate status of its
parishes; other denominations meeting a set of general qualifications
would be incorporated and supported with tax funds. The lengthy and
complicated provisions of this plan were more restrictive than those in
the Fundamental Constitution of 1669, but their intent and a number of
specific phrases recall the tolerant program devised for Carolina by
John Locke and the Earl of Shaftesbury. Moreover the qualifications for
ministers in the new establishment came largely from the Anglican
Book of Common Prayer.[45]

The establishment of Protestantism in South Carolina lasted only
until 1790 when a new constitution created a situation of religious
freedom and separation of church and state. The provisions of 1778 are
important, however, because they demonstrate the reluctance of the
legislators, most of them Anglicans, to divorce politics from religion.
The churchmen of South Carolina, like their brethren throughout the
South, believed in the civil utility of religion.

In many respects the establishment in South Carolina was stronger
and more secure at the time of the Revolution than ever before. Competent clergymen filled the low country parishes, the two churches in
Charles Town were well adorned and well attended, the laity were
satisfied with the structure and operation of the state church, and the
dissenters were not openly hostile to it. In contrast to Virginia and
Maryland, the religious situation in South Carolina was stable and
harmonious.

Disestablishment came because the settlement of the backcountry
gave the dissenters a large numerical majority and the American Revolution created a political situation in which change was necessary. The

Church of England failed to make an effective appeal to the backcountry dissenters, but it is doubtful that they could have been converted in any case. The forces that brought about its downfall were larger than the state church could have been expected to control.

William McLoughlin has suggested "that the role of religion in the Revolution was to create religious liberty for Protestantism in order to provide the cultural cohesion needed for the new nation."[46] This summary fits the situation in South Carolina and appears to work for the rest of the South as well. The Church of England lost its privileged status so that the new states might achieve the unity necessary for their continued existence. All in all, a not unfitting role for a church originally shaped by the reason-of-state values of Elizabeth I.

CHAPTER 5

THE CHARACTER OF
THE CLERGY

"A sound Divine and a good Preacher, which join'd with an examplary good Life and Conversation, rendered him much beloved and esteemed in this place...," declared the *South Carolina Gazette* in 1747 at the untimely death of Robert Betham, assistant minister of Saint Philip's Parish. Describing the minister they hoped to receive in 1761, the vestry of Saint Helena's Parish asked for a "Gentleman of a Studious Turn and regular, Uniform deportment, who will maintain the authority of the Church without being austere or rigid to the dissenters."[1] Taken together these statements provide a good description of what the Anglican laity in South Carolina wanted their clergymen to be: conversant with the doctrines and forms of the Church of England, able to communicate effectively from the pulpit, moral in their personal behavior, and tactful in dealing with parishioners as well as with the numerous dissenters in the province. Clergymen who met these standards were effective in their function, and they strengthened the church as a whole. The reverse was also true: inept or immoral ministers weakened the establishment and usually drove people to the dissenters.

Anglican clergymen in the South had a reputation for worldliness and impropriety, and there are examples in South Carolina to support the worst of those charges.[2] Atkin Williamson, a Church of England minister who came to South Carolina in the seventeenth century, was certainly a drunkard and may well have christened a bear during one fit of inebriation.[3] By 1728 the local reputation of the Church of England ministry was so bad that one parish vestry referred to "the Vulgar Notion and reproach that anyone is good enough for the plantations and that they are a Clergyman's last Recourse and dependence."[4] On the other hand, there were ministers who performed very well, men such as Robert Betham.

There were bad ministers and there were good ministers, but what was the overall quality of the clergy? Did they behave well enough to make the establishment an effective institution? Another issue has to do with change over time: did the quality of the clergy alter as the state church developed during the eighteenth century? The only way to answer these questions is to examine the careers of the 124 clergymen who began service in the parishes of South Carolina from the arrival in 1696 of the first minister associated with the forces that would bring about the establishment of the Church of England in 1706 to the arrival in 1775 of the last minister prior to its disestablishment in 1778.[5] The seventy-nine years in question are divided into three periods that correspond with major eras in the history of the established church to facilitate a comparison of the ministers in each period.

The first period extends from 1696 to 1719 and may be called the establishment era. A total of twenty-six clergymen arrived in these years, among them some very capable people. Particularly impressive was Francis Le Jau, a native of France educated at Trinity College in Dublin, Ireland, and an SPG missionary. An intelligent and dedicated man, Le Jau rejoiced at the natural beauty of South Carolina and lamented the materialism and cruelty of the settlers, whom he nevertheless served with kindness, patience, and humility. He was loved and respected by laymen and clergy alike. A prominent parishioner described his death as "an Unspeakable loss to this unhappy Collony as well as to the parish under his immediate Care."[6] The two commissaries appointed by the bishop of London, Gideon Johnston and his successor William Tredwell Bull, performed very well, although Johnston was somewhat given to vindictiveness and self-pity. Other effective ministers were Samuel Marshall, whose arrival in 1696 began the Anglican development of the colony; Samuel Thomas, the first SPG missionary; and Robert Maule, Thomas Hasel, Gilbert Jones, and Nathaniel Osborne, all SPG missionaries who arrived after the establishment of the church. Rather than discuss the behavior of these men in detail, it is useful to look at the activities of one of their colleagues, the Reverend William

Guy, who serves as an example of an effective minister and whose career illustrates the hardships that many faced.

Guy came to South Carolina in 1712, having been sent by the SPG to assist the rector of Saint Philip's Church in Charles Town and to run a school as well. By the time he arrived the schoolmaster position had been filled by someone else, but Guy made a good impression on people in the colony; because of the pressing need for ministers he was actually elected rector of the newly created Saint Helena's Parish despite the fact that he was a deacon rather than an ordained clergyman. Returning to England with recommendations from his parish and leading officials in the colony, he secured both ordination and a place on the SPG payroll as a missionary.[7]

During the next five years William Guy had a series of adventures that may well have made him wonder about his choice of a career. Sailing to South Carolina in the summer of 1714 he warned the captain about some moral lapse and the officer responded by physically roughing him up. In April of the next year the Yamasee Indians launched their attack on South Carolina and Saint Helena's Parish was their first target. Guy escaped death by fleeing to a vessel in Port Royal harbor. With the Indians in temporary control of his parish, he became a refugee in Charles Town, where he made himself useful keeping up the spirits of other displaced persons. White settlers did not return to Saint Helena's for some time after the war, and Guy, now married and with a pregnant wife, found himself out of a job. The SPG offered him a post in Rhode Island, where its missionary in Newport was having difficulty serving the Anglicans scattered around Narragansett Bay. Guy served in Saint Philip's until a new minister arrived for that church and then sailed for New England, arriving in June 1717. He served Rhode Island conscientiously enough, selling his slave to pay expenses rather than nagging his parishioners for fees; but his wife, a native of South Carolina, longed for a warmer climate, and when the parishioners of St. Philip's asked him to return, he accepted happily. The SPG concurred and provided £50 sterling for moving expenses. Again the Guys took ship, arriving outside the Charles Town bar in November 1718. While the vessel waited for a pilot, Guy went ashore in a small boat: suddenly a pirate ship appeared and captured the vessel in which his family remained. Three days later the pirates returned the passengers unharmed, but they kept all the Guys' possessions. Meanwhile, Guy learned that Saint

Philip's actually was not vacant; the parishioners were heartily sick of their scandalous minister, but he was still legally the rector. A disheartened William Guy moved to Saint Andrew's Parish on a temporary basis and waited to hear from the SPG about his future.[8]

Guy's affairs eventually turned out well. He became the rector of Saint Andrew's and continued there for the next twenty-one years in relative peace and contentment. He got along well with the parishioners, the SPG continued his missionary salary, and he believed the country parish was healthier than Charles Town. During his first year on the job he baptized thirty children, some of them black, and converted one adult dissenter. He built the number of communicants to above thirty, a level at which it remained for years. There were many more parishioners. In the early years he reported that dissenters formed a majority of the parish inhabitants, but either the situation changed or he revised his estimate. In 1746 he gave the number of white families at 180 and claimed that 163 of them were members of the Church of England, although only 36 people took the sacrament. He listed 2,600 slaves as heathens: as with most Anglican clergymen he baptized an occasional black, but made little headway in converting the masses of slaves.

While he attended to the needs of his parishioners, Guy also served the church in other ways. Between 1725 and 1733 he acted as agent for the SPG in the collection of several philanthropic bequests left by members of the colonial laity, and for a time in the 1740s he and Alexander Garden jointly administered the legacy of Richard Ludlam, an Anglican clergyman who left his estate for the purpose of founding a school in the parish of Saint James, Goose Creek. In 1730 Guy returned to Rhode Island for several months and held services for Anglicans there, and four years later he sat on the first ecclesiastical court held in South Carolina. Guy suffered from several serious illnesses over the years and returned to England for his health in 1725. Despite an increasingly infirm body, he often visited neighboring parishes when they lacked clergymen. He died in 1751.[9]

The hardships of William Guy's early career were extreme but not extraordinary. The rigors of an ocean voyage, the dangers of a semi-wild environment, and the uncertainties of parish tenure were common hazards for Anglican clergymen in the early eighteenth century in South Carolina. Guy's response was also typical: he faced his own problems and met his responsibilities to Saint Andrew's Parish in a way that was competent if not spectacular; it brought credit to himself and to the church. Most other ministers behaved in a similar fashion, but their reputation was tarnished by the misdeeds of a significant minority. Among those who did not measure up to what was expected of them were at least three clergymen who failed to adhere to the liturgy of the Church of England. Two of these were Frenchmen, Claude Philippe de Richebourg and John La Pierre, who exasperated Commissary Johnston and Francis Le Jau by using Calvinist practices derived from their Huguenot background. However, the parishioners of these men were French settlers for the most part, recent converts to the Church of England with nominal loyalty only. Had de Richebourg and La Pierre been more orthodox, they would have been less popular.[10] The situation was different in the case of Ebenezer Taylor, a Presbyterian minister in South Carolina recruited into the Church of England by Commissary Johnston. Taylor traveled to England to be ordained, and on his return, with Johnston's help, was elected rector of Saint Andrew's Parish, but his parishioners were never happy. In 1716 they charged him with a number of liturgical faults, including "entering into a long and unmannerly Expostulation with God Almighty, after the Method of the meanest and most ignorant of the Presbyterians." They also claimed he abused and attacked them and was given to "railing in his Sermons." Finally he was accused of parsimony, specifically in neglecting his attire for reasons of economy and in halting church business by quarreling with the vestry over money.[11]

Several other ministers were guilty of tactless or impolitic behavior. At the time of the establishment of the Church of England, Edward Marston, who was the rector of Saint Philip's Church, attacked Anglican legislators from the pulpit because they did not share his High Church attitudes about the independence of the clergy from political control. The politicians responded by removing him from office. Principles aside, Marston was extremely irascible.[12] John Maitland was offensive in a less grand manner, but it did equal harm to his ministry: he was critical of his parishioners to such an extent in the Sunday sermons that they simply stopped coming to church.[13] Other ministers were excessively materialistic. This was true of Ebenezer Taylor, but the classic example was William Dunn, who asked the SPG to send his salary in merchandise: six dozen pairs of women's lambskin gloves, six reams of the finest writing paper, various dressmaking materials, "Roles & weirs for head Dresses Fashionable," and "12 pair of Leathern cloggs for Women." The clergyman hoped to make a 100 percent profit on this line of women's wear and notions.[14]

Laxity with respect to form, tactlessness, and materialism were all something less than acceptable from the standpoint of articulated standards but they were not scandalous activities, at least in the instances cited. By comparison there were four ministers between 1696 and 1719 who committed acts perceived as being immoral and who brought notoriety to themselves and scandal to the church. The first of these was Richard Marsden who came to South Carolina from Maryland in 1706. He was personally charming and so popular a minister that the people of Saint Philip's Church were unhappy when Commissary Johnston replaced Marsden as their minister. Marsden later got himself deeply in debt and absconded without paying his creditors, a pattern he was to repeat in a number of other colonies.[15] In 1710 James Gignilliat, a French SPG missionary, married a rich widow in his parish, then forced her out of the house and lived handsomely on his newly acquired wealth. Gignilliat resigned his clerical position, but the episode reflected badly on the church. Commissary Johnston claimed that legislation that would have benefited the establishment was tabled because the politicians were unhappy over the Gignilliat affair.[16] Alexander Duncan, who was not an SPG missionary and who arrived in the colony on his own after the Yamasee War, was guilty of drunkenness and other unspecified character faults.[17] Finally there was William Wye, the rector who kept William Guy from serving Saint Philip's Church and a thorough scoundrel. He falsified the letters of recommendation that allowed him to obtain an SPG appointment; and he rented and then stole three horses and a chaise just before coming to South Carolina. In the colony his misdeeds included marrying "a young man. . . to his Mothers Sister, whilst she lay in bed, being delivered the night before of a Bastard Child."[18]

Anglican clergymen in South Carolina between 1696 and 1719 functioned in a difficult environment and many of them did it rather well, yet the ministry as a whole had a bad reputation. The four ministers who were scandalous in their behavior and to a lesser extent those who were marginal in their performance detracted from the reputation of the majority. Why there was so much scandal is not entirely clear. It was a worldly age, however, and to a certain extent loose-living clergymen reflected the standards of their time. Then too the better ministers probably had more opportunities in England and chose to remain at home so that the less respectable members of the profession were more apt to show up in the colonies. In any case the situation did not soon improve.

The second period covers the years from 1720 to 1749, essentially the era of Alexander Garden. As the bishop's commissary, Garden dominated the established church during these years and as the rector of Saint Philip's Church he also acted as a model clergyman. At his retirement his parishioners presented the commissary with an engraved silver plate in testimony to his "Exemplary life, and constant Labours, in the cause of Virtue and Religion." Sometime later David Ramsay wrote that under Garden "a profession of religion was no slight matter. It imposed a necessity of circumspect conduct regulated in all aspects by the prescribed forms of the church."[19]

Lewis Jones, Garden's contemporary, also had an excellent reputation in the province. Jones began service in Saint Helena's Parish in 1726, when the Port Royal area was still recovering from the damage done during the Yamasee War. Four years later Jones had an opportunity to move to a richer parish close to Charles Town, but he refused because there was no other cleric within eighty miles of St. Helena's and "the small congregation which I have collected here, and have been at some pains to Cultivate, would soon be dispersed." By continuing at his frontier post, Jones subjected himself to a series of hardships. He traveled at regular intervals to the remote islands of his parish, covering thirty miles round trip and sometimes holding services in a Presbyterian meetinghouse. In 1742 he and his family fled from an imminent Spanish attack and took shelter in a barn for sixteen days. At the death of their rector in 1745, the church officers informed the SPG that Jones' nineteen years of service had "Gained him the esteem of every body that knew him."[20]

Another outstanding clergyman of this period was Samuel Quincy, an SPG missionary in Georgia who came to South Carolina as Garden's assistant in Saint Philip's. His modern fame rests on a volume of South Carolina sermons that were published in Boston in 1750. Richard Beale Davis called Quincy "an abler writer and perhaps an abler pulpit preacher" than Garden and one of "the most effective of the southern Anglican preachers who directly opposed the Great Awakening." Quincy's sermons emphasized the reasonable quality of Christianity: ". . . nothing is prepared to our Belief that is contrary to the Sense and Reason of Mankind." They are written in a rational manner and they lack the bitterness that Commissary Garden could not suppress.[21]

Garden, Jones, and Quincy were among forty-five ministers who arrived in South Carolina between 1720 and 1749. About sixteen of these men we know very little, in most cases they served for only short periods of time, and it is unlikely that their collective performance made much impact on the reputation of the established church. Available records indicate that nineteen men, including Garden, Quincy, and Jones, performed creditably. Three other ministers failed to meet the standards we have applied but avoided notoriety. One of these was Joseph Bugnion who was unable to speak English and therefore ultimately unacceptable to a majority of the parishioners in Saint James, Santee; another was Charles Boschi, a convert from Catholicism, who was an ineffective preacher; and finally there was Thomas Morritt, who employed himself "in Merchandizeing and Planting to the Neglect of his Ministerial Duty."[22] The remaining seven ministers behaved in such a way as to bring substantial discredit upon themselves and on the established church.

Francis Merry, an SPG minister who arrived in St. James, Goose Creek, in 1721, was the first offender. Repeated public drunkenness made Merry "an open scandal to his profession," in the words of Commissary William Tredwell Bull, and St. James dismissed him within a year.[23] An even worse episode occurred in 1727 when Brian Hunt, another SPG missionary, performed a "Collusive & Clandestine" marriage that united a wealthy heiress with a young man against the express wishes of her guardians. Hunt's motive appears to have been financial gain, and the affair created an uproar in the province that was only alleviated when the SPG suspended him. The Anglican clergy made it clear that these scandals hurt the church: "the ill behavior or fault of any one Clergyman seldom misses of being improved into a Scandal & Prejudice agt Religion, the Church & the whole order of the Clergy by their enemies."[24] One may assume that enemies meant the dissenters, and, unfortunately for the Church of England, they had more ammunition the following year. John Winteley, another SPG missionary, was, as one parishioner put it, "A Whoremonger and a drunkard." Christ

Church Parish dismissed him from their service, but not without considerable difficulty.[25]

Happily, the growing discontent of the Anglican laity with the behavior of its ministers coincided with an increased capacity on the part of the establishment for internal discipline. When Alexander Garden became commissary in 1728, his commission included the power to conduct ecclesiastical courts for the purpose of trying errant ministers. Acting under that authority, Garden convened a court in 1734 that tried, convicted, and suspended from office John Fulton, a habitual drunkard who had succeeded Winteley in Christ Church Parish.[26] The potential for ecclesiastical discipline may well have helped to alleviate the need for it: Garden never again tried a resident minister. Problems remained, nonetheless. Edward Dyson served briefly in a South Carolina parish before becoming the chaplain of a royal garrison at Port Royal. Garden claimed Dyson was a "notorious Drunkard," and lamented that his powers as commissary did not extend to the military position that Dyson held.[27] Another clergyman named Lawrence O'Neill entered the province in 1734 and officiated briefly before a letter from Bishop Gibson put a stop to his career. The details are obscure: probably O'Neill was not licensed to serve in the colonies. In any case he was an unsavory character who spent some time in the Charles Town jail before leaving the colony.[28] Last but hardly least was Stephen Roe, whose tenure in Saint George's Parish from 1737 to 1742 was unexceptionable. Later, however, it was learned that Roe had a wife in England, an upsetting disclosure for the church since he had pretended to be a bachelor and had courted the daughter of a prominent parishioner. The province was well rid of Roe: at his next post in Boston he became a public disgrace by fathering a child with his landlady's daughter.[29]

Clerical behavior was a significant problem during the Garden era. The four notorious ministers between 1696 and 1719 were 15 percent of all Anglican clergymen, and their frequency was almost exactly matched by the seven clergymen between 1720 and 1749 who composed 16 percent of the clergy. The Church of England was established and settled, but one out of every seven Anglican ministers continued to behave in an immoral fashion. Small wonder that the Anglican laity believed that "the plantations . . . are a Clergyman's last recourse."

During the years between 1750 and 1775 the character of the Church of England in South Carolina underwent a change, and the quality of the clergy changed with it. Commissary Garden's commission lapsed in 1748 and no other commissary was ever appointed. The SPG had already stopped providing missionaries for newly created parishes, and it gradually stopped supporting the ministers in old parishes. Increasingly, the responsibility for recruiting and disciplining ministers devolved on the parishes themselves. Under these altered circumstances the overall caliber of clergymen seems to have improved markedly.

A total of fifty-three clergymen began careers in the established church during the years between 1750 and 1778, the revolutionary era. Among the most distinguished was Richard Clarke, Garden's successor in Saint Philip's, who published several theological tracts and delivered sermons that were long remembered in Charles Town both for the depth of their learning and the appealing manner of their delivery. After Clarke returned to England, a number of prominent Carolinians sent their children to be educated by him.[30] Charles Woodmason, itinerant Anglican clergyman in Saint Mark's Parish from 1766 to 1770, is well known for his rapport with the Regulators and his impressive accounts of backcountry life. He was a controversial figure, but an effective and dedicated minister.[31] Robert Smith, rector of Saint Philip's after 1757, was the unofficial leader of the Anglican clergy in the last years of the established church. He seems to have been the principal founder of the Society for the Relief of the Widows and Orphans of the Church of England that began operation in 1762. Smith was a staunch American patriot and was exiled by the British because of his partisanship and his influence within the colony. After the war he organized a private school that later merged with the College of Charleston, and in 1795 he became the first bishop of South Carolina.[32]

At the opposite extreme there were several ministers who distinguished themselves in a negative manner. Michael Smith, an Irish clergyman and SPG missionary who arrived in South Carolina in 1753, traveled about Prince Frederick's Parish with a woman who, he claimed, was his nurse but who also shared his bed. Smith was married but he paid little attention to his wife, ignoring her during an illness of which she died, and also neglected his children.[33] William Peaseley, an SPG missionary and married, was dismissed from Saint Helena's Parish in 1756 for visiting a woman in the parish frequently and at late hours.[34]

Because there was no commissary to make periodic reports to the bishop of London and few missionaries wrote letters to the SPG, we know less about the ministers in these years than in earlier periods. Of the other forty-eight, another fifteen seem to have been capable while there is little evidence about the individual careers of the remaining thirty-three. Nonetheless, it seems clear that this group of ministers fulfilled the expectations of their parishioners better than had their predecessors. Charles Woodmason, writing in 1765 while still a layman, praised the "Candour, Prudence, and regular demeanour" of the ministers in the province at that time, who, he claimed, were "the best Sett of Men, that Carolina were ever blest with at One Time." Woodmason also asserted that in the past the establishment had "greatly suffered" because of immoral ministers and he specifically mentioned Peaseley and Smith.[35] Presumably he knew of no others in the nine years since Peaseley's dismissal. Nor do available records for the period from 1765 to 1778 reveal evidence of notorious behavior on the part of any Anglican clergymen, excluding, of course, the political activities of those ministers who failed to support the revolutionary movement. In particular William Tennent's lengthy and well-documented speech on behalf of disestablishment makes no mention of clerical impropriety.[36] Scandal by its nature generates comment and the lack of evidence is significant. Very probably Smith and Peaseley were the only scandalous ministers in the revolutionary era; if so an important change had occurred. Notorious ministers were only 4 per cent of all ministers in the last years of the established church, about one-fourth as numerous as in the first two periods. (See Table 1.)

Table 1
Scandalous Ministers as a Percentage of All Ministers

	Total Ministers	Ministers Involved in Scandal	Percentage Scandalous
1696-1719	26	4	15.4
1720-1749	45	7	15.6
1750-1775	53	2	3.8
All Periods	124	13	10.5

The basic cause of the improvement in the Anglican ministry in the years after 1750 was the growing independence of the provincial church. Independence meant freedom from control by authorities in England,

and it is illustrated by the striking decline in the number of SPG missionaries entering the province. From 1696 to 1719 the missionaries were 58 percent of the clergy as a whole; from 1720 to 1749 they were 69 percent; but from 1750 to 1776 they were only 13 percent. To a great extent, during the last period, parishes hired their own ministers, and they were apparently able to attract better men. On the other hand, despite an elaborate process involving written recommendations and an oral interview, the SPG had been unable to weed out the undesirable clergymen from its candidates. Nine of the thirteen scandalous clergymen in South Carolina were sent by the SPG; missionaries constituted 69 percent of the unworthy clerics while they were only 43 percent of the ministry as a whole. Small wonder that when they sought to replace the Reverend William Peaseley, the vestry of Saint Helena's wrote that "an application to the Bishop of London or the Universities seems more agreeable to the generality of the Parish than applying to the Society."[37] (See Table 2.)

Table 2
SPG Missionaries as a Percentage of All Ministers

	Total Ministers	SPG Missionaries	Percentage SPG
1696-1719	26	15	57.7
1720-1749	45	31	68.9
1750-1775	53	7	13.2
All Periods	124	53	42.7

Aside from the behavior of its missionaries, Anglicans in South Carolina resented the SPG because it exacted a measure of control over the provincial church as a reward for the salaries paid to missionaries, and at times its concern for the welfare of clergymen conflicted with the interests of the parishioners. In particular the SPG opposed the practice of hiring ministers on an annual basis, a means by which the parishes were able to maintain control over their clergymen. Under the Establishment Act of 1706, an elected minister had a freehold right to his parish, and there was no legal way to remove him. Alexander Garden's commission gave him the right to try ministers and suspend guilty ones from their posts, but that authority lapsed with the office of commis-

sary. During the 1740s parishes began to postpone the election of ministers and by the 1750s the practice was widespread; as a result Prince
Frederick's Parish was able to rid itself of Smith and Saint Helena's
Parish fired Peaseley. It seems likely that this capacity for discipline
discouraged other like-minded clergymen from seeking positions in the
colony.[38]

The SPG also hired a large number of clergymen from Ireland, Scotland, and the continent of Europe.[39] The colony had a prejudice against
the Irish and the Scots, and it may have disliked the fact that so many of
the European ministers were members of other denominations prior to
becoming members of the Church of England.[40] In any case there was a
significant change in the backgrounds of the ministers once the parishes
gained control of hiring. We know the national origin of 46 percent of
all ministers, spread rather evenly across the three time periods. Among
this group clergymen from England, Wales, and the colonies amounted
to 54 percent between 1696 and 1719, and 61 percent between 1720 and
1749, but 81 per cent between 1750 and 1775. Clergymen who had
served other denominations prior to being ordained in the Church of
England were 19 percent in the establishment period, and 20 percent in
the era of Alexander Garden, but only 6 percent in the revolutionary
era. (See Tables 3 and 4).

The independence of the established church after 1750 allowed the
parishes to choose ministers whom they liked and to replace them when
necessary, but this freedom would have been useless had it not been
accompanied by adequate incentives to attract worthy clergymen. During the first two periods the salary provided by the SPG was an important part of a clergyman's income in South Carolina. It was originally
£ 50 sterling and then dropped to £ 40 in 1734 and sometime later to £ 30.
Meanwhile the provincial salary began at £ 50 in local currency in 1706
with a stipulation that it would increase to £ 100 in three years. The
value of currency was always much less than sterling, however, so
that missionaries depended heavily on their SPG income. In 1722 the
provincial salary was stated in proclamation money that was pegged at
75 percent of sterling, a substantial improvement. Missionaries continued to receive more income than nonmissionaries up until 1756 when
the government added £ 30 to the income of the latter. After 1756 the
basic salary of all rural ministers was about £ 110 sterling. Ministers in
Saint Philip's Church had always been better paid than other clergy-

Table 3
National Origins of Ministers, in Percentages

	England	Wales	Colonies	Scotland	Ireland	Continental Europe	Total
1696-1719 (N=13)	46.2	7.7	0	0	30.8	15.4	100.1
1720-1749 (N=18)	50.0	5.6	5.6	5.6	5.6	27.8	100.2
1750-1775 (N=26)	69.2	7.7	3.8	7.7	3.8	7.7	99.9
All Periods (N=57)	57.9	7.0	3.5	5.3	10.5	15.8	100.0

Table 4
Ministers Affiliated with Other Denominations

	English Protestant	Foreign Protestant	Catholic	Protestant and Catholic	Percentage of all Ministers
1696-1719	1	3	0	1	19.2
1720-1749	1	5	1	2	20.0
1750-1775	1	2	0	0	5.7
All Periods	3	10	1	3	13.7

men, and the same was true of Saint Michael's after it became the second Anglican church in Charles Town. In the 1760s and 1770s the basic salary for ministers and assistant ministers in those churches was £ 200 sterling.[41]

Ministers received various perquisites as well, in particular a parsonage and glebe, the latter being land alloted for the use or income of the incumbent. There were also irregular gifts. The parish of Saint John's, Berkeley County, for example, gave its first minister a horse and saddle in 1708; and in 1721 it raised funds to provide a new minister with a slave couple and some cattle. Service fees also provided income that varied greatly. At first few fees of any kind were collected, but as the province grew in wealth and population, the income to some ministers was substantial. In 1762 marriages with banns were worth 15s., with licenses 110s.; burials in the churchyard 9s., on plantations 15s. Christenings, as one minister put it, "depend on the Benevolence of the People, whose generosity is very diffusive on those as well as other occasions.[42]

During the last period of its existence, the established church could provide lucrative employment. Charles Woodmason reported in 1766 that the rector of Saint Philip's and his assistant each received fees equaling the amount of their salaries and therefore earned about £400 yearly. Woodmason also claimed that four ministers had built up "Genteel Fortunes since being in the Province." James Stuart, erstwhile rector of Prince George's Parish, applied for compensation as a Loyalist in 1784, claiming a loss of £200 sterling based on a salary of £108 11s, on rental of a parsonage for £15 a year, and on fees of about £80.[43] He may have exaggerated in the hopes of larger benefits, but clearly there were strong economic incentives for clergymen to come to South Carolina.

Substantial economic benefits were necessary to attract good clergymen in part because immigrant ministers found the South Carolina environment so unhealthy. Despite the fact that most clergymen arrived in the colony in their late twenties or early thirties, they often did not live long. Of the 123 for whom data is available, 35 of them, 29 percent, died before completing five years of service in the colony. The rate of death within five years of arrival was relatively constant over the three periods; 35 percent from 1698 to 1719, 27 percent from 1720 to 1749, and 29 percent from 1750 to 1775. An English clergyman who accepted a South Carolina parish may well have thought he was entitled to high risk compensation.

Clerical behavior improved in the years before the Revolution because the SPG withdrew from the colonies, and the parishes gained control of the hiring and firing of their ministers. Such power would not have been effective if the low country had not become populous and wealthy enough to provide an income package that would attract and keep capable clergymen. Having the freedom to choose their own ministers, the capacity to provide them a good living, and the power to fire them if they misbehaved, the Anglican laity of South Carolina were able to maintain a more effective ministry than that which had been provided by English benevolence.

The character of the clergy in South Carolina was roughly the same as in the southern colonies as a whole. About 10 percent of the Anglican ministry in South Carolina and the South behaved in an unsavory manner and detracted from the reputation and effectiveness of the Church of England. On the other hand, a number of clergymen served with distinction and the average minister was capable and well behaved. Historians who dismiss the importance of Southern Anglicanism would be well advised to look at the activities of the ministry as a whole rather than at its worst examples.

The improvement of the clergy after 1750 appears to have been unique to South Carolina and the result of local conditions. After parishes began to hire and fire their own ministers, the clergy as a whole became more English in their nativity and more committed in their allegiance to Anglicanism. Fewer of them were outrageous in their behavior. In this instance the colonial Church of England functioned better as it diverged from English practices and imperial ecclesiastical authority and came instead under the control of the local Anglican laity.

CHAPTER **6**

RED, BLACK, AND ANGLICAN

Nowhere in the eighteenth century was the multiracial quality of English America more evident than in South Carolina. The earliest white colonists had settled in the midst of a number of Indian tribes, among them the Westos, the Shawnee (or Savannahs as they were called), and the Yamasee; and later settlers had extensive contacts with larger tribes living in the west, the Creeks, Chickasaws, Choctaws, and Cherokees. The Carolinians traded for deerskins and for Indian slaves, and the resulting commerce was an important element in the provincial economy. For their part, the Indians became dependent on the English goods that improved their lives; to secure them they hunted extensively, made war among themselves for captives, and became embroiled in conflicts between the colonists and the Spaniards in Florida and the French in Louisiana. Blacks first came to the colony with the Barbadian sugar planters who were among the early settlers. As an agricultural economy took root, particularly with the successful cultivation of rice, the colonists imported African slaves in large numbers. In 1720 the Negroes outnumbered their masters by nearly two to one, and on the eve of the Revolution slaves formed 60 percent of South Carolina's population.[1]

The presence of so many heathens in South Carolina was a challenge to the Church of England. Anglicanism was catholic in spirit, opening its arms to all those who had mastered the fundamentals of Christianity, and the established church was a natural vehicle for the conversion of Indians and Negroes. Moreover a missionary spirit had developed within the Church of England after the Glorious Revolution, one concrete embodiment of which was the formation in 1701 of the Society for the

Propagation of the Gospel in Foreign Parts. The SPG saw the nonwhite residents of South Carolina as an opportunity for Christian benevolence and instructed its missionaries to convert them while ministering to the white population. The effort was one of the few instances in which the English attempted to bring the races closer together, if only in worship. In the ensuing pages we sh₍ ˀ₎ see exactly what was attempted and why it did not succeed.

Thomas Nairne was the man who first interested the SPG in the heathens of South Carolina, and the object of his concern was the Indians. Nairne was a planter and frontiersman who lived near the Yamasee Indians and was aware that they had been instructed in Christianity by Spanish priests. He believed that something should be done to continue their religious education and convinced his friend, Robert Stevens; Stevens wrote Bishop of London Henry Compton who encouraged the Society to appoint the Reverend Samuel Thomas as a missionary to the Yamasees. Thomas arrived in the colony in 1702, but instead of going among the Indians, he settled at the Cooper River plantation of Sir Nathaniel Johnson, the governor of South Carolina, where he provided religious services for Johnson and his neighbors. Nairne was preoccupied for a time, fighting with the Carolina forces that destroyed Spanish hegemony over the Indians of northern Florida, but eventually both he and Stevens complained to the SPG about Thomas's failure to fulfill his mission. Nairne also pointed out that a much larger number of Indians, many of whom had been exposed to Christianity for more than 100 years, were now dependent on South Carolina. If the English did not provide spiritual care that was equal to that of the Spaniards, wrote the frontiersman, "What a good fight have we been fighting to bring so many people from something of Christianity to downright Barbarity & heathenism."[2]

The SPG was annoyed with Samuel Thomas, but he returned to London in 1705 and made an effective defense not only of his own behavior but also of the spiritual needs of South Carolina as a whole. Thomas claimed that the frontier warfare had made the Yamasee villages unsafe and that, in any event, the language barrier made missionary work among the Indians impossible. He went on to assert that the English plantations offered an outstanding religious opportunity. There were few ministers among the whites and Thomas claimed, with some exaggeration, that his own efforts "did excite. . . a vehement thirst after God's Ordinances ministerially dispensed" on the part of the Cooper River planters. Moreover, the black slaves were as much in need of Christianity as were the Indians and better suited to receive instruction; according to Thomas, 80 percent of the Negroes could speak English and "many of 'em are desirous of Christian knowledge."[3] The SPG was apparently impressed by these arguments; it rehired Samuel Thomas and committed itself to providing missionaries for the parishes of South Carolina. The SPG also broadened the scope of its activities with respect to heathens. In 1702 when Richard Willis, dean of Lincoln, preached the first anniversary sermon to the SPG he claimed that its purpose with respect to the colonies was "to settle the State of Religion as well as may be among our *own People*. . . and then to proceed in the best Methods. . . toward the *Conversion* of the *Natives.*" On a similar occasion in 1706, John Williams, bishop of Chichester, presumably reflecting the influence of Thomas's report, added Negro slaves as a further field for missionary endeavor.[4] Samuel Thomas died on his return to South Carolina, but other clergymen arrived in the colony and began to implement the goals of the SPG.

In the letters of these early missionaries, a marked interest in the character and mores of the Indian population is evident. The clergymen perceived the Indians as virtuous, but they were critical of native culture, in particular of what they saw as a lack of sustained economic activity on the part of the red men. Francis Le Jau, the first SPG missionary in Saint James Parish, Goose Creek, described the Indians near him in terms of the noble savage: "They make us ashamed by their life, Conversation, and Sense of Religion quite different from ours; ours consists in words and appearance, their [*sic*] in reality." He claimed to "admire their sobriety, patience, contentment in their Condition and no care for time to come but to provide Corn against Winter." Later, however, he noted that "they have no Ambition." Benjamin Dennis, an SPG schoolmaster in Le Jau's parish, visited an Indian town where he was irate at a baby tightly bound "in a small thing made of small canes." He also found the Indians lacking in industry, but noted that what little they had was equally shared. Robert Maule, who came to Saint John's Parish in 1707, was particularly struck by the contrast between virtue and idleness. He praised the Indians as "Lovers of Justice and Equity" and noted that the heads of families were deferred to and respected by children and relatives. All, however, were "much Inclined to Idleness and Prodigality." Instead of saving their corn they ate it immediately and then lived on "fruites, Rootes, and other Eatables as the Wood can afford them.[5]

The missionaries were interested in Indian customs in part because they hoped that primitive religious practices would prove that Christianity was a natural faith as well as a revealed religion. On the lookout for such evidence, they were able to find it. After long discussions, Maule concluded that the Indians believed in "those two great Articles of Natural Religion, the being of God and Imortality of the Soul." Le Jau was more aggressive in his use of evidence. When the Indians living near him held a dance during which the men and women were separated for three days, he asked one man to explain the separation: "He told me 'twas to remember a time wherein Man was made alone and there was no Woman: but after, God took somewhat out of Man and made the Woman: asking what it was God took; the Man put his hand on his breast and somewhat there, and then called it a Bone: My wife presently named a Rib, the Indian smiled and said Yea." On another occasion he watched an autumn religious festival in which forty Indians, "trimd painted and dres'd in their fineryes," were led by three young men in a serpentine dance, which began near a miniature house erected on poles. When Le Jau asked an elderly Indian about the significance of the ceremony, he was told that the three men were sons of one man "from whome all the rest came" and that the little house was a ship. He suspected that "they had some Tradition abt. Noahs Ark and his 3 Sons." Le Jau also eagerly passed on a rumor that some tribes practiced circumcision. Fifteen years later another French SPG missionary, Francis Varnod, serving in the frontier parish of Saint George's, found similar evidence of natural religion among the Indians, in particular the belief in a supreme being, a tradition about the flood, and the practice of circumcision. Indeed Varnod seems to have believed the Cherokees originated in the Middle East: "They are divided into ten tribes, . . . & I perceive they have not a few Hebrew or rather Phoenician words. . . .[6]

Despite the supposed proximity of Indian religious beliefs and Christian doctrines, the missionaries were unable to bring about any conversions. Le Jau claimed that "their Souls are fit Materials which may be easily polish't . . . ," yet he could not get any Indians to live with him for the purpose of instruction or even to send their children. Benjamin

Dennis was similarly unsuccessful in convincing Indian parents to place their children in his school.[7] The Indians were apparently content with their own religion, or at least saw nothing in Christianity that seemed appealing. A group of Indians told Robert Maule that they had no desire to join the white man's religion since the white man cheated, lied, and drank too much. Maule himself cited "the Wicked Lives and Scandalous behavior of many professing Xianity . . . who have sometimes been guilty formerly of such gross enormities, as even the more Modest Heathens themselves have been ashamed of."[8] The Indians may also have been aware of the missionary attitude toward their culture and recognized that conversion would have required them to change more than their religion.

The reluctance of the Indians to become Christians was one reason that Gideon Johnston, the bishop of London's commissary in South Carolina, took George, the son of a Yamasee chief, to London with him in 1713. The idea was that George would become a Christian in the English capital and then return to South Carolina to serve as a living model for other Indians to emulate. Probably Johnston was also aware of the splash created by the four Iroquois chiefs who had sojourned in London in 1710. In any case the SPG agreed to pay for the education and maintenance of the "Yamasee Prince." George suffered from homesickness and his education went slowly, but finally he learned enough Christian doctrine to allow his baptism by the bishop of London. Unfortunately for the commissary's plan, he and George arrived back in South Carolina in the summer of 1715, during the Yamasee War when the colonists and the Indians were doing their best to exterminate each other.[9]

The causes of the Yamasee War help to explain why the Anglican missionary effort was so ineffective. Unlike most conflicts between Indians and white settlers, this one had little to do with the land hunger of the English; instead it was the exploitative nature of the Indian trade and the unscrupulous behavior of the traders that drove the Yamasees and their allies to attack the colony. Their dependence on English technology lessened the bargaining power of the Indians, and the traders improved their already superior position by manipulating the natives with rum and cheating them in a variety of ways. By 1715 the Yamasees were deeply in debt to the English despite the fact that the men spent most of their time hunting deer or making war on other tribes in order to get captives whom they could sell as slaves. The Carolinians kept

Indian women and children as slaves to work for them, the men they sold to other colonies; their extensive involvement in Indian slavery illustrates the attitude they took toward their business associates.[10] Le Jau found that many of his parishioners "can't be persuaded that Negroes and Indians are other than Beasts, and use them like such." In the woods within two miles of his house, the clergyman found a female Indian slave in 1710, scalped and left for dead at the orders of the Indian trader who was her master. "By their Whispers & Conduct," he learned that people did not want him "to urge of Contributing to the Salvation, Instruction, and human usage of Slaves and free Indians."[11]

The Church of England clergy were aware of what was happening to the Indians. In 1713, Le Jau commented on the fact that the Yamasees had declined from 800 fighting men to 400. Warfare was the cause, and he suspected there was "no other Necessity for those Nations to Warr against their Neighbours but that of making slaves to pay for the goods the traders Sell them, for the Skins trade do's not flourish as formerly." The Reverend William Tredwell Bull of Saint Paul's Parish contrasted the growing prosperity of the white colonists with the declining state of the natives: the whites were beginning to enjoy "a more Gentile way of Living," exemplified by "Gayety of Dress & handsome furniture of Houses" while the Indians "either thro'd their Natural Laziness, or more properly I think, the extortion & Knavery of the Traders can hardly procure ordinary Cloathing to cover their Nakedness." Whatever sympathy the missionaries had for the Indians seems to have been destroyed by the ferocity of frontier war. There is nothing of the noble savage in the report of the Church of England ministers as they describe "the Invasion of Savages (to wm pity & compassion are unknown) who have no other notion nor expression of Courage than the exquisiteness of the torture & prolonging the Deaths they inflict upon their Captives, they seem to have nothing but the shape of Men to distinguish them from Wolves & Tygers."[12]

There were occasional reports from missionaries after 1715, but for the most part the SPG effort with respect to Indians ended with the Yamasee War.[13] Part of the reason may have been a changed attitude on the part of the SPG and the clergymen: one cannot, after all, propagate the Gospel among wolves and tigers shaped like men. Also the long and costly fighting had depopulated many parishes and it took time for the settlers and their ministers to reestablish themselves. Then too the Indians had suffered a drastic defeat, and the remnants of those tribes, like the Yamasees, which had lived close to white settlements now moved further west: assuming that the Anglican clergy were still interested in sharing their religion with the barbarous foe, the separation made it more difficult.

Even if there had been no war, however, it is unlikely that the missionaries sent by the SPG would have converted many Indians. Effective missionary work required learning the language of the natives; it required time and patience to overcome their lack of interest; and it required some detachment from the concerns of the white settlers. The SPG clergymen were settled in parishes that were part of the established church and their primary responsibility was for the spiritual welfare of the colonists. They had neither the time nor the freedom of action that was necessary to convert the Indians to Christianity. What was needed were special missionaries who could devote full time to the Indians. In 1705 Thomas Nairne had developed a plan by which the Indian traders of South Carolina would have been taxed to support six missionaries to the Yamasees. Nairne envisioned that the missionaries would be tough, dedicated men who would live among the Indians and learn their language. He pointed out that they would be "disinterested from all ye wrangle of trade" and therefore able to improve Indian-white relations by explaining the grievances of the natives and reporting on their activity and temper. Nothing ever came of Nairne's proposals, probably because they were unacceptable to the politicians of South Carolina who were heavily involved in the Indian trade.[14]

The SPG might have provided men like those called for by Nairne; it had sent Samual Thomas for that purpose. After Thomas's report, however, the Society decided that the white colonists were a more fitting object of benevolence and it never shifted from that decision. Stimulated by letters from Le Jau, Bishop Compton urged the SPG to send two missionaries to the Yamasees in 1712, but the SPG decided it could not afford to do so. In 1725 Francis Varnod, a missionary who studied the Indians and admired them, offered to live with the Creeks for a year in order to learn their language. The SPG appears to have done nothing, perhaps because it was more impresssed with the analysis of Varnod's contemporary, Richard Ludlam of Saint James, Goose Creek, who found the Indians "wholy adicted to their own barbarous & Sloathful Customs."[15]

The SPG missionaries were more successful with the Negroes than with the Indians. Francis Le Jau wrote about his activities in some detail. In December 1708 he set aside one weekday for the instruction of slaves, white servants, and poor whites. The results were limited, probably because few bondsmen were available for instruction during the week; Le Jau persisted and he developed a set of guidelines for the conversion of slaves. He would not baptize a slave without the permission of his or her master. He also required an oath from the candidate that was designed to counter the idea that baptism would alter the temporal condition of the slaves: "You declare in the Presence of God and before this Congregation that you do not ask for the holy baptism out of any design to free yourself from the Duty and Obedience you owe to your Master while you live, but meerly for the good of Your Soul and to partake of the Graces and Blessings promised to the Members of the Church of Jesus Christ." Finally there was an oath that bound a married slave to his or her spouse "till Death does part you," which reflected Le Jau's concern about the lack of sexual fidelity among the Negroes. He also disliked the fact that slaves attended "feasts, dances, and merry Meetings" on Sundays and warned the Christian blacks to "spend not the Lord's day in idleness" lest he "cut them off from the Communion."[16]

Shortly after his arrival in South Carolina, Le Jau expressed the opinion that "the Negroes are generally bad men, chiefly those that are Scholars." He apparently did not teach reading to the Goose Creek blacks, but some of them possessed that skill. One literate slave, "a very sober and honest Liver" in Le Jau's opinion, read a book describing the apocalyptical judgments that would visit a sinful world, and under that influence he began to make obscure but dire-sounding prophecies. Other slaves spread rumors that he had been visited by an angel, had heard voices, and had seen signs. This was not the type of religious activity that Le Jau wanted, and he moved quickly to silence the prophet and squelch the stories. He also became more skeptical about whether Negroes should read: he claimed that an elderly slave told him that instead of reading "he wou'd rather choose hereafter to practice the good he could remember."[17]

In the summer of 1710 Le Jau began holding special instructional sessions for Negro and Indian slaves after his regular Sunday services. About fifty bondsmen attended and gradually they learned to recite Anglican prayers, the Apostles' Creed, and the Ten Commandments. Le Jau eventually baptized some of the slaves and he rejoiced when they became living advertisements for the program: They "behave themselves very well, and do better for their Masters profit than formerly, for they

are taught to serve out of Christian Love & Duty." Eventually ill health
forced the missionary to discontinue the special Sunday meetings, but
his former pupils came to regular services and even listened from the
outside when it was too crowded for them to enter the church. Le Jau
continued to be gratified at the behavior of the black Christians, claiming that they had given up sexual promiscuity and dancing and that they
did not engage in rebellious activity.[18] After a time he began again to
catechize slaves; early in 1712 he was working with at least twenty and
sometimes twice that number. The program, however, seems to have
produced comparatively few church members: between 1710 and 1715
Le Jau reported baptizing only nineteen Negroes, this in a parish that had
2,000 slaves in 1720. Still, on the eve of the Yamasee War eight of the
seventy communicants in Saint James, Goose Creek, were black.[19]

Ebenezer Taylor, an SPG missionary in Saint Andrew's Parish, produced more church members than Le Jau, but the work of conversion
was actually done by lay people. The slaves lived on a plantation
belonging to Alexander Skene, secretary of the colony of Barbados, and
they were taught by Skene's sister, Mrs. Haig, her husband, and a
couple named Edwards. In 1716 Taylor claimed to have baptized fifty
blacks and earlier he reported giving Holy Communion to fourteen.
Religious activity on the Skene plantation continued for some time. By
1728 the property was part of Saint George's Parish, and in that year the
rector, Francis Varnod, baptized three Negro children belonging to Skene
and Mrs. Haig and reported that nineteen of their slaves were among his
communicants.[20]

The other early missionaries were less successful than Le Jau and
Taylor. Thomas Hasel baptized two black slaves in 1711 in Saint Thomas
Parish who had been taught to read and instructed in the basics of
Christianity by their master and mistress. If other planters would teach
their slaves, particularly the children born in the colony who were
"civilized" and fluent in English, Hasel believed much could be accom-
plished. Only a few slave owners were willing to make the effort,
however, and gradually the missionary became discouraged. In 1712 he
was instructing more than twenty slaves himself, but a few years later
he wrote that it was "extremely difficult to infuse into them the Notions
and Principles of Religion as also to teach them to read." John Whitehead, a schoolmaster in Charles Town, found most people opposed to
the conversion of slaves. He did baptize one Negro and he convinced a

few owners to send black children for instruction. He taught some of them to recite the catechism and to embellish their answers with scriptural quotations, and he had them perform in Saint Philip's Church in order to impress the congregation. William Tredwell Bull could find no one in Saint Paul's Parish who would allow him to instruct his slaves. Instead he purchased four slaves himself and began teaching them English and Christianity in the hope that the planters would be won over by example.[21]

Opposition to missionary work among African slaves was widespread in South Carolina. Commissary Gideon Johnston, rector of Saint Philip's Parish, was indignant about the "ill masters who not only neglect to instruct . . . their slaves but scoff at those who attempt it and give them likewise strange ideas of Christianity from the scandalous lives they lead." Mr. Haig, on the Skene plantation, claimed that some of his neighbors laughed at him for instructing slaves in the Christian religion. Some of this was due to what would be today called racism: Francis Le Jau reported that a lady in his parish was concerned about the prospect of meeting her slaves in heaven and "a young Gent had sd . . . that he is resolved never to come to the Holy Table while slaves are Recd there."[22] For the most part, however, the opposition grew out of a concern for the continuation of slave labor. At first slave owners raised the possibility that baptism would make the slave free. When this point was quickly denied, an economic argument took its place. Owners pointed out that religious instruction would take slaves out of the fields and they professed to believe that Christian slaves would not be so efficient as heathen slaves.[23] As the slave population increased and slave resistance became more common, owners began to fear that Christianity would lead to rebellion. Slaves meeting for worship, for example, might use the occasion for other purposes.[24]

The basic position of the Church of England was that a Christian master had a moral duty to promote the religious development of his slaves. The missionaries also argued that the process would be economically beneficial since the Christian slave would serve out of love rather than duty.[25] This last claim was tactically unsound since it moved the discussion from the realm of morality, where the ecclesiastic could claim a certain authority, to that of practicality, where the planter's judgment was supreme. Moreover certain elements within the church argued that economic concerns should take precedence over moral ones.

In 1711 William Fleetwood, bishop of Saint Asaph, preached a sermon
to the SPG in which he argued strongly that the planters had a moral
duty to provide for the instruction of their slaves, but only insofar as it
consisted with good business. "I would not have any one's Zeal for
Religion (much less my own) so far outrun their Judgment..., as to
cause them to forget that we are a people who live and maintain ourselves by *Trade*; and that if Trade be lost, or overmuch discouraged, we
are a ruined Nation: and shall ourselves in time become as very Slaves,
as thos I am speaking of, tho' in a nother kind: I would not...be
understood...to plead for any other Liberties or Privileges, than what
are reconcileable with Trade and the Nation's Interest, a little perhaps
abated."[26]

Bishop of London Edmund Gibson was somewhat tougher in a pastoral letter sent to the colonies in 1727. He urged that Christian masters
should think of their servants not "upon the same level with labouring
Beasts, but as *Men*-Slaves and Women-Slaves" possessed of souls, and
attend to their religious instruction. If the planter lost some profit by
giving his slaves time off to learn about Christianity, Gibson asserted
that God would reward him in some other way. Whether or not by
design, Gibson also addressed a fear of slave insurrections that was
growing in South Carolina. The bishop argued that on the plantation as
in the state Christianity would make the governed easier to handle: "It is
certain that the Gospel every where enjoins not only Diligence and
Fidelity, but also *Obedience*, for Conscience Sake....And, in Truth,
one great Reason why Severity is at all necessary to maintain Government, is the *Want* of Religion in those who are to be governed, and who
therefore are not to be kept to the Duty by any Thong but *Fear* and
Terror...."[27]

Experience, however, gave the lie to Gibson's claim that Christian
slaves would be more docile. As early as 1724 there were reports that
converts to the Church of England had been involved in "Secret Poison-
ings & bloody Insurrections." The issue came into the open in 1737
when the *South Carolina Gazette* carried a letter from Antigua describing several slave conspiracies that had been uncovered. The leaders of
one were Negroes who had been taught to read and write and instructed
in Christianity according to the wishes of Bishop Gibson. They had sworn
members to secrecy and administered the sacraments "according to the
Rites of the Bishop's Church." According to the writer, this afforded "a

Speciman of what may be expected from Converting Negroes." At that point every white male on the island over sixteen years was doing guard duty every fourth night. A few months later a South Carolina author, probably Commissary Alexander Garden, took issue with the Antigua writer and defended "the Christian and holesome Admonitions" of the bishop. Sympathizing with the melancholy condition of the islanders, this writer nonetheless felt that conversion of the slaves was not the cause of the attempted insurrection; rather "'tis the Want of *Religion* and the *Usage* they meet with," which brought the bloodshed. Religion was in fact a better means of dealing with the problem than were slave patrols. Moreover, the master could find it difficult to give an account of his own soul if he denied the word of God to his slaves. The South Carolinian ended on a note as ironic as it was tragic. "I could say more on this subject, especially in Relation to the Right we have of making them what they are, but prudence and our Safety forbids."[28]

Two years after this debate the *Gazette* reported an incident that suggested the effects of Christianity on slaves were more ambiguous than either of these writers believed. Two blacks were captured in the spring of 1739 after escaping from their masters and fleeing, probably towards Florida. One was whipped, but the other suffered a harsher punishment, the thought of which apparently reminded him of his religious training: ". . . the said Caesar was executed at the usual Place, and afterwards hung in chains at Hang-man's Point opposite to this Town, in sight of all Negroes passing and repassing by Water: Before he was turned off he made a very sensible Speech to those of his Colour, Exhorting them to take warning by his unhappy example; after which he begged the Prayers of all Christian People, himself repeating the Lord's Prayer and several others in a fervent and devout manner."[29]

The Church of England ministers in South Carolina advocated the conversion of slaves, but their attitudes toward the blacks were similar to those of the laity. In 1711 Benjamin Dennis reported "discoursing with one of the Negroes, . . . a very sensible fellow," and gave an account of the conversation; this is one of the few instances in which a missionary wrote about a slave as a fully capable human being. In the other infrequent instances where a black appears as subject rather than object, his intelligence is belittled, his behavior is condemned, or he is damned with faint praise. Le Jau spoke out against extreme cruelty on the part of masters but he wrote about blacks in a patronizing manner. In striking contrast to their attitude toward the Indians, the missionaries appear to have been totally uninterested in the culture of African slaves. An example of a general attitude comes from a letter written in 1744 by Thomas Thompson, missionary in Saint Bartholomew's Parish, to Philip Bearcroft, secretary of the SPG. Thompson was pleased that Mrs. Bearcroft appreciated a young, black boy named Toby that the minister had sent to England: "I beg leave to offer my very humble respects & hearty thanks to Mrs. Bearcroft for having any thought of me, and for the care which I know She has of her little Negro. I have at last got a mocking bird & shall send it when a proper opportunity offers...."[30] The clergy were also slaveholders themselves. The Establishment Act of 1704 assumed that parish ministers would be supplied with a few slaves and most of them acquired more.[31]

The prejudice with which the clergy approached the Negroes as black people and as slaves must certainly have detracted from their efforts to treat them as heathens and convert them to Christianity. A minister, for example, might disagree with the community belief that conversion was too expensive and dangerous but he could understand and appreciate the values on which that judgment was made. Under these conditions he might well put his energies into projects that would receive more community approval, particularly since he was dependent on the public for much of his income. Nor, as we have seen, was the Church of England as a whole rigorous in its commitment to the Christianization of slaves. It has sometimes been contended that an Anglican bishop in the American colonies might have increased the number of Christian slaves by exerting pressure on the laity.[32] It seems very unlikely that the Church of England would have tried to force slave owners to do something they were strongly opposed to doing: on the one hand, the church did not believe in risking prosperity for the sake of morality, on the other hand, its own morality did not exclude racism or slavery.

Under these conditions the Anglican program made little progress during the 1730s. The bishop of London's pastoral letter had no effect on the attitudes of the laity, and one newly arrived missionary reported that most of his colleagues believed that the further conversion of slaves was impractical because of the bad behavior of Christian blacks. In response to the SPG's continuing interest in the subject of missionary work among the slaves, several clergymen called for a law making it compulsory for planters to provide for the instruction of their servants.[33]

In Saint George's Parish the number of Christian slaves grew, presumably as a result of the efforts of the Skene family. In 1741 there were 85 black members of the Church of England in that parish, although the minister pointed out there were 3,287 heathen slaves. In other parishes there was a handful of black Anglicans. William Guy in Saint Andrew's reported baptizing a slave or two almost every year. Other ministers baptized fewer slaves and some none at all.[34]

The Anglican effort to convert slaves in South Carolina was at a near standstill on the eve of the Great Awakening. That it did not remain so was due to the efforts of an Anglican minister who was also the Church of England's most bitter critic, the Reverend George Whitefield. After creating a stir in the American colonies in the fall of 1739, Whitefield retired to Georgia where he produced a series of public letters that set the terms for his later conflicts. One of these, *A Letter to the Inhabitants of Maryland, Virginia, North and South Carolina*, dealt with the issue of slavery. Whitefield was not opposed to the institution itself, but he claimed that masters should treat their slaves decently. Some slaves, he said, were treated worse than dogs or horses. In particular Whitefield, like the Church of England, argued that slaves should be converted to Christianity; he parted company with the Anglican establishment, however, by offering his own ministry as a superior service. Responding to the well-known argument that Christian blacks became worse slaves, he blamed their instruction: "They were baptized and taught to read and write, and this they may do, and much more, and yet be far from the Kingdom of God." "There is," said Whitefield, "a vast Difference between civilizing and christianizing." The difference, of course, was whether or not the subject was brought to the point of spiritual rebirth. Whitefield challenged anyone to produce a slave who had experienced the "New Birth" and was a worse servant.[35]

Whitefield attacked the character of the South Carolina clergy as well as their doctrines, and the immense popularity of his preaching put a great deal of pressure on the established church. Commissary Alexander Garden defended the Church of England and its programs. With respect to slavery, his first response came in the summer of 1740 in a document published as *Six Letters from the Rev. Mr. Garden to the Rev. Mr. Whitfield* [sic]. The commissary began by suggesting that Whitefield should have reprinted Gibson's letter about slavery rather than writing one of his own. Garden ignored Whitefield's assertion that the orthodox clergy did not actually convert the slaves they taught. Instead the commissary forcefully defended the planters from Whitefield's charges that they did not treat their slaves well: "The Generality of Owners use their Slaves with all due Humanity, whether in respect of Work, of Food, or Raiment." Garden did agree that little was being done for the souls of the slaves. Not the deliberate action of the planter was at fault, however, but "the want of one certain uniform Method of teaching them." Without elaboration, the commissary suggested that this "will soon be established with success."[36]

Garden was alluding to a school for Negroes that he hoped to establish in Charles Town. He had first written to the SPG about the project in May 1740, at a time when there was a strong possibility that Whitefield would preempt the field of slave instruction. In April the evangelist had purchased 500 acres of land on the Delaware River to be used as a center for Negro instruction. The project came to nought, however, in part because its cosponsor, William Seward, was murdered six months later by a Welsh mob. Whitefield manifested his intentions in the letter written to southern slave owners in January 1740. That letter was published in Philadelphia, South Carolinians knew of its existence in February, and Garden penned a rebuttal in July. It is very likely that Garden knew of the contents when he made his own proposals to the SPG, and that the proposed Charles Town Negro School was a direct result of the challenge of evangelical good works.[37]

Garden's plan, his "one certain uniform method" for the conversion of slaves, was that American-born blacks under the age of ten would be taught by other American slaves carefully educated for that purpose. He had conceived the idea some time earlier and had hoped that plantation owners with more than eighty slaves would voluntarily give up one bondsman to be educated as a teacher and employed to instruct other blacks. Garden had found no master willing to participate of his own accord, however, and the legislature was unwilling to consider making the action mandatory. Now the commissary hoped that the SPG could purchase a number of young slaves so that they could be trained as teachers. The SPG was indeed amenable, and it empowered Garden and two other ministers to purchase two suitable blacks. Accordingly, on April 4, 1742 the SPG became the owner of Harry and Andrew, aged fourteen and fifteen respectively. The two boys came from the estate of the recently deceased Alexander Skene; together they cost just under £60 sterling.

Under Garden's vigorous management the Negro school gradually became a reality. Andrew proved to be an academic disappointment, but Harry made progress under the commissary's tutelage. In March 1743 Garden advertised for donations to build a school in Charles Town where young slaves might be instructed. Six months later the school opened, and shortly thereafter Harry was teaching thirty students. In a year the number of pupils had doubled; the SPG had supplied spelling books, copies of the *Book of Common Prayer*, and Bibles for the Christian neophytes. Garden visited England in 1746 and reported that twenty-eight children had graduated from the school. At that time it had seventy students, fifty-five children taught during the day and fifteen adults who attended night classes. The commissary claimed that black parents were anxious to have their children instructed, and he felt the method had proven a successful one that might be emulated elsewhere.[38]

The Anglican Negro school also proved successful with respect to the battle against evangelical religion. While it was being organized, a planter named Hugh Bryan, a partisan of Whitefield's, engaged in a form of slave instruction that seemed infinitely dangerous to the gentry of South Carolina. Believing himself to be guided by a divine spirit, Bryan began to meet with slaves at large evening gatherings in Saint Helena's Parish. In February 1742 the spirit told him that a slave insurrection would occur before April and that the blacks would devastate the province and win their freedom. Bryan made the prophecy public in order to warn the white population of South Carolina about the consequences of its sins. Already alarmed at the assembling of slaves, the Commons House resolved that Bryan's predictions could "prove of the most dangerous Consequences to the Peace and Safety of this Province" and ordered that he be taken into custody. On March 1, however, Bryan wrote the House and asked pardon for his behavior. He now believed that his spirit was a minion of Satan rather than God. A grand jury condemned Bryan's prophecies and cited Hugh and his brother, Jonathan, for assembling blacks and preaching to them without authority. The public reacted first with relief and later with amusement as further stories of Hugh's religious delusions were spread about the province.[39]

Bryan's behavior put the evangelical party on the defensive. In April the *Gazette* carried a letter from two dissenting ministers, both of them

Whitefield's supporters, which praised the bishop of London's efforts on behalf of slave instruction and recommended his pastoral letter to members of their own persuasion. Despite the fact that the piece was couched in a humble and respectful tone, it received an aggressive reply. The next week a writer asked the two ministers why they asserted that their names would have little weight with "some Gentlemen of the Establishment." Why was this an opportune moment for praising the Anglican effort? When recommending "Attempts of this nature," did the clergymen mean only regular and countenanced programs or that "every idle and designing Person" should be free to pursue other activities: "vis. gathering Cabals of Negro's about him, without public Authority, at unseasonable Times, and to the Disturbance of a Neighborhood; and instead of teaching them the Principles of Christianity, filling their Head with a Parcel of Cant-Phrases, Trances, Dreams, Visions, and Revelations and some-still worse, and which prudence forbids me to name?"[40]

The Negro school was also used as a symbol of fiscal integrity against the alleged misuse of funds at Whitefield's Bethesda orphanage. In 1743 and 1744 a running battle occurred in the *South Carolina Gazette* between those who saw the orphanage as an outstanding example of good works and critics who claimed that it was an abuse of public charity. The critics called for a public accounting of income and expenditures, and when the accounts of the Negro school were published shortly thereafter it was not hard to make the connection.[41]

Despite its partisan purposes the Charles Town Negro School continued for many years. Garden was enthusiastic about his project. When the original schoolhouse blew down in 1752, he quickly had another built. Richard Clarke, who succeeded the commissary as the rector of Saint Philip's Church, also managed the school in a capable manner and reported that seventy children were receiving instruction in 1755. The Reverend Robert Smith took over in 1759 and reported that there were over fifty students. The school seems to have continued in operation until 1768, when the teacher was unable to carry on. The end of Harry's academic career is recorded in the vestry book of Saint Philip's Church: "Ordered that Harry, the Negroe that keeps School at the Parsonage (for repeated Transgressions) be sent to the Work house, And to be put into the Mad house, there to be kept till Orders from the Vestry to take him out." Although he had been teaching for twenty-five years, Harry was only forty years old. One would like to know more about his transgressions, whether or not they reflected mental disturbance, and if so whether it was related to his job. It may be that there was a great deal of stress involved in being a slave teacher of slaves in eighteenth century Charles Town. Even though the ostensible purpose of the school was to train teachers, Harry was not replaced and the school ceased to exist.[42]

In the parishes outside of Charles Town, Christianization made erratic progress in the years after the Great Awakening. In 1751 the Reverend Robert Stone received the thanks of several of his parishioners in Saint James, Goose Creek, who believed their slaves were more tractable as a result of his efforts to teach them Christianity. James Harrison, who succeeded Stone, took advantage of the congenial environment to become the most successful of all the SPG's missionaries with respect to the conversion of slaves. In 1766, after being in the parish fourteen years, Harrison reported that 150 slaves were members of his church and 30 of them were communicants. His parishioners were apparently happy: one of them gave Harrison a Negro girl in appreciation of his efforts at spreading the Gospel among the slaves.[43] In other parishes, however, things were much as they had been; the missionaries baptized a few slaves, but the owners were not sympathetic to the idea of religious instruction for blacks. The Reverend Charles Martyn reported from Saint Andrew's Parish in 1753 that his parishioners believed conversion made slaves "become lazy and proud, entertaining too high an Opinion of themselves, and neglecting their daily Labour." Twelve years later an Anglican clergyman named Isaac Armory resigned his position in Saint John's Parish in Colleton County because he believed that teaching slaves about Christianity was part of his job and his parishioners disagreed.[44]

Because of the Charles Town Negro school and the activity in Goose Creek, there were probably more Christian blacks in South Carolina on the eve of the Revolution than ever before. Nonetheless, they were only a tiny fraction of the slave population and the prevailing sentiment among slave owners was hostile to the conversion of slaves. As the closing of the Negro school suggests, the Anglican effort had resulted in the baptism of a number of slaves, but it had not altered the prevailing pattern of heathenism.

The basic reason that the Church of England did not convert the Indians of South Carolina to Christianity was that the Indians did not wish to become Christians. With respect to slaves, however, the situation was different, since it was not the blacks who chose to remain in a heathen condition, but rather their owners who made the decision for them. Despite the best efforts of the clergy, the Anglican gentry as a whole remained convinced that religious instruction for their slaves was not a desirable thing. Pleasing their patrons among the laity was a higher priority for the clergy than doing missionary work among the heathens; therefore, the process of Christianization went on in only a halting fashion.

In addition to the disinterest of the Indians and the prejudice of the slaveholders, the self-interest of the Church of England set limits on the effectiveness of missionary work. The SPG pushed for the conversion of Indians and slaves but in the context of propagating the Church of England as well as the Gospel. When the SPG shifted its emphasis from the Indians to the white colonists, it chose, in effect, to promote Anglicanism rather than Christianity, and the moderate position of the Church of England on the question of religious instruction for slaves was designed to insure that benevolence did not bring ill will. The church was so willing to placate the white colonists that the program of slave instruction was slowly dying when the Great Awakening threatened Anglican hegemony and created a need for "good works" to balance the conspicuous outpouring of faith generated by Whitefield. Out of this danger to the established church came a new program for the education of slaves, but when the threat subsided, so did the effort. The determination of the planters that their slaves remain heathen was, throughout this period, met by a lack of determination on the part of the Church of England that they become Christians.

CHAPTER 7

THE ASPIRATIONS OF THE LAITY

In some ways the Church of England in South Carolina was a product of outside forces. The Carolina proprietary played a role in founding the institution and the SPG helped to maintain it for almost fifty years. Still, it was the Anglican citizens of the colony who fought for establishment and supported the church with tax revenues and private donations; moreover it was they who shaped the English institution to suit their own American tastes. What, one wonders, did they gain? What needs—spiritual needs certainly, but also social, political, and intellectual needs—did the state church fulfill for the people who supported it? It is a difficult question, in part because there is little direct evidence about the attitude of Anglicans toward the church. Moreover, it seems probable that few members of the laity were aware in any precise manner of the forces that motivated their action. Most people are not. It is possible, however, to infer something about the significance of the church for the laity by looking at the various ways in which the people interacted with the institution. If we know how individuals behaved in the context of religious practice, we can perhaps understand why religion was important to them.

There was a worldly quality to the Church of England in South Carolina that has often been remarked upon by modern commentators who suggest that religion was not very influential in the colony. For the most part, however, worldliness seems to have conditioned religious worship rather than detracted from it. A good example is the exhortation with which Colonel Daniel Horry is reputed to have encouraged his men to resist the British attack in 1776: "Fight stoutly, my lads, for those brave fellows who were killed yesterday at Sullivans Island are now in heaven, riding their chariots like hell, by´G——d." The remarks were certainly profane, but not really irreligious; indeed the use of the religious idiom suggests that Christianity was a common bond among the soldiers.

Another aspect of worldliness was the materialism expressed in the adornment of churches and churchgoers. Penuel Bowen, a New England clergyman visiting Charles Town after the revolutionary war, found a luxury that pleased him. The two Episcopal churches in the city were "without and within quite superb and grand. . . . The furniture is rich & good & the organs large & full." Bowen described the congregations as well suited to their environment: "The Assemblies of people are large & splendid and well-behaved too." In Charles Town Anglican worldliness was associated with comfort and gentility, but in the rural parishes it was sometimes more crude. In 1747 the pastor of Saint Bartholomew's Parish complained that his congregation was accustomed to coming in and out of the church during services in order to refresh themselves with water and punch. He also found it common for brides to be visibly pregnant at the time of their marriages; occasionally he felt compelled to provide a chair so that an expectant mother could sit during the ceremony.[1]

Despite such worldliness, however, there was also in the Church of England a measure of simple piety. Early in the eighteenth century, Mrs. Thomas Broughton wrote to her son in terms that indicate a profound religious commitment as well as a touching maternal concern:

> my Dear Natt the consarn for your soul lies heivily upon my heart, lest the present injoyments of this World should take up all your thoughts and affections. Consider my Dear child I beg of you, that there is an eternity acoming that Merrits as well as requires your chefest cair, I have often desired you to look over your catichisem and consider what vows and promises was made for you in your baptism which it is now high time for you to think of renewing at the lord's table. . .,which still more strictly oblege you not to live in the neglect of known duty, nor commission of any evel, remember you depend on the allmighty for all things, and it is impieous to live without acknowledging that dependence by praying to him, and praising of him.

Equally unaffected and heartfelt is the plea of the Saint Helena's Parish vestry in 1730, after it learned that the SPG was thinking about transferring their minister to another parish: "We beg your Honrs to consider that we are a remote Parish, and that we can't hear the word of God in the way we profess or Enjoy the Benefits of the Sacraments upon the most extraordinary Occasions without going 80 or 90 Miles, and if any of us should die while our Parish is unprovided; tho we are Christians we must be buried like dogs; these are very Melancholy considerations."[2] The letters of Eliza Lucas also indicate that she was a sincere and pious Anglican. In 1742 she wrote to a younger brother who had recently entered the army on behalf of the "xtian scheme" lest he be tempted away from "the dictates of rason [sic] and religion." Later she comforted another brother who suffered from a fatal disease by sharing her thoughts on "a well grounded hope of blessed immortality." Eliza's husband, Charles Pinckney, was also a devout Anglican and together they impressed their own religious views on their three children. The young Pinckneys attended church and later memorized the opening prayer and read the sermon text in their own Bibles. Out of this environment Charles Cotesworth Pinckney grew to be an outstanding lay supporter of first the Church of England and later the Protestant Episcopal Church.[3] A number of other Charles Town families in the years before the Revolution seem to have been equally rigorous in their religious commitment.[4]

Even for the most devout of Anglicans, the church must have been important for secular reasons, in particular because of its significance with respect to social class. In 1750 Peter Manigault wrote from London to his mother in Charles Town explaining the purchase of a lace coat: "One Sunday Evening, I went with Billy Drayton to hear the celebrated Mr. Foster, a well-known clergyman. I was drest quite plain, My Friend had a Laced Waistcoat and hat, he, or rather his Laced Waistcoat, was introduced into a pew, while I, that is My plain Cloathes, were forced to stand up, during the whole time of divine Service, in the Isle." As Manigault learned, the Church of England not only recognized and respected the structure of social classes, but it also acted to reinforce it. Church support of social distinctions also occurred in South Carolina. Frederick Dalcho wrote that in the years before the Revolution Stephen Bull was accustomed to entertain the parishioners of Prince William's Parish after services each Sunday. Bull mingled with "the more respectable part of the congregation while his overseer, by his direction, and at his expense, liberally entertained the rest." As the guests regaled themselves, the difference between the gentry and the commoners was reinforced, and the host emphasized his own predominant role in the community. The established church gained along with the social hierarchy: "Seldom less than 60 or 70 carriages, of various descriptions were seen at the Church on the Lord's day."[5]

Anglican clergymen ministered to the poor and to those of modest means, but they maintained a special relationship with members of the gentry class. An episode from the early history of the church illustrates a general phenomenon. Robert Maule complained in the spring of 1711 that the small wooden house he was living in was cold in winter and hot in summer. He doubted that the parishioners would build a proper parsonage since most of them were poor and there was "not one leading Man among them by whose Influence & authority this or any other Charitable work might be promoted." Maule was on the verge of moving to another parish when the arrival of Colonel Thomas Broughton convinced him to remain where he was. Broughton was the son-in-law of Sir Nathaniel Johnson, "that great Instrument of Settling the Church here," and he himself was "a hearty lover of our Church." Broughton quickly began to get things done: "This pious Gentlemen has not only subscribed very generously himself but being a Person Universally Esteemed has by his Interest and Influence over the rest of ye parish prevailed with Several others of them also to Subscribe for the Purchase of the house and Settlement."[6]

Maule's gain was Francis Le Jau's loss. Broughton had left Le Jau's parish, Saint James, Goose Creek, to move to his "fine seat" in Maule's parish (Saint John's). About the same time Le Jau had buried a Colonel John Gibbs, and he was left with "no leading man or men of authority." The effect was serious: "I must arm my self with patience and for want of a potent friend must submit to see neither my church nor house finish'd, nor my Subscriptions paid." Meanwhile Broughton proved to be a real boon to Maule. A church had long been under construction in Saint John's, and under the direction of this "very Worthy Gentlemen" the exterior was completed and the interior elaborately furnished.[7] Maule benefited from Broughton's aid, but the relationship probably was not one-sided. Certainly the clergyman's respect for his patron must have been well known in the parish, and Maule's praise must have strengthened Broughton's position as a "leading man."

There was a symbiotic quality to the relationship between the clergy and the gentry, but the status of the ministers was usually secondary. "A certain Gentlemen and a Lady" showed their contempt for Gideon Johnston's office by bribing the parish clerk to alter his manner of delivering psalms. Johnston declared himself unwilling to be "a mere nose of wax . . . to be instructed every moment by his People," and he won the support of the vestry for his position.[8] Still the attempt illustrates the attitude of some members of the laity. The problems of the clergy were largely economic; few of them had enough property to be accepted on an equal basis by the wealthy members of their parishes. Peter Manigault understood the situation very well and exhibited what were probably the prevailing values: "They tell me good Friend Cousin Betsy is to be married to Parson Keith. If she likes him I have no objection to the Match, but I would have her consider, that Gentlemen of his cloth wear their Clothes longer than other Sort of People, & that there is no great Diversion in sewing a Horsehair Button on a greasy black Waistcoat."[9]

The alliance between the Church of England and the upper class in South Carolina was strengthened by the interest of the church in promoting education and other charitable activities. Social welfare in England was left largely to private philanthropy, to the benevolence of the aristocracy, in particular to the charitable urges of the wealthy mercantile and professional elites. Trusts and corporations, the legal apparatus of English modernization, were the forms through which private charity was put to work ameliorating the problems caused by economic change, social inequality, and ill fortune. The outpouring of funds for schools, hospitals, orphanages, and other benevolent enterprises was immense.[10] Accustomed to philanthropic action, the Anglican clergy in South Carolina looked to the "great men" for benevolence and they found a number of provincial elites willing to emulate their English counterparts. Education in particular benefited from this patronage.

The SPG itself was a charitable corporation made up of prominent Englishmen interested in promoting not only religion but also benevolence in general and education in particular. Among the earliest missionaries sent to Charles Town was Thomas Hasel, who was to have served as a schoolmaster before he was recruited to serve as a priest. Gideon Johnston later encouraged the passage of a law that created a free school in Charles Town in 1712, and John Whitehead taught in the school until the Yamasee War brought it to a halt. The SPG also sent a missionary to open a school in Saint James, Goose Creek, but the school did not operate for long.[11]

A more permanent school in Charles Town resulted from the efforts of Governor Francis Nicholson, himself a member of the SPG. Nicholson encouraged the Anglican clergy to ask the SPG to appoint a schoolmaster, and the SPG sent the Reverend Thomas Morritt who arrived early in 1723. Some time was lost while Nicholson convinced the legislature to give Morritt a salary and to provide a schoolhouse, but in June the school began to operate. In the fall of 1724 there were forty-five students, twenty of whom were studying Latin. A year later Morritt reported that there were more than fifty students; one of them had come from Philadelphia, another from the Bahama Islands, and ten were supported by the charity of the province. According to their instructor, some of the students who had arrived barely able to read were now able to translate chapters of the New Testament into Latin.[12]

Even before Morritt's school was operating, the gentry of South Carolina were beginning to take an interest in benevolence. In 1715 Richard Beresford was selected to act as an agent for South Carolina in England. Facing two ocean voyages, he made a will providing an annual sum for the care and education of his three-year-old son, John, and further providing that until John was twenty-one the income from Beresford's estates in Carolina would go into a fund to be administered by the vestry of Saint Thomas Parish for the purpose of creating a school. While in England Beresford married Dorothy Melish who brought a dowry of £800 sterling. By 1722 his slaves had increased from 50 to 100 and his plantations from two to seven. In the interval Dorothy died, leaving Beresford with a second son, Richard Jr.

All this became of interest to the Church of England in 1722 when a tree limb fell on Beresford's head and killed him. The vestry of Saint Thomas and the Reverend Thomas Hasel undertook to collect the legacy, but that proved to be a difficult task. Friends of the family questioned the validity of the will since it made no mention of the younger son. The case was carried to England and the parish asked the SPG for aid. The SPG's counsel advised that Beresford's change of circumstances voided the will and along with it the provision for a school in Saint Thomas. The court decided differently, and Hasel reported in 1727 that the vestry had received £3,000 as the profits from Beresford's estate in the previous year. Steps were being taken to purchase land, and the remaining money was to be put out at interest in order to create a fund that would support a school.[13]

The Beresford "free school," as it was called, began operation in 1729 and continued to educate children until the Revolution. It was located for a time on a plantation close to the church but eventually moved into a new two-story brick building. The proceeds from Beresford's estate were loaned at 10 percent interest, and the resulting income paid for the schoolhouse, provided a salary for the schoolmaster, and maintained a number of poor children. The financial situation became precarious for a time when local planters borrowed from the fund, got themselves elected to the vestry, and eased their own repayments. The legislature prohibited the practice in 1736, however, and at the same time incorporated the vestry for the purpose of administering the fund. The school, meanwhile, was an acknowledged success. In one sense, however, Beresford's wishes were frustrated. He had intended that it would provide instruction in language, mathematics, and science, as well as the basics of reading, writing, and arithmetic. Despite the hopes of Thomas Hasel and his successor, the Reverend Alexander Garden, Jr., the more advanced subjects were never offered. In practice the Beresford "free school" seems to have concentrated on preparing poor children to carry out lowly tasks with diligence and dispatch. In 1763 Garden wrote that eight indigent children were being supported by the fund and educated "so as to fit them for Apprentices"; at the same time he noted that the vestrymen were pleased to see the many graduates who were now "sober industrious Christians & useful members of Society."[14]

Other well-to-do Anglicans left money for philanthropic purposes, but the results were less successful than in the case of the Beresford trust. George Boyle died in 1718 and left most of his estate to the SPG. Saint John's Parish in Berkley County, where Boyle had lived, wanted the SPG to use the money for a free school, but the SPG was unwilling to do so unless the parish would make a contribution of its own. In the meantime the money, estimated at £1,200, remained in the hands of George Pawley, son of the original executor.[15] The SPG was again a beneficiary when John Whitmarsh of Saint Paul's Parish died in April 1723. Whitmarsh had ordered that £1000 in Carolina currency go to Saint Paul's within a year of his death, one-half of the money to be given to the SPG for the purchase of books for the poor children of the parish. The vestry was to spend the remaining £500 for educational purposes within the parish.[16] In the spring of 1725 the SPG deputized the Reverend William Guy of Saint Paul's Parish to collect its legacies. Guy approached Pawley, but the planter was unable to pay at the appointed time in September 1726: Pawley received an extension, but the economy took a downturn, and he fled to the frontier to escape his creditors. Pawley paid small sums at intervals, however, and finally in 1731 Guy remitted the remainder of the legacy to the SPG. He had even managed to win a dispute over several barrels of rice and earn the SPG an additional £167.[17] The Whitmarsh legacy was more difficult. By the time Guy became involved, the vestry of Saint Paul's had done nothing about collecting the £1000 and Mrs. Whitmarsh had remarried. The clergyman pushed the vestry to obtain an accounting of the late Whitmarsh's estate; the actual assessment was done without Guy's knowledge, and it showed a net value of only £361 17s. Guy and the vestry exchanged tart letters, but the results did not change. It was finally January 1733 when Guy turned over £153 5s. to the SPG.[18]

Another educational project was initiated in 1728 at the death of the Reverend Thomas Ludlam, who left his entire estate to the SPG for the purpose of founding a charity school in the parish of Saint James, Goose Creek. A very efficient local planter named William Dry, who was anxious to have the school near his plantation, handled the administration of Ludlam's estate, which produced something more than £200 sterling in money and land of equal value. The SPG then empowered William Guy and Alexander Garden to administer the fund, and they increased the principal to £600 sterling by 1741. At that point the parish and the SPG reached an agreement by which the former would provide land and build a school and home for the schoolmaster, and the latter would pay an annual salary of £100 out of the proceeds from Ludlam's estate. Cooperation, however, soon broke down. The parish started work on a school and it drew up a proposal for a law that would govern the institution. The SPG failed to act on the law for some time and then objected to the fact that the trustees would have power to hire and fire the schoolmaster. By 1750 the fund was capable of supporting a teacher but the school was incomplete, and the law had not been passed.[19]

The development of private philanthropy in South Carolina had an importance that transcended the specific projects for which it was used. It grew out of a larger process of social maturation that was taking place in the colony. By the third decade of the eighteenth century the provincial economy was well established (if still subject to fluctuations), the revolution of 1719 had created a firm political base, and society itself was coming of age. As part of the process, local elites emulated their English counterparts and demonstrated social responsibility by using their newly earned fortunes to ameliorate the lot of those less fortunate. It seems likely that good will was one motive for such benevolence, but members of the gentry also engaged in philanthropy in order to demonstrate or insure their own status. In a fluid social structure one might become a member of the elite by doing the things that elites do. Of particular significance is the role that the Church of England played in all of this: it acted both as a social welfare agency for the unfortunate and as a vehicle by which the fortunate identified themselves.

South Carolina was still youthful, however, and the provincial atmosphere was not always congenial to philanthropy. The vestry of Saint James, Goose Creek, for example, asked the SPG to empower private individuals to administer the Ludlam legacy because the vestrymen of Saint Thomas Parish had used the Beresford trust for private gain. Another controversy in Saint Thomas was reported by the *South Carolina Gazette* in 1732. Captain Richard Harris died leaving £100 in currency for the free school and one-half of his estate to a granddaughter. Harris's wife, Hanna, was infuriated: she got the will away from the executor, tore it into small pieces, and began to sell cattle, horses, and slaves. A chancery suit was instituted to protect the beneficiaries![20]

Describing the spiritual character of Charles Town Anglicans in 1786 for a correspondent back home in Boston, Penuel Bowen wrote that they were "easy & tolerable, polite without cultivating the principle—religious without feeling."[21] What he meant is not entirely clear, perhaps that the South Carolinians lacked religious commitment. On the other hand, "religious without feeling" suggests an approach to religion that was rational rather than emotional. This quality was very much a part of the Church of England in South Carolina. Rationalism was emphasized by the earliest clergymen who came to the province and over time it became one of the most important things separating members of the Church of England from their counterparts in the dissenting persuasions.

A faith in rational persuasion and in the reasonableness of Anglican beliefs was evident in the efforts of early clergymen to win over those people who dissented from the state church. Francis Le Jau believed the Anglican product would sell itself: "I dont seek to meddle with the Dissenters in matters of Controversy, but upon occasion and chiefly when asked I declare the words of Jesus Christ with the doctrine and practice of our Church, they wanted most of them to be better informed." Robert Maule asked the SPG to send tracts "rationally written in vindication of Infant Baptism." Arguments given in conversation were useful, said Maule, but people were apt to forget: "Whereas had they such little Tracts prudently dispersed among them, and which they might at all time have an opportunity of perusing at pleasure the Truths contained in them might probably be so tenaciously fixed in their Memories as nothing cou'd easily obliterate them." The SPG did send pamphlets, and the ministers found them useful, so much that rival clergymen confiscated them whenever possible. Le Jau decided that the tracts might also aid "the Settling of those of our Communion; who being dayly tormented with the Silly Argumt & Nauseous Reflections of those Hereticks upon our Holy Church might ignorantly Entertain some Scruples."[22]

Anglicans believed that a rational approach to religion was one of the important things that separated their church from other denominations. Francis Le Jau made the point when he described the three Baptist "teachers" in South Carolina in 1713: they were "very obstinate, and hardly capable to form a right judgment of things for being Illiterate." Yet Le Jau was insecure: they were "cunning and Artfull," and while "Any person of sense" was immune to their persuasions, the "simple and Ignorant" were "sometimes ensnared by their tricks." The Church of England won a victory when one of these men gave a discourse on predestination and a member of the audience, given to fits of depression, went home and hanged himself. Le Jau called the event a "Dismal Accident" but he described it with grim satisfaction: such were the dangers of emotional religion.[23]

As the dissenting interest became more powerful in South Carolina, proponents of the Church of England dwelt increasingly on the irrational character of their opponents. In the fall of 1724, Sir Francis Nicholson wrote to the bishop of London about the arrival of three new Presbyterian ministers in Charles Town. According to Nicholson, the newcomers "infuse Ante Monarchical Principles into the people and are Setting up for an Independt Government both in Church and State. . . ."

The clergy echoed Nicholson's views, but they also mounted a more fraudulent and more vicious attack. They wrote about a Huguenot family named Dutartre, living in Saint Dennis Parish, who had embraced a bizarre set of religious ideas under the influence of an itinerant Moravian preacher. One of them proclaimed himself a prophet and began living in sin with his sister-in-law, allegedly under divine direction. The matter came to the attention of a local peace official, who attempted to arrest the adulterers. The Dutartres resisted this attack on their holy community and mortally wounded the officer, but his posse killed one member of the family and captured the rest. Reporting these events and the trial and execution of the offenders, the Church of England clergy used the Dutartres as a justification for limiting the activities of all dissenters. They asked the SPG to help ensure that "fanatick teachers" not be "pour'd into other colonies in America from New England or. . . Scotland," and that colonial governors be given the power to prevent "all future propagation of such pernicious principles within their Governts."[24]

Over time this antipathy to the dissenters waned, or at least it was less often expressed, as Commissary Garden encouraged a policy of accommodation between the established church and its rivals. Rationalism remained a distinguishing characteristic of the Church of England, and it was a point of pride for Anglican communicants. In 1742 Eliza Lucas urged her brother "to live agreeably to the dictates of rason [*sic*] and religion" and explained how the two authorities complemented one another: "The Divine goodness. . . furnished you with both reason, which is his natural revelation, and with his written word supernaturally revealed and delivered to mankind by his son Jesus Christ."[25] This emphasis on reason, and its counterpart, a rejection of emotion, was a central issue in the Great Awakening. George Whitefield and his followers charged the Church of England with offering only an empty formalism and an arid intellectualism and were themselves accused of excessive emotionalism, which for Anglicans seems to have been any emotion at all. The struggle over these and other issues was bitter and prolonged, but the Great Awakening ended with the congregations of the established church essentially intact. There is no reason to believe that the Church of England consequently put less emphasis on reason; the reverse is probably true.

This faith in rational religion, this rational faith as it were, was a significant aspect of Anglicanism in South Carolina. It probably did create a coolness and even a detachment on the part of the worshiper who apprehended the world in Newtonian terms, trusted in a natural order and the benevolence of a reasonable God, and was more concerned to understand than to feel.

Rationalism was an important part of Anglican identity, helping to set the member of the Church of England apart from a Baptist or Presbyterian and at the same time acting as a positive force in his religious life. By emphasising reason, however, which all men hold in common, the Church of England inadvertently suggested that particular religious practices were of secondary importance and thereby threatened its own claims to special treatment. The danger is illustrated again by Eliza Lucas, who, devout Anglican communicant though she was, defined the Christian religion as "such as is delivered in the scripture without any view to any particular part."[26] This ecumenical attitude was common in South Carolina, and it was the primary reason that the Church of England clergy gave up attempting to limit the activities of the dissenters. Rationalism also moved in the direction of elevating reason over revelation, in short, to deism. There is less evidence in the early years that people in South Carolina openly questioned the assertions of Christian revelation, but as the doctrines of deism were put forth in England they quickly appeared in the cultural provinces. Concrete evidence of this came in 1732 when Thomas Whitmarsh began weekly publication of the *South Carolina Gazette* and created a forum for public debate within the colony. Perhaps because the opportunity was new, local writers quickly generated a spate of controversy over religious issues.

The newspaper had been publishing about four months when an unnamed poetaster in an engaging combination of ribaldry, piety, and common sense advanced the thesis that there was no difference in the services offered by the Anglican cleric and the dissenter. Both the "long Surplice" and the "short Cloak" could marry and be married: "Nay yet more, can induce the most *gravely precise* To believe a *brisk Girl* 'tween the Sheets, is no Vice. Let none of us doubt, in their guidance to Heaven But (our Duty well done) their Virtues are even."[27] Several months later a prose writer printed an addendum to an essay on pride and took full revenge against his inept and haughty clergyman.

> How odd a Spectacle... to see a Minister descend from the pulpit, wrapt in the dear Contemplation of his Abilities, and receive the

cold Compliments due to a flat discourse, with such an Air of
Serenity, that one would think he enjoy'd the highest Satisfaction
in having obliged his Audience either by saying little or nothing to
the Purpose, or by unmercifully twisting the Subject, 'till he has
explain'd the Meaning quite away?[28]

These attacks, while doubtless annoying and perhaps embarrassing to
the Anglican clergy, did not constitute a threat to the Church of England. More serious was the support for religious rationalism that was
manifested in the fledgling newspaper.

In May 1732, the printer of the *South Carolina Gazette* gave notice
that he was taking subscriptions of 7s. 6d. for reprinting a sermon,
entitled *The Traditions of the clergy destructive of Religion: With an
Enquiry into the Grounds and Reasons of such Traditions*, that had been
delivered by William Bowman, vicar of Dewsbury, at a visitation at
Wakefield in Yorkshire, held in June 1731. Two hundred subscriptions
were needed for publication, and they were apparently found; the editor
Whitmarsh reported in October that "some particular Persons" were
displeased because he had reprinted Bowman's piece. Whitmarsh revealed something about the identity of his attackers when he pointed out
that in Great Britain the work was not looked on as "a Libel against the
Church of *England* and her Ministers," since Bowman was later given
dispensation to hold two livings. A month later an anonymous author
declared that Bowman's success had nothing to do with the validity of
the deism that he was espousing: princes were pleased by the idea that
religious institutions were not sacred since that meant that they could be
altered to suit political necessity.[29]

The controversy over Bowman generated a larger one that dealt with
the subject of religious toleration. A self-styled "Moderator" opened the
question by urging his readers to have charity for all religious ideas that
did not threaten them physically. At one point he used a culinary metaphor to illustrate the necessity of freedom of conscience.

Every Man, who is in earnest in his Religion, must chuse his own
Priest, as well as his own Cook, accordingly to his Sentiments
and his palate: and if he can find neither Priest nor Cook to his
Mind, he must be content to say his own Prayers and dress his
own Victuals.[30]

"Moderator" was soon answered by an anonymous Anglican writer who impugned his opponent's character and disparaged his writing ability, logic, and knowledge of the Bible. This writer also claimed to be tolerant: he would accept all religions that were Christian, reverent, and decorous, "The sacred Name of Charity" could not be made "to serve the vile Purposes of *Infidelity* and *Profanness*." He said the Bible may have left a freedom to choose one's minister, but certainly not an obligation. The prayers of the Church of England were made for all men, but he would not molest those who would use their own.[31]

The provincial defender of the faith was himself soon challenged. A third party joined the fray, claiming that the churchman was not a true Christian but rather a "furious Zealot." "Moderator" also responded to his attacker by denying that he intended to demean the clergy by likening them to cooks. He did feel that metaphor might be congenial to some ministers who were "equally skilled in making good Sermons and entertaining their *Parishioners* with a Jigg," and claimed that "among the Right Reverend Doctors, who support their Orthodoxy with a Coach and Six," there were those who favored "the upper End of a Table, as well as *the upper End of Government*." "Moderator" closed his final effort with a declaration that he would not again become involved in such a dispute.[32]

"Moderator's" reticence is understandable. The issue between the combatants was a narrow one and the attack moved quickly from principles to persons. Each side favored toleration for rival opinions, but the churchman saw Anglicanism as the standard of truth while "Moderator" and his ally had more catholic tastes. The vehemence of the churchman doubtless stemmed from the fact that the broader view hardly justified the expense of a state church or the privilege it gave to one body of clergymen. In fact it seems very likely that Commissary Alexander Garden was the man who defended the Church of England against both Bowman and "Moderator." In 1731 Garden had warned the clergy to be on the lookout for signs of deism in their parishes, and he had offered his own library to help them prepare to defend orthodoxy.[33] Garden would have been the logical person to pressure Whitmarsh, and the writing style of the Church of England pieces is similar to his. In his vehemence, however, Garden probably misjudged the temper of his parishioners.

It seems likely that the people of South Carolina would continue to worship in their accustomed way regardless of the views of Bowman or of "Moderator," neither of whose ideas were far removed from the situation that existed. There was no bishop in South Carolina, only a small percentage of Anglican churchgoers partook of the sacraments, and the government offered a broad toleration for religious ideas. The threat to the establishment felt by the churchman was probably more imagined than real. The basic reaction to the quarrel seems to have been boredom and annoyance. One writer commented that if "Moderator" had said a man "might" choose his priest rather than "must," it would have satisfied 75 percent of the population. He felt that plain sense and plain writing would have been more instructive than elaborate learning and logic. The latter, in fact, was simply out of place in the provincial scene: "To hear a Country Parson explaining the Hebrew Text to his Congregation, or a Lawyer talking Latin to an *American* Judge, are both subjects of Ridicule. And 'tis as ridiculous to see a Pedant exercising his stiff and formal Talents in a trading Town."[34]

Tolerant, irreligious even, attitudes were not serious threats to the established church when they appeared occasionally in the provincial newspaper, but when they manifested themselves at the local level they could make life miserable for a parish priest. In the years after the Great Awakening, Levi Durand, rector of Christ Church Parish, was vexed by a small number of wealthy men, nominally Anglicans, whose ideas smacked of deism, anticlericalism, and simple profanity. Jacob Bond, "Esqr," the leading figure of the parish, told a crowd of people gathered at a funeral that "it was impossible to offend God, and that he did not take notice of what little Dirt we took from one another." Durand claimed in 1751 that his church warden only attended services once each year, but was an improvement over an earlier one who stole from the collection plate and made off with five yards of linen ordered for a surplice.[35] Despite the presence of "Infidelity, Prophaneness, Heresy, Blasphemy and the most Offensive Breaches of Common Morality," Durand was at first determined to remain, as he put it, "in one of the dark corners of the world,... amidst a perverte and Crooked Generation."[36] After a time, however, he decided that things could only get worse and moved in 1752 to Saint John's, Berkeley. Two years later the luckless cleric experienced the same problem. A parishioner named William Anderson made light of Durand, laughing at him during several services because of a sermon in which the minister attempted to prove the divinity of the scriptures by showing the fulfillment of prophecies.

There may have been mitigating circumstances, however. In his own defense, Durand asserted that the parishioners were familiar with the sermon, some of them having heard it four or five times.[37]

Among the things that the Church of England offered to its parishioners, nothing was as important as stability. The doctrines and practices of the church were traditional, rooted as they were in medieval Christianity; the political and social values of the church stressed the importance of established authority; and the avoidance of emotional excess encouraged the individual to maintain control over himself. This conservatism, however, did not lead to a static view of society; the Church of England, at least by the eighteenth century, had adapted itself to the process of English social and political modernization. It did not oppose change, but rather worked to see that change occurred in an orderly and predictable manner and with due regard to vested interests. The capacity of the Anglican establishment to function in this manner was understood and appreciated by the laity of South Carolina, as the following makes clear.

Sometime in May 1727, the Reverend Brian Hunt, a clergyman of the Church of England, united in matrimony Gibbon Cawood and Robert Wright. Despite the fact that Hunt was the rector of Saint John's Parish in Berkeley County, he performed the ceremony in Charles Town, at midnight in the home of the bride's mother. Mrs. Cawood was not present, nor were any other relatives. Gibbon was the daughter of the late John Cawood: she was sixteen years old and until her marriage was the legal ward of Andrew Allen and Charles Hill, two local merchants. Gibbon and Robert had asked the guardians for permission to marry and the answer had been no.[38]

Hunt's motive for performing the marriage was apparently financial. For five years his correspondence with the SPG had revolved around economic problems. At one point Hunt asked the SPG to ignore a London print seller who might demand part of his salary in payment of a debt. He also asked the SPG to send him some Bibles that he hoped to be able to sell at a profit. Despite the fact that Saint John's provided him with five slaves, Hunt could not make ends meet.[39] Previously, in 1726, he had performed a marriage ceremony for William Yeomans and Mary Le Sieur after the governor refused them a license because of evidence that William already had a wife. Hunt had the couple take up temporary residence in his parish and then he published the banns under assumed names. In the case of Gibbon and Robert, he had the couple rent rooms in his parish, which, though never used, established Hunt's right to marry the couple. He published the banns using correct names, but on obscure religious holidays when only a small group of his friends were in the church to act as witnesses.[40]

The marriage of Gibbon and Robert caused an outcry in the province. The bride's guardians asked Governor Arthur Middleton to take action, and after conferring with the clergy he referred the two merchants to the SPG. Allen and Hill explained to the Society that Hunt's action would produce "the most destructive Consequences." In this instance they had lost all hope of securing a marriage settlement for Gibbon, and it seemed likely that her handsome estate would soon be gone. Hunt's fellow clergymen were unanimous in disapproving the "Collusive & Clandestine" marriage. The Reverend William Guy wrote that it had "given great Scandal & offence" within the province and that the establishment would suffer unless something were done. The Reverend Francis Varnod believed "an incredible deal of mischief" had been done to the Church of England: "This renders the hatred of her open Enemies more implacable, & is a terrible stumbling block to her weak members as also to those that begin to think well of her. In a word it gives such a deep wound to Religion in this place that it seems to me almost incurable."[41]

The SPG acted quickly to prevent the church from falling into disrepute. After receiving the letter from Gibbon Cawood's guardians, it immediately voted to suspend Hunt's salary. Informing the merchants of this, the SPG also declared that the bishop of London would soon be sending a new commissary to South Carolina who would investigate the situation and prosecute Hunt if possible. After taking this action the SPG must have been gratified to learn more about Hunt's character from the vestry of Saint John's who claimed that he had begun with "lesser Indecencies and transcient levities & follies" before graduating to "gross repeated vices," including drunkenness, quarreling, defaming, lying, insolence, abusive language and troublemaking. In any event the SPG rebuke served its purpose; early in 1728 the clergy happily announced that Allen and Hill in particular and the province in general were now satisfied.[42]

Meanwhile Brian Hunt was confined to the Charles Town jail, on a charge that is now not clear. He used the time to write letters that he hoped would defend his reputation and improve his fortunes. He asserted that the marriage was not illegal, and that the bride and groom and their families were happy. Other clergymen, according to Hunt, had acted in an irregular manner, and the charges against his own character were prompted by vindictiveness. Allen and Hill, "the two infamous Pedlars," were motivated only by money.[43] Hunt's apology does not generate a great deal of sympathy, but there is an element of surprise at his predicament that seems both genuine and justified. He had performed an equally questionable marriage a short time before the Cawood-Wright affair and nothing had happened. Why all the fuss this time?

The answer, of course, lies in the hierarchical structure of South Carolina society. When Mary Le Sieur chose to marry a suspected bigamist, neither the governor nor her parish priest would be a party to the match, but once performed the marriage was a matter of scorn more than outrage. Gibbon Cawood's case was different because her father was a wealthy man and a great deal of property was at stake. John Cawood had made adequate provision for his daughter, giving her a substantial legacy and sound guardians, but through the actions of the Reverend Hunt those preparations had been frustrated. Cawood also had been a leading figure among the Anglican community: he was a member of the SPG, and his will provided £43,000 to adorn Saint Philip's Church.[44] If the Church of England could deal so harshly with Cawood's affairs, what might other men expect?

The Hunt episode went to the heart of what the Church of England was and what was expected of it. It was expected to be a stable institution that would promote orderly behavior throughout society. For the most part the clergy understood these ends and acted in accordance with them, seeking help from the gentry on that basis. Hunt's actions, however, called all that into question. If a priest of the Church of England acts like this, one can hear a parishioner say to himself, in the fashion of an ignorant, Anabaptist preacher, of what use is a tax-supported established church? It was this question that moved that Anglican clergy and the SPG to make amends as soon as possible.

The striking aspect of the interaction between the Church of England and the laity in South Carolina was the degree to which the established church served the interest of the provincial upper class. The clergy treated the gentry with deference and acted to promote social relationships that supported its interest and prerogatives. In return, the ministers called on the lay elite to undertake benevolent projects and act in a responsible manner. At the same time that it taught the upper class to behave in the best tradition of the English gentry, the Church of England also taught the lower class to respect and obey their economic superiors.

The religious doctrines and practices of the church also had a class bias. Anglican theology was pitched to a sophisticated and well-educated audience; it fit within the framework of traditional Christian belief, but it was congruent with the scientific world view of the eighteenth century. Anglican worship took place within handsome and well-furnished churches, and it utilized an elaborate ritual, creating an atmosphere of richness and formality that complemented the clothing and manners of well-to-do planters and merchants.

The state church, nonetheless, was a universal church. If the rich were favored, the poor were not ignored. Anglican philanthropy provided education facilities and other forms of aid for the underprivileged, and all classes worshipped together. The utopia of the Church of England was a harmonious world in which orderly relationships existed among men and between man and God.

CHAPTER **8**

THE AUTHORITY OF
THE LAITY

The Church of England offered its members a comfortable religion: the environment was aesthetic, the practices were traditional, and the beliefs were reasonable. There were also social benefits for the well-to-do, since Anglican clergymen stressed the importance of social rank and treated the gentry with deference. In return for these services, an Anglican establishment called upon the laity to shoulder responsibilities, the most important of which involved service on the vestry. In South Carolina vestry service was particularly significant since counties were not important as administrative units, and the parish was the center of such local government as existed. The parish vestry that was annually elected by the Anglican parishioners was an important organ of both the established church and the government. Exercising an authority that was traditional as well as statutory, the vestry intervened in the lives of the inhabitants regardless of their religious persuasion and underlined as it did the hegemony of the established church.

The term vestry comes from a room in English churches that was used to store clerical vestments and church records. These rooms were also used for parish meetings, and the meeting itself became known during the Elizabethan period as the vestry. At vestry the parishioners listened to reports by churchwardens, who were responsible for church property, and periodically chose new wardens from among themselves. During the sixteenth and seventeenth centuries, the open vestry, consisting of all parishioners who cared to attend, gave way to the closed or select vestry, composed of a small group of men who exercised the power that had belonged to the parishioners as a whole. The select vestry was normally made up of members of the parish gentry and it filled vacancies by cooptation.

The duties of English vestries were defined by custom more than law. The canons of 1604 say nothing about vestries, but spell out in great detail the duties of churchwardens. Under the canons of 1604 the churchwardens, among other duties, were to provide bread and wine for the communion, maintain the parish register, and keep the church in repair. They were also to report parishioners who were guilty of immorality, unorthodox religious opinions, or prolonged absence from church. All these duties became concerns of the vestry as it supervised the activities of the wardens. In addition English vestries also acquired a set of civil responsibilities during the sixteenth century, the most important of which involved maintaining the parish roads and administering relief to the poor.[1]

The English vestry was a hardy institution that transplanted well to the New World. All Anglican churches in the colonies used the vestry system as a means of governing themselves. In the North, where the Church of England was not established, the vestry served only as an ecclesiastical institution, but it broadened the traditional duties by raising money for the church and acting as its legal agent. These vestries set a model for those of the Protestant Episcopal Church. In the southern colonies, where church and state were united, the vestry was similar to that of England, functioning as a civil institution as well as an ecclesiastical one.[2]

American vestries differed from English ones in the control that they exercised over the clergy. In England a parish minister was usually nominated by a local nobleman or by the bishop; he was never chosen by the parishioners or by the vestry. In the colonies the American laity, acting through the vestry for the most part, asserted its right to select the minister of the parish. This claim was often frustrated in fact, but it was seldom given up. The SPG, which provided missionaries for northern parishes, limited the freedom of the vestries; yet northern churchmen continued to play a part in the process, and sometimes they selected men that the society then hired as missionaries.[3]

The vestries of Virginia were a model for most Southern Anglicans. According to law in the Old Dominion, the vestry was free to choose a clergyman, who was then inducted by the governor, after which he was the rector and could be removed only by an ecclesiastical court. Virginia vestries were wary of granting tenure to their ministers; they simply gave up presenting them for induction and offered yearly contracts instead. The attorney general of England weakened this position in 1703, however, when he ruled that the governor could induct a clergyman who had not been presented after a year of service. Over the years a succession of royal governors protected clergymen from abuse by their vestries, and finally in 1748 the House of Burgesses passed a measure that granted automatic induction after a year of service. The power of Virginia vestries declined after mid-century, but they remained free to choose any clergyman they wished and to dismiss him during the first year. In North Carolina vestries also hired their own ministers, albeit with increasing opposition from royal governors. Only in Maryland, where the clergy were part of proprietary patronage, did Anglican vestries lack substantial control over the selection of their ministers.[4]

In other respects the powers of southern vestries were similar to those of English vestries. They cared for the church, kept order among the congregation, and provided for the parish poor by assessing taxpaying inhabitants. Vestries in Virginia and North Carolina even followed the old English practice, albeit irregularly, of processioning the parish so that boundaries would be well known to the inhabitants. Southern vestries were not generally responsible for the upkeep of roads; that function of the English vestry was normally assigned to the county courts. There were also some duties that were distinct to the New World. In Virginia and Maryland, for example, Anglican vestries played an important role in the regulation of tobacco production, and in North Carolina they administered the bounty on wild animals.[5]

The Anglican vestry was a major institution in the colonial South, but in some areas it declined after the middle of the eighteenth century. The Virginia House of Burgesses not only limited to one year the period that clergymen could serve without induction, but they also passed a measure, rejected by the council, that would have required vestry elections every three years. The growing population of the Old Dominion and increased religious diversity appear to have motivated these and other curbs on the power of the oligarchical vestries. At the same time the appearance of newspapers in Virginia made the vestries less important for communicating laws, proclamations, and notices to the people. A related development occurred in North Carolina where the assembly gradually stripped the vestries of their civil functions and turned them over to secular institutions better suited to getting the job done.[6]

On Easter Monday, 1772, the "inhabitants and freeholders" of Saint Philip's met and elected two men to serve as churchwardens and seven men to act as vestrymen during the ensuing year. The nine men were remarkable in their capacity for leadership. Charles Cotesworth Pinckney was also serving in the Commons House and would continue to do so until the American Revolution. After a distinguished military career, he would serve as a delegate to the federal convention, and be the vice-presidential candidate of the Federalists in 1800 and their presidential candidate in 1804 and 1808. Also serving in the Commons House were Charles Pinckney and Thomas Loughton Smith, the latter heir to one of South Carolina's greatest fortunes. Gabriel Manigault was sixty-eight years old in 1772, and his service in the assembly and as Public Treasurer was long in the past. Manigault, however, was still considered to be the richest businessman in South Carolina. John Poag, another merchant, was elected to the Commons House from 1768 to 1771, and Thomas Smith had probably served in the 1760s.[7]

A week after the election the churchwardens and vestrymen met together for the first time as a body. They took the oaths of conformity to the Church of England and then proceeded to the business at hand. The vestry considered several applications for the position of parish doctor, and it chose a new man despite the fact that the old doctor wished to continue. It was also decided to assess £9,000 in currency from the parish in order to pay the cost of poor relief. With these general decisions out of the way, the vestry voted to aid three persons in need.

Aiding the indigent of the parish was a traditional duty of the Anglican vestry, and the colony of South Carolina in 1712 had authorized the vestries to assess the taxable inhabitants of their parishes to provide for the poor.[8] The demand for relief increased as the colony grew in population, and in Charles Town the administration of poor relief became a major problem. In 1734 the vestry of Saint Philip's petitioned the government for a workhouse and a hospital, citing the "number of Idle, vagrant and vitiously [*sic*] inclined People, either brought in by Shipping, Or On Various Pretences, resorting hither from diverse parts of the Provinces and by Drinking and other sorts of Debauchery Speedily reducing themselves to Poverty and Diseases. . . ." By 1738 the workhouse was finished and "all the poor. . . on the Parish" went to their new home.

During the 1760s, probably owing to the French and Indian War, the burden of relieving the poor in Saint Philip's Parish increased greatly. The annual assessment, which had been £1,000 or £2,000 in prewar decades, climbed to £8,000 and above. The vestry of Saint Philip's sought to lighten its work load by enlisting aid from the vestry of Saint Michael's Parish, the second Charles Town parish, created in 1761. At a strained meeting between the two sets of church officers, those from Saint Michael's made it clear that they did not feel legally obliged to participate in the care of the poor and would not do so.[9] The vestry of Saint Philip's left unsatisfied and continued to do the job alone. In 1766 it complained to the government that the workhouse was filled with seamen and slaves and that all the poor could not be accommodated. Moreover, the punishment of slaves created an unpleasant environment for the indigent sick. The vestry also claimed that poor people from all over the province came to Charles Town, creating an intolerable financial burden for the inhabitants of the city. Acting on these sentiments, the church officers and the Reverend Robert Smith proceeded to the workhouse a few days before Christmas and examined the condition of the inmates. There were eighteen men, thirty women, and nineteen children living in the workhouse; despite the fact that there were "barrack rooms" still empty, the vestry ordered four men, seven women, and four children to leave on the grounds that they were selling rum and involved in "disorderly living."

The church officers elected in 1772 did not visit the workhouse, at least not officially, and we have no record of anyone they might have turned out. Nor do we know of anyone to whom they denied aid, although they may well have done so; we do know that in fifty-five instances they did help unfortunate people, and they did so in strikingly individual ways. In nineteen of these cases they gave aid on a continuing basis. Mrs. Pratt and her family, for example, received a monthly allowance of £6, and Mrs. Ducket was given £4 on the same basis. Peter Tully, apparently a former soldier, received summer clothing and the right to live in the work-house. Elizabeth Graham, a child, was boarded with her aunt for £3 per month. A number of people already receiving aid had their allowances increased, and the vestry even asked the wardens to look in on John Cardin and his wife and add forty shillings to their monthly allowance if necessary.

One time or limited duration aid, often given for what was called "present relief," was more common than monthly allotments. Mrs. McKelvy received aid more than once, but only while her husband was in jail. Mrs. Gardner and her child received summer clothing. Mary John got £10 for present relief, as did a number of people. An interesting case was David Duncan, "an industrious man," who was hit by a trunk thrown from the upper window of a house. Duncan was badly injured and no doctor in Charles Town could help him so the vestry provided twenty guineas for him to travel to Edinburgh, Scotland, in search of medical expertise. Travel money to leave town was a frequent form of relief. The vestry apparently believed it was economical to pay for the removal of anyone who would be a permanent recipient of aid if allowed to stay. It paid for one man to go to Ireland, sent another to George Town, and helped Joanna Shilling and her mother get to Saint Bartholomew's Parish, "to which they belong." The church officers even borrowed £500 to assist 173 indigent Irish immigrants to travel into the backcountry where they hoped to settle.

Poor relief was the most time consuming activity of Saint Philip's vestry, but it also gave considerable attention to the church and the congregation. The vestry authorized the digging of a new well at the old parsonage, and it agreed that the church wardens should draw an order on the Public Treasurer for £4,000 in order to build a new parsonage. It also made arrangements for repairs to the church and signed a three-year contract to have the organ tuned and kept in working order. Dealing with another kind of problem, the vestry prohibited the further erection of tombstones in the church-yard cemetery, probably owing to a lack of space, but agreed that markers might be laid flat or leaned against the cemetery fence. The vestry acted when Henry Purcell, assistant rector of the parish, complained that during the funeral of Charity Johnston, he attempted to speed up the burial and was verbally abused by three men. C. C. Pinckney, the church warden, was instructed to look into the matter, and his report apparently supported Purcell because the vestry voted to lay the matter before the grand jury.

The other vestries in South Carolina functioned in much the same way as that of Saint Philip's, although relief of the poor was a much less burdensome task in the rural parishes. Probably for that reason, most vestries met only two to four times a year as compared to the ten or more meetings that were usual in Saint Philip's. Rural vestries also levied taxes to support the indigent, however, and they intervened in the lives of the unfortunate in just as thorough a fashion.[10] Examples from Saint Helena's Parish will illustrate the point.

The parish assessment for poor relief in Saint Helena's was only £100 in 1737, about 10 percent of that in Saint Philip's that same year. Only an occasional instance of aid found itself into the minutes of the vestry meetings. In 1767 three people were "on the parish" in a continuing manner: Prudence Albergoti was receiving £30 a year, John Leach twenty shillings a week, and an orphan child was being cared for by John Myers who was receiving £10 monthly for doing so. When it could, the vestry acted to keep individuals from becoming a public burden. In 1734 the vestry ordered the churchwardens to take Catherine Thomas, pregnant with child, to a magistrate so she might name the father. Assuming she did name the man, he would be forced to give security for the maintenance of the child. When there was no other recourse, however, the vestry found orphans a home. In 1754, William Sommers, "a poor Orphan Child at this Parish," was apprenticed to Sarah Mathews in Beaufort at the age of four, to remain in service until age thirteen. The vestry paid Mrs. Mathews £15 annually for her expenses.

Maintaining and improving parish property was a constant occupation of Anglican vestries. The Commons House usually appointed special commissioners to oversee the building of churches, but all repairs were done under the supervision of the vestries. Not only churches, but also parsonages, chapels, and glebe lands were the responsibility of the vestry, and oftentimes the work was time-consuming. The vestry of Christ Church, for example, wrestled with major repairs to its church and parsonage during much of the 1730s. The laxness and inefficiency of some vestries were a trial to parish rectors, as is illustrated by the unhappy experience of William Orr in Saint Paul's Parish in the 1740s. The still remaining parish churches of Saint James, Goose Creek, and Saint Michael's testify to the effectiveness of other vestries.

Vestries also became involved in the administration of philanthropic bequests. The Beresford Free School in Saint Thomas Parish was controlled by the vestry of that parish and for the most part in an effective manner. The Reverend Lewis Jones trusted the vestry of Saint Helena's enough to leave it a sum of money for educating poor children of the parish. Successive vestries administered that fund according to the wishes of their late rector for more than twenty years.

South Carolina vestries also rented pews to members of the congregation. During the seventeenth century pew-renting became an important source of income in some English parishes. The practice was carried to the colonies and became particularly significant in the North where churches did not receive public support. In the South the income was incidental, and the practice was less common.[11] For the most part pews were distributed by lot to families who paid a standard fee; in other cases preferred pews went to parishioners who paid higher prices. Prince Frederick Parish in 1732 assigned sixteen pews to families who subscribed £25 for the new church, while Christ Church parish in 1734 allowed subscribers to choose their own pew in an order determined by the value of their subscription. Pews in the Charles Town churches were particularly sought after. Even among the comparatively opulent urban society, however, there was a sense that the price of going to church ought not be unlimited. Saint Michael's in 1766 auctioned eighteen new pews to those who offered the highest annual rent and received bids ranging from £30 to £75. There were enough complaints about the prices, however, so that the vestry reduced the rents to a low of £20 and a high of £35.

Most of the money for the established church came from the provincial treasurer. Vestries had funds from the collection plate at their disposal and they were allowed to assess the inhabitants for the relief of the poor, but that was all. Unlike other southern vestries, those of South Carolina were not allowed to tax their parishioners for parochial charges, a concession made to the dissenters early in the century. The cost of new churches and of major upkeep on old ones was paid from the "General Tax" levied and collected at the provincial level. During the 1760s the parochial charges paid from this fund averaged 2.5 percent of total disbursements. Clergymen were paid from a "General Duty" and their salaries constituted about 11 percent of all revenue from all duties during the period from March through September 1765. The nature of the records makes an accurate accounting difficult, but it seems clear that the total cost of the established church to the public was well under 5 percent of all expenses, at least during the decade of the Stamp Act.[12]

South Carolina vestries were also active in the selection and control of the parish minister. The parishioners as a whole selected the rector, but the vestry usually located a candidate for the position. In the early

years of the establishment this was generally done by writing to the
SPG, but later the process became more informal. In 1766 the vestry
of Saint Helena's, for example, agreed that Thomas Middleton, a
wealthy member of their body, should write to his brother, who was
probably in London and could advertise the fact that the parish wanted
a clergyman. Twenty pounds sterling had been raised by subscription
to defray the travel expenses of a suitable candidate. When a clergyman proved unsuitable to a parish, it was always the vestry that took
action to force him out. The vestry of Saint Helena's discharged William Peaseley in a crisp message that alluded to failures in his conduct,
and the vestry of Prince Frederick's Parish documented the exploits of
Michael Smith in a convincing manner and took the necessary steps to
get rid of him.

The power that the vestries wielded over the minister was hardly
unlimited. The SPG, the commissary, the legal rights of an incumbent
clergyman, and the scarcity at different times of clergymen in general all
frustrated the will of vestrymen. The power of the vestry increased with
time, however, as the established church became more independent,
and it was maximized by the skill and resourcefulness of individual
vestries. The election of an incumbent as rector could not occur unless
the vestry asked the church commissioners for a precept for that purpose. Unhappy experiences with some inducted ministers led the vestries to stop asking for elections, and they were apparently supported by
the parishioners. As more and more clergymen served on year to year
contracts, however, the power of the vestries was enhanced since it was
they who dismissed unpopular clergymen lacking the legal rights of
parish rectors. The power of South Carolina vestries waxed at mid-
century almost exactly as that of Virginia vestries waned.

Parish government in South Carolina was also enhanced by an activity of churchwardens that was unique to that colony. In 1719 the government made the parishes of the established church the electoral units
for the Commons House. The churchwardens were designated the man-
agers of the elections, and they functioned in that capacity for the rest of
the colonial period. Just as the administration of poor relief emphasized
the hegemony of the Church of England, so also did the election of
legislators. The churchwardens gave notice at the parish church two
weeks prior to the election, and they announced the results at the same

location. The connection between church and state was obvious to all even as they took part in a secular political process.[13]

The English vestry was traditionally staffed by lesser members of the gentry who, at their best, felt a sense of social responsibility and exercised a benevolent authority over the inhabitants of their parish. In the southern colonies the situation was similar. There was more democracy in the selection of vestrymen and social status was more fluid, but parish officials were usually members of the elite and in general they exercised responsible leadership. Virginia vestries originated in an election of twelve men by the parishioners. Vestrymen then filled vacancies by cooptation, and by the early eighteenth century the vestries were closed corporations made up of representatives from the leading families of the Old Dominion. The Virginia vestry was "the stepping stone of politics, a school for government." Young men learned leadership and social responsibility while serving on the vestry and went on to exercise it in the House of Burgesses. In the fifty years between 1690 and 1740, more than half of Virginia's legislators served at some time on a parish vestry. The power of the Virginia vestry declined in the years after 1750, but its character remained essentially the same.[14]

In other southern colonies the vestry system was similar to that of Virginia, but less powerful and prestigious. A Maryland vestry was composed of six vestrymen, two of whom were elected each year, and an incumbent minister who always served as a seventh member. The vestry selected two men from outside its membership to serve as churchwardens. Maryland parishioners often chose vestrymen with previous experience, and they sometimes elected men of wealth and political power. The extent of overlap between vestry membership and legislative service is yet to be determined. A North Carolina vestry consisted of twelve men elected by the parishioners. Elections were held at irregular intervals, in part because of the opposition of dissenters. The vestry chose two of its own members to serve as churchwardens. In Saint Paul's Parish, Chowan County, and Saint John's Parish, Carteret County, the vestrymen were well above average in wealth and they held numerous local political positions. Most of the colonial legislators from these counties had experience on the Anglican vestry. The vestrymen who served were economic and political leaders, but the North Carolina parishes had some difficulty finding men who would accept the office. The same problem also existed in Maryland, where it was compounded by the failure of many vestrymen to attend meetings.[15]

South Carolina law called for the Anglican inhabitants of each parish to elect annually, on Easter Monday, seven men who would serve as vestrymen and two men who would be churchwardens. In general these church officers were members of the colonial elite, and had a knowledge of the world and a habit of command. Vestry service was a habit in some influential families, among them the Barnwells of Saint Helena's Parish.

John Barnwell was one of the men who laid the groundwork for South Carolina's power and prosperity in the early eighteenth century. An Irish immigrant, he amassed extensive land holdings in the Port Royal area when it was largely untamed and made it safe as one of the colony's most successful Indian fighters. His son, Colonel Nathaniel Barnwell, served as a churchwarden in Saint Helena's Parish in 1727, was elected to the vestry in 1731, and served more than thirty terms through 1772. In 1738 Nathaniel was joined by his brother, John, who served nearly thirty terms through 1773. A third Barnwell, Nathaniel, Jr., was elected to the vestry on Easter Monday in 1772, and a fourth, John, Jr., became a vestryman in May of that year to fill a vacated position. Four Barnwells on a seven-man vestry were too many for the inhabitants of Saint Helena's. An unprecedented comment in the minutes for Easter Monday, 1773, stated that "a great number of the Parishioners met at the Church" and elected new vestrymen, who included Nathaniel, Jr., and John, Jr., but not the senior members of the Barnwell family. Colonel Nathaniel Barnwell, whose home had been the scene of many vestry meetings and who owned ninety-one slaves, was no longer a church officer. His son, John, Jr., continued on the vestry, however, and also served in the Commons House and later the state senate. In 1808 Barnwell County was named in his honor.

The Barnwell family was remarkable in its sustained service to the parish of Saint Helena's, but other vestrymen were also stable in their leadership. More than 75 percent of the vestrymen (churchwardens are not included in this data) served for more than one term and the average length of service was five and one-half years. Between 1728 and 1778 about a dozen men refused to serve after being elected either as vestrymen or churchwardens, and it was normal for one or two members of a vestry to miss a meeting. Neither of these circumstances appears to have hampered the effectiveness of the vestry. Saint Helena's Parish had the most stable vestry among the parishes for which we have records. Prince Frederick's Parish was at the other extreme, yet even there more than half of the vestrymen served more than once, and the average length of service was three and one-half years. Prince Frederick also had its own version of the Barnwells. John White, a leading planter and sometime Commons House member, served on the vestry for more than twenty years, and so also did Anthony White, probably his relative.[16]

Political leadership in South Carolina was demonstrated by election to the Commons House. The frequency with which membership in the Commons House overlapped with service as a vestryman or churchwarden is an indication of the importance attached to the state church. We have the records for seven parishes in 1772 that collectively elected sixty-five church officers, of those men seventeen (26 percent) were at some time chosen by voters to serve in the Commons House. Of the seventeen, however, eight came from Saint Michael's and Saint Philip's, the two parishes of Charles Town. Nearly 50 percent of the urban church officials were considered Commons House material while less than 20 percent of the rural vestrymen and churchwardens were in that category.[17]

A similar pattern emerges from an analysis of all men elected to the Commons in 1772. Nineteen of the forty-eight men elected to the Thirty-first Royal Assembly (40 percent) served as church officers at some time in their career, but thirteen (68 percent) were associated with the vestries of Saint Philip's and Saint Michael's. Vestry service appears to have been a high status position, but service in Charles Town attracted many more influential people than did duty in the rural parishes.

Service on a vestry in South Carolina does not appear to have been a rung on the ladder of political advancement. Only six of the nineteen parish officers elected to the Commons in 1772 served the church prior to serving the state. In a few cases they undertook the responsibilities at almost the same time, and often vestry service followed legislative service. The vestry was not a training ground for politicians; it was a responsibility that political and economic leaders were expected to accept.[18]

Vestrymen and churchwardens in South Carolina were usually members of the Church of England, but occasionally dissenters served as parish officials. The government character of the vestry encouraged this ecumenical approach, and so also did the policy of accommodation that was inaugurated by Commissary Alexander Garden. Something similar occurred in Virginia in the western counties where dissenters were in the majority. The civil functions of the Anglican parish made it necessary to have a vestry even if few members of the Church of England lived in the area.[19] The fact that dissenters did serve in South Carolina and the limited nature of such service are indicated by a conflict that occurred in Prince Frederick Parish.

On Easter Monday, April 11, 1757, the parishioners of Prince Frederick voted for vestrymen and churchwardens, and the existing wardens tallied the votes. An objection was raised, however, that four voters did not conform to the Church of England. The laws were read and a discussion about eligibility ensued. Those objected to asserted that they were freeholders and that they had served as church officers, although they did not claim to be Anglicans. The crowd was apparently on their side because the wardens accepted the contested votes "to silence the Clamour." After the election, Colonel John White complained to the governor about the illegality of what had taken place, and the churchwardens ordered a new election on April 25, at which church officers were finally chosen. The second election produced the same results as the first, but apparently now the dissenters were not allowed to vote and the complaints ceased. Colonel White, who raised the issue of eligibility, was not reelected in 1757 after nearly twenty years of service; neither was Anthony White who had served almost as long. It seems likely that dissenters had voted before and that the defeat of the Whites was responsible for the complaint. It is significant, nonetheless, that the complaint led to the disfranchisement of the nonconformists. Dissenters did sometimes serve and they had probably voted more often, but the vestry was still an Anglican institution.

Anglican vestries in South Carolina were powerful institutions and remarkably democratic in comparison with those of England and other southern colonies. In addition to administering the property of the church, they also exercised a great deal of control over the parish minister. They levied taxes for the needy and decided who should be helped and in what manner. Annual elections did not prevent some men from continuing in office for three decades, but they did mean that the vestry could not ignore the parishioners.

Service on the vestry, in South Carolina and elsewhere, was a high status position, and the incumbents were generally capable men. Nowhere did southern churchmen come closer to acting out the role of the English landed gentry than when they served on the parish vestry.

CHAPTER **9**

CONCLUSION

For nearly three quarters of a century the Church of England was the established church of South Carolina. During that period the population of the colony grew from perhaps 5,000 to about 125,000, and South Carolina expanded from a narrow strip of coastline to an area roughly that of the present state. The rice and indigo cultivated by 75,000 slaves made it the richest colony on the mainland of North America. By the time of the American Revolution, South Carolina was a prosperous, stable, and largely self-governing society, despite its racial division into white and black, its religious division into Anglican and dissenter, and its geographic division into low country and backcountry. The Church of England was almost nonexistent in the backcountry, and it offered very little spiritual comfort to the black majority. It served Anglicans well nonetheless, and its economic, political and social effects were felt by everyone in the colony.

Viewed as a state church, the Anglican establishment of South Carolina was distinguished by its moderation. Moderation is perhaps a strange way to describe an institution born into a political dispute between religious parties and the sibling of a law that gave Anglicans a monopoly on legislative power. Yet one year after approving the Establishment Act of 1704, Anglicans passed a measure that ensured the right of dissenters to practice their religion. The law that excluded dissenters from serving in the assembly was repealed in 1706, albeit because a veto promised to be forthcoming in England. More impressive evidence of moderation was the elimination of parish taxes that was achieved in 1710. Dissenters still supported the established church through export and import duties, but they paid no direct taxes. After a few years of bitter partisanship that resulted in the creation of a state church, the Commons appears to have decided that religious toleration would benefit the economic and political development of the colony.

While no new legislation restricted the rights of dissenters after 1704, some officials associated with the Church of England acted in an immoderate fashion. Just as Sir Nathaniel Johnson struck at dissent in 1704, Sir Francis Nicholson attempted to harrass noncomforming ministers two decades later, only to learn that the Commons House would not support him. Another zealot was Commissary Gideon Johnston, who hoped to pressure non-Anglicans into joining the Church of England and who attempted to use the conversion of the Reverend Ebenezer Taylor as an object lesson. Commissary Alexander Garden was wiser, or perhaps he learned from the experience of his predecessors, and he realized that a policy of accommodation would better serve the interests of the Church of England. Garden was sensitive to the feelings of the dissenters, and when one of their number did take Anglican orders, the commissary encouraged the SPG to send him to another colony. In retrospect it seems clear that the established church benefited by avoiding controversy and concentrating on its own problems. The positive example of a well functioning church probably was the most effective means of proselytism.

The established church was also moderate in its latitudinarian approach to doctrine and forms. The Reverend Samuel Thomas, the first missionary sent by the SPG to South Carolina, used a relaxed liturgy, apparently to encourage the dissenters, and that style appealed to the Anglican laity. Some later clergymen, particularly those who were former Huguenots, were not rigorous in their adherence to the *Book of Common Prayer* and the rules of the Church of England. Commissary Johnston attacked what he called "playing fast and loose with the Canons and Rubrick," and Commissary Garden denounced the Reverend John La Pierre for baptizing a child in an irregular manner. Both officials, however, recognized that some flexibility was required by the colonial environment, and Garden even criticized the Reverend Andrew Leslie for being too strict in enforcing the rules about godparents. Eliza Lucas Pinckney was a member of the Church of England but she spoke of Christianity as her religion. She was attracted to the state church not because of its ceremonies, but because of its emphasis on reason and moderation. Low Church practices and a latitudinarian approach to doctrine appealed to the Anglican laity and made it easier to coexist with the dissenters.

More consistent than the theme of moderation was the quality of lay control that characterized the establishment. From 1704 to 1778, the Anglican laity made it clear that they wished to determine the nature of their church and hire and fire their ministers. At the provincial level, lay power was exercised by the Commons House. That body made its attitude known when it inserted in the first establishment act a provision for a commission of lay persons with the power to remove immoral clergymen from office. Sir Nathaniel Johnson, whose Anglicanism followed High Church forms, was upset with this departure from English practice; authorities in the mother country found it unacceptable. The lay commission created in 1706 lacked the power of removal, but it did oversee the elections of clergymen and provide a degree of central authority. In this and later pieces of legislation, the Commons House continued to exercise lay power and provide for its exercise by others. The legislators controlled the structure of the state church and provided it with financial support; at the parish level, to a remarkable degree, they put the people in charge.

The most significant power of Anglican parishioners in South Carolina was the right to elect or reject a clergyman, and thereby to bestow or deny the status of rector and the tenure that came with it. No aspect of the colonial church was so foreign to English clergymen as their need to win the approval of the people they served. Commissary Johnston, for example, was surprised and shocked that his appointment by Henry Compton, bishop of London, could be nullified by the preference of the parishioners for the Reverend Richard Marsden. Most of the time, however, parishioners exercised their power by not using it. Borrowing a tactic from the vestries of Virginia, they refused to elect clergymen to avoid giving them tenure. The early clergymen found this appalling and so did the SPG, whose missionaries were controlled by parishioners who had accepted the charity of the SPG. The intervention of the SPG and of the commissaries resulted in the election of most clergymen until 1750; but when the church became independent of English control, the year to year contract became a standard practice and few ministers could call themselves rectors. The relatively high quality of the clergy in the period after 1750 indicates that popular authority over tenure was a better method of controlling ministers than was the SPG's selection process combined with disciplinary authority exercised by a commissary. Direct democracy decided the fate of a minister, but the remaining affairs of a parish were administered through representative government. The vestries of South Carolina were elected annually, and it seems clear that they represented the popular will. The vestry acted as the executive of the parishioners in its relationship with an incumbent clergyman, it administered the buildings and property of the church, and it dealt with a host of other matters of interest to the parish. The vestry also levied taxes for the support of the poor and divided the proceeds among the needy. The churchwardens administered elections to the Commons House. In these ways members of the Church of England stretched their influence into matters that affected Anglicans and dissenters alike.

Exactly why the Anglican laity in South Carolina were so insistent on controlling their established church is not clear. It might have been related to the character of the clergymen and the fact that they were usually unknown in the colony prior to starting service; on the other hand, the Carolinians had had very little experience with ministers when they passed the Establishment Act of 1704. "What has the Bp of London to do with us?" said the parishioners of St. Philip's in 1710, manifesting an apparent hostility to both ecclesiastical hierarchy and outside control. Probably their concern was not based on local experience, or even on that of Virginia, which provided an example of a lay-controlled church. One senses in the attitude of South Carolina Anglicans an awareness of the role that the hierarchy of the Church of England had played in the political and religious controversy that beset England in the seventeenth century and a determination to avoid those problems in the colony. In religion as well as politics, South Carolinians shared with other Americans a desire to run their own affairs.

In addition to moderation and lay control, which were forces that came from within the colony, the state church benefited greatly from the benevolence of the Society for the Propagation of the Gospel in Foreign Parts. During its early years, the established church faced an insecure situation. The dissenters were bitter about the fact of establishment and the manner in which it was carried out, and they were an important political factor in the colony. Moreover, it is not clear that the Anglican laity had the material resources and the religious zeal to bring the church to life without outside aid. By recruiting missionaries, sending them to the colony, and providing a substantial income, the SPG helped to overcome the hostility of the dissenters and the indifference of many Anglicans. Once the clergymen were in the province, they were able to generate more support for the state church and help it to become self-sustaining. The local benevolence that appeared during the governorship of Sir Francis Nicholson suggests that local Anglicans took pride in the church and were capable of supporting it. The SPG did not always choose its missionaries well; its involvement in South Carolina lasted longer than was necessary or even healthy for the church; but the Society played a major role in giving the establishment a chance to succeed.

The support of the SPG in its early years, a moderate approach to doctrine, forms, and dissent, and a large amount of control by the laity—these were the factors that made the Church of England successful in South Carolina. The best evidence of success is the fact that it was able to survive, grow, and develop for almost seventy-five years. After the revolution of 1719, there was no serious threat to the existence of the state church until the American Revolution. From 1704 until 1778, new parishes were created, churches built, and clergyman hired at a rate that seems to have met the religious needs of the low country. The quality of the clergy was generally good, and it improved as the establishment reached its final form and the laity asserted control over their ministers. In Charles Town, the hub of activity in South Carolina, Saint Philip's and Saint Michael's churches were impressive with regard to their architecture, their music, the learning of their clergy, and the size and wealth of their congregations.

Only in the backcountry did the established church fail. A few clergymen showed concern about the backcountry settlers and also an ability to communicate with them effectively, but the church as a whole ignored backcountry society. While it had poor people among its members, the Church of England operated in alliance with the upper class. Anglican clergymen for the most part relied on the gentry to give them aid and support, and the backcountry society had no such people. Given the existing denominational attachments of the settlers, it seems unlikely that the Church of England could have become the dominant force in the backcountry. It did not try very hard, however, and the price of failure was disestablishment.

A comparative perspective helps in understanding the strength of Anglicanism in South Carolina. In Virginia and Maryland, there were strong Anglican establishments in the eighteenth century, but both colonies were wracked by religious discontent on the eve of the American Revolution. One cause of Virginia's troubles seems to have been the intolerance of the Anglicans who were determined to suppress the growing dissent. Another problem was the lack of trust between the clergy, who believed that lay control was operating in an irresponsible manner, and the laity, who felt their ministers were not subjected to enough discipline. In Maryland the laity were largely without power in their church, and they came to see it as an agent of British imperialism. Having attacked their own state church, Anglicans were in a weak condition to defend it from the dissenters.

North Carolina also offers an instructive comparison. The Church of England received official status there in 1702, but it was never strong. One reason was the large number of Quakers and Presbyterians in the colony; another was the absence of an Anglican upper class willing and able to support the Church of England. Despite its weakness, the established church was immoderate: Anglican legislators made it difficult for dissenting clergymen to perform marriages and refused to let them run schools. Lay control was important in North Carolina, but it was weakened by the Vestry Act of 1764, which gave the right of presentation to the governor. Governor William Tryon promoted Anglicanism and some progress was made, but the state church became identified with the mother country rather than the colony. Still unrooted by the time of the Revolution, the established church toppled easily.

In contrast to its neighbors, South Carolina had a relatively strong and active laity, a policy of moderation toward dissenters that neutralized their hostility, and a degree of lay control that allowed Anglicans to administer the church effectively and encouraged them to identify with it. Because of these factors, the Great Awakening had few lasting effects in the low country, there was no Parsons' Cause, and little friction existed between clergy and laity. A stable, peaceful, and successful established church existed in the low country; it was disestablished because it failed to win the backcountry, but was spared the internal strife that affected its sister churches.

The strength of Anglicanism in South Carolina allowed the state church to be an important force in the colony. Its significance is difficult to measure exactly because it performed a variety of functions and because much of the evidence is indirect. The impact of the Church of England, nonetheless, was broader and more pervasive than generally has been assumed.

The Reverend William Tennent, the Presbyterian proponent of disestablishment, complained about the economic burden of the state church on the dissenters. By creating a state church, Anglicans shifted the cost of their religion to the taxpayers of all denominations. Anglican churches and parish houses were built largely with public funds, and the salaries of ministers, beyond the support that came from the SPG, were also paid from the provincial treasury. The savings to an individual Anglican were not great, nor was the cost to an individual dissenter, but the cumulative effect amounted to a major subsidy for the Church of England. On the other side of the balance sheet was the view, expressed by the proprietors on a number of occasions, that religious freedom would bring economic benefits to the colony by promoting immigration and commerce. It is likely that the economic benefits of establishment were a stronger cause of discontent than they were a motive for the creation and maintenance of the state church.

The political role of the church was greater than its economic role. The context of establishment argues for a short range political goal on the part of the founders who created a religious standard and used it to remove their enemies from the legislature. When this grab for power failed, however, Anglicans continued to support the state church. Probably their longer term motivation came from the support the Church of England would give to social and political authority in a youthful and changing society, composed of a mixture of peoples and a servile laboring class and beset with foreign enemies. If so, they were not disappointed, for Anglican clergymen did encourage obedience to leadership in general and respect for Anglican leaders in particular. At first the clergy saw English authority as being paramount, as in 1719 when they supported the proprietors against the people, but eventually their full allegiance went to the colonial gentry, as their response to the American Revolution suggests. Dissenters as well as Anglicans probably appreciated the civic usefulness of this kind of established church. The disestablishment of the Church of England reflected the political power of dissent and the compelling ideology of religious freedom, but the idea of a Protestant establishment that would give tax support to all denominations reflected the happy experience of South Carolina with a state church that had promoted stability by clothing political leadership with legitimacy. The social role of the church was related to its political function. The establishment of the Church of England, its structure, and the teachings and behavior of the clergy—all reinforced the status, prerogatives, and power of the Anglican gentry. Even when they readmitted dissenters to the assembly, Anglican elites remained on the parish vestries by themselves, where they made important decisions affecting the lives and property of their neighbors, dissenters as well as Anglicans. Anglican clergymen taught respect for established authority in general, but the authority figures they obeyed and to whom they deferred were their patrons, the Anglican gentry. Sunday worship had class overtones. The gentry wore their best clothes, visited with one another, and in Charles Town at least, enjoyed an excellent organ played in an artful manner. All this was part of the style by which they distinguished themselves from the less fortunate. While it strengthened the power of upper class Anglicans, the church also taught them to exercise it in the interest of society as a whole; political leadership, social responsibility, and benevolence were the price of respect.

Certainly, however, the social vision of the Anglican laity extended beyond class hegemony. A respected and powerful upper class was not an end in itself, but rather a means to a larger goal, an orderly and stable society that provided for all, albeit in differing proportions. The episode of Gibbon Cawood's marriage illustrates the degree to which Anglicans saw their church as a vehicle for effecting what they thought of as sound and reasonable relationships among members of a society. The world view of the Anglican gentry was self-interested and prejudiced according to religion, class, and race, but it also involved the concept of a good society, the achievement of which was a major responsibility of the Church of England.

Because of its involvement with the upper class, the church was compromised in its relations with poor whites, black slaves, and Indians. It served the entire community, and a cross section of society attended Sunday services, yet its style and point of view were that of the gentry. Its attitude toward the unfortunate was benevolent and patronizing when they behaved and intolerant and hostile when they did not.

Anglican clergymen found it difficult to understand the religious needs
of lower class whites and harder still to meet them, as Charles
Woodmason's diary illustrates. Towards blacks and Indians the attitude
of the church was similar; a sense of Christian benevolence called for
the conversion of nonwhites, but it was coupled with a belief in their
inferiority and a larger concern for the welfare of the white colonists.
Even the Reverend Francis Le Jau seemed to worry more about the
sexual morality of his Christian slaves than about their souls, and he had
little regard for their intelligence and ability. The clergy were more
impressed with the Indians, but they quickly turned against them when
the Indians struck at their white oppressors. The interests of the Anglican gentry marked the boundary of Anglican benevolence.

Despite its failures, the Church of England was the major cultural
force in South Carolina. Through worship services, sermons, and religious instruction, the Anglican clergy kept the colonists in touch with
their Christian heritage. On a more sophisticated level, the theological
learning and intellectual activity of the clergy allowed South Carolinians to read local debates about Calvinism, deism, and Whitefield's
"New Birth." Commissary Garden's exchanges with George Whitefield
were read outside the colony, and they made South Carolina an integral
part of a major development in colonial culture. Outside the field of
religion, the clergy played a paramount role in educating the youth of
South Carolina. Many ministers taught reading and writing, the SPG
provided several full time schoolmasters for the colony, and Anglican
philanthropy endowed a number of schools that served Anglicans and
dissenters alike. Without the Church of England, South Carolina would
have been far poorer in religious learning and secular education.

In addition to its economic effect, its political and social roles, and its
cultural contribution, the Church of England met the religious needs of
a large number of people. South Carolina Anglicans were not intense in
their beliefs nor emotional in their worship; this relaxed manner reflected a belief in reason and restraint rather than a lack of faith. A
stylized liturgy, a well-appointed church, and an optimistic theology are
all valid forms of religion. The Church of England was more than a
spiritual institution, yet there are few types of religion, perhaps none,
that are not also involved with economics, politics, and social class.
There were also irreligious persons among the laity, but the inclusive
nature of a state church made that difficult to avoid. In general, the

Anglicans of South Carolina were not more hypocritical than most people then or now; they supported the Church of England because its doctrines conformed to their views and its form of worship suited their taste.

The Church of England was disestablished in South Carolina in 1778, but its influence did not end. It was succeeded eventually by the Protestant Episcopal Church, whose active laity and elected bishops made it a republican institution as compared with the Anglican church of England. The change was related to the American Revolution, but it was based on the experience of South Carolina and other southern colonies, as well as that of the northern Anglican churches, which taught Americans that the laity should exercise a large amount of power within the church.

The social values of the Church of England seem to have been carried forward by the Protestant Episcopal Church and incorporated into the regional culture of the South. According to Avery Craven, antebellum southern society was conditioned by a "rural way of life capped by an English gentleman ideal."[1] Certainly there was more to this than religion, yet the English gentry was the model to which the upper class colonial aspired, and the Church of England helped him to achieve that goal. Long after Anglicanism was gone, southern elites who sought the same status as their ancestors learned to practice leadership, responsibility, and benevolence. The membership of the Protestant Episcopal Church was relatively small, but it included a disproportionate number of the upper class. In a certain sense it kept alive not only Anglican religious customs but also the tradition of gentry leadership so important to the Church of England.

Appendix

MINISTERS OF THE ESTABLISHED CHURCH OF SOUTH CAROLINA, 1696-1775

1696-1719

Name	Began Service in South Carolina	Native Country	SPG	Other Denominations	Parish	Years of Service	Cause of Termination
Samuel Marshall[1]	1696	England	no	...	St. Philip's	3	death
Edward Marston	1700	England	no	...	St. Philip's	8	removal
William Corbin	1700	England	no	...	St. James, Goose Creek	3	resignation
Kendall[2]	1702	...	no	...	...	0	...
Samuel Thomas	1702	England	yes	...	St. James, Goose Creek	4	death
William Dunn	1706	Ireland	yes	...	St. Paul's	2[3]	resignation
Francis Le Jau	1706	France	yes	Huguenot	St. James, Goose Creek	11	death
Richard Marsden	1707	...	no	...	St. Philip's; Christ Church	2	resignation
Alexander Wood	1707	...	yes	...	St. Andrew's	3[4]	death
Robert Maule	1707	Ireland	yes	...	St. John's, Berkeley	9[5]	death
Henry Gerrard[6]	1707	...	no	...	St. John's, Berkeley	0	resignation
John La Pierre	1708[7]	...	no	Huguenot	St. Dennis	20	resignation
Gideon Johnston	1708	Ireland	yes	...	St. Philip's	8	death
John Maitland	1708	...	no	...	St. Paul's	3[8]	death
Robert Forbes[9]	1708	...	no	...	...	0	...

Name	Year	Origin	Religion	Licensed	Parish	No.	Reason for departure
Thomas Hasel	1709	England	...	yes	St. Thomas and St. Dennis	35	death
James Gignilliat	1710	France	Huguenot	yes	St. James, Santee	1[10]	resignation
Claude Philippe de Richebourg	1712	...	Catholic; Huguenot	no	St. James, Santee	7	death
Ebenezer Taylor	1712	...	Presbyterian	yes	St. Andrew's	4	resignation
William Tredwell Bull	1712	England	...	yes	St. Paul's	11	resignation
Gilbert Jones	1712	Wales	...	yes	Christ Church	9	resignation
Nathaniel Osborne	1713	...	...	yes	St. Bartholomew's	2	death
William Guy	1714[11]	...	...	yes	St. Helena's; St. Andrew's	35	death
John Whitehead	1714	...	...	yes	St. Philip's	2	death
Alexander Duncan[12]	1717	...	...	no	St. John's, Berkeley	0	death
William Wye[13]	1717	Ireland	...	yes	St. Philip's	2	removal
			1720-1749				
Peter Tustian	1720	England	...	yes	St. George's	1	resignation
Alexander Garden	1720[14]	Scotland	...	no	St. Philip's	33	resignation
Francis Merry	1720	England	...	yes	St. Helena's; St. James, Goose Creek	3	dismissal

Name	Began Service in South Carolina	Native Country	SPG	Other Denominations	Parish	Years of Service	Cause of Termination
Albert Pouderous	1720	France	no	Catholic; Huguenot	St. James, Santee	11	death
Moses Clark	1720	...	yes	...	...	0	death
Benjamin Pownal	1722	England	yes	...	Christ Church	2	resignation
Brian Hunt	1723	England	yes	...	St. Johns, Berkeley	5[15]	resignation
Richard Ludlam	1723	...	yes	...	St. James, Goose Creek	5	death
Francis Varnod	1723	France	yes	...	St. George's	13	death
David Standish	1724	...	yes	...	St. Paul's	4	death
John Warden	1725	...	no	...	Christ Church	1	death
Lewis Jones	1726	Wales	yes	...	St. Helena's	18[16]	death
John Winteley	1727	...	yes	...	Christ Church	2	dismissal
John Lambert	1727	...	yes	...	St. Philip's	2	death
Thomas Morritt	1728	...	yes	...	Prince George's; Prince Frederick's; Christ Church	8	resignation
Daniel Dwight	1729	Colonies	yes	...	St. John's, Berkeley	19	death
Edward Dyson	1729	...	no	...	Christ Church	0	resignation
Andrew Leslie	1729	...	yes	...	St. Paul's	11	death
John Fulton	1730	Ireland	yes	...	Christ Church	4	dismissal
John James Tissot	1730	...	no	Huguenot	St. Dennis	33	death

Name	Year	Country		Religion	Parish	No.	Reason
Stephen Coulet	1731	France	no	Catholic, Huguenot	St. James, Santee	1[17]	death
Joseph Bugnion	1732	Switzerland	no	German Reformed	St. Peter's, St. James, Santee	3	dismissal
Timothy Millechamp	1732	England	yes	...	St. James, Goose Creek	14	resignation
David Collodon	1733	...	no	Huguenot	St. James, Santee	0	death
Thomas Thompson	1734	...	yes	...	St. Bartholomew's; St. George's; St. John's, Colleton	14	resignation
Robert Gowie	1734	...	yes	...	St. Bartholomew's	0[18]	death
Lawrence O'Neill	1734	...	no	...	Christ Church	1	resignation
John Fullerton	1735	...	yes	...	Christ Church	0	death
John Fordyce	1736	...	yes	...	Prince Frederick's; Prince George's	15	death
Peter De Plessis	1736	England	no	Huguenot	St. James, Santee	6	death
Stephen Roe	1737	...	yes	...	St. George's	5	resignation
William Orr	1737	...	yes	Presbyterian	St. Philip's; St. Paul's; St. Helena's; St. John's, Colleton	18	death

Name	Began Service in South Carolina	Native Country	SPG	Other Denominations	Parish	Years of Service	Cause of Termination
Robert Small	1738	...	yes	...	Christ Church	1	death
Levi Durand	1741[19]	England	yes	...	Christ Church; St. John's, Berkeley	24	death
William McGilchrist	1741	...	no	...	St. Philip's	4	resignation
Samuel Quincy	1742	...	yes	...	St. John's, Colleton; St. George's; St. Phillip's	7	resignation
Alexander Garden, Jr.	1743	...	yes	...	St. Thomas and St. Dennis	40	death
Henry Chiffelle	1744	Switzerland	no	Huguenot	St. Peter's	14	death
Charles Boschi	1745	...	yes	Catholic	St. Bartholomew's	4	death
Robert Betham	1746	England	no	...	St. Philip's	1	death
Alexander Keith	1746	...	no	...	Prince George's; St. Philip's; St. Stephen's	27	resignation
William Cotes	1747	...	yes	...	St. George's	5	death
Richard St. John	1747	...	yes	...	St. Helena's	3	resignation
Robert Cuming	1749	...	yes	...	St. John's, Berkeley	1	death
Robert Stone	1749[20]	England	yes	...	St. James, Goose Creek	2	death

1750-1775

Name	Year	Origin			Parish	No.	Reason
William Langhorne	1751	...	yes	...	St. Bartholomew's; St. George's	8	resignation
William Peaseley[21]	1751	...	yes	...	St. Helena's	5	dismissal
John Rowan	1751	...	no	...	St. Paul's; St. James, Santee	4	resignation
James Harrison	1752	England	yes	...	St. James, Goose Creek; St. Bartholomew's	32	resignation
Charles Martyn	1752	England	yes	...	St. Andrew's	18	resignation
Michael Smith	1753	Ireland	yes	...	Prince Frederick's	3	dismissal
Richard Clarke	1753	England	no	...	St. Philip's	6	resignation
John Andrews	1753	England	no	...	St. Philip's	3	resignation
Robert Baron	1753	...	yes	...	St. Bartholomew's	11	death
Alexander Baron	1754	Scotland	no	...	St. Paul's; St. Helena's	5	death
Jonathan Copp	1756	Colonies	no	...	St. John's, Colleton	6	death
Robert Smith	1757	England	no	...	St. Philip's	23	resignation
Samuel Fayerweather	1757	...	no	Independent	...	3	resignation
Samuel Fenner Warren	1758	England	no	...	St. James, Santee	31	resignation
Robert Cooper	1758	Wales	no	...	St. Philip's; St. Michael's	18	death

Name	Began Service in South Carolina	Native Country	SPG	Other Denominations	Parish	Years of Service	Cause of Termination
Winwood Serjeant	1759	...	no	...	St. Philip's; Christ Church; St. George's	8	resignation
John Tonge	1759	England	no	...	St. Paul's	14	death
Abraham Imer	1760	Switzerland	no	Reformed	St. Peter's	6	death
Joseph Dacre Wilton	1762	England	no	...	St. Philip's	5	death
Offspring Pearce	1762	...	no	...	Prince George's; St. George's	20	resignation
John Green	1762	...	no	...	St. Helena's	3	death
George Skeene	1762	...	no	...	Prince Frederick's	4	death
Samuel Drake	1762	...	no	...	...	4	resignation
John Evans	1764	...	no	...	St. Bartholomew's	6	death
Isaac Armory	1764	England	no	...	St. John's, Colleton	1	resignation
John Hockley	1765	England	no	...	St. John's, Berkeley	2	resignation
William Dawson	1765	Scotland	no	...	St. John's, Colleton	2	death
Samuel Hart	1765	...	no	...	St. Michael's; St. John's, Berkeley	14	death
John Fevrier	1766	...	no	...	St. Helena's;	0	death
Charles Woodmason	1766	England	no	...	St. Mark's	4	resignation

Name	Year	Country			Parish	Number	Reason
James Crallan	1767	England	no	...	St. Philip's	1	resignation
Paul Turquand	1768	England	no	...	St. Matthew's	18	death
John Lewis	1769	...	no	...	St. John's, Colleton; St. Paul's	15	death
Richard Farmer	1769	...	no	...	St. John's	0	death
Robert Purcell	1769	England	no	...	St. Philip's	6	resignation
James Pierce	1769	England	no	...	St. Helena's	2	death
Thomas Panting	1770	England	no	...	St. Andrew's	1	death
Samuel Frederic Lucius	1770	...	yes	...	Coffee Town	13	death
James Foulis	1770	...	no	...	St. David's	0	resignation
John Bullman	1770	...	no	...	St. Michael's	4	dismissal
Edward Ellington	1770	...	no	...	St. Bartholomew's; St. Helena's; St. James, Goose Creek	20	resignation
Henry Purcell	1770	England	no	...	St. George's; Christ Church; St. Michael's	32	death
John Ernest Christopher Schwabb	1771	Germany	no	...	St. Andrew's	2	death
John Villette	1772	...	no	...	Prince Frederick's	...	...
Thomas Walker	1772	...	no	...	St. Mark's	1	resignation
William Miller	1772	...	no	...	St. Bartholomew's	0	death
James Stuart	1772	...	no	...	Prince George's	5	resignation

Name	Began Service in South Carolina	Native Country	SPG	Other Denominations	Parish	Years of Service	Cause of Termination
Edward Jenkins	1772	Wales	no	...	St. Barthomew's St. Michael's; St. Philip's	16	dismissal
Alexander Findlay	1773	...	no	...	St. Stephen's	10	death
Charles Frederick Moreau	1773	...	no	Huguenot	St. Helena's; St. Philip's	7	resignation
William Percy	1773	England	no	...	St. Michael's; St. Philip's	13	resignation
John Dundass	1774	...	no	...	St. John's, Colleton	0	death
Benjamin Blackburn	1775	...	no	...	St. John's, Colleton	0	death

NOTES

Works abbreviated below are cited in full in the list of Abbreviations.

1. Except where otherwise noted, data given here is taken from Frederick Lewis Weis, *The Colonial Clergy of Virginia, North Carolina and South Carolina* (Boston, 1955). Length of service has been calculated by subtracting the beginning year from the year of termination; 0 indicates less than a full year.

2. Stevens to SPG, November 1705, RSPG, A, 2, no. 156; "Documents concerning Rev. Samuel Thomas, 1702-1707," *SCHGM* 5 (1904): 47-49.

174

3. Le Jau to SPG, February 18, 1709. *Le Jau*, p. 50.

4. Le Jau to SPG, February 9, 1711, *Le Jau*, p. 85.

5. Hasel to SPG, December 27, 1716, RSPG, B, 12: 160.

6. Trott to SPG, September 13, 1707, RSPG, A, 3, no. 152; Maule to SPG, January 23, 1715, RSPG, A, 10: 77.

7. La Pierre to SPG, June 24, 1710, RSPG, A, 5, no. 132.

8. "An Account of . . . St. Paul's . . . in Mr. Bull's of 20 January 1715," RSPG, A, 10: 124-25.

9. Le Jau to SPG, September 18, 1708, *Le Jau*, p. 45.

10. Gignilliat to SPG, July 15, 1711, RSPG, A, 6, no. 105.

11. Le Jau to SPG, July 4, 1715, *Le Jau*, p. 141.

12. Thomas Broughton to SPG, September 26, 1717, RSPG, A, 13: 135-37.

13. Hasel to SPG, December 20, 1717, RSPG, A, 13: 138-40; Bull to SPG, January 27, 1719, RSPG, A, 14: 61-63.

14. Bull to the Reverend Thomas Mangey, May 12, 1720, FP, 9: 92.

15. Hunt to SPG, May 6, 1729, RSPG, A, 22: 239-40.

16. Jones to SPG, February 19, 1726, RSPG, A, 19: 84.

17. Garden to Gibson, November 8, 1732, FP, 9: 266-67.

18. Garden to Gibson, November 13, 1734, FP, 9: 314.

19. Vestry of Christ Church to SPG, April 12, 1741, RSPG, B, 9, no. 143a.

20. *HAPEC*, p. 258.

21. *The Minutes of the Vestry of St. Helena's Parish, South Carolina, 1726-1812*, ed. A.S. Salley (Columbia, S.C., 1919), pp. 73-86.

ABBREVIATIONS

CSC	*Colonial South Carolina: A Political History, 1663-1763,* by M. Eugene Sirmans (Chapel Hill, N.C., 1966).
DAB	*Dictionary of American Biography,* ed. Dumas Malone (New York, 1928-1936).
FP	Fulham Papers, Lambeth Palace, London, Eng.
HAPEC	*An Historical Account of the Protestant Episcopal Church in South Carolina from the First Settlement of the Province to the War of the Revolution,* by Frederick Dalcho (1820; reprint ed., Charleston, S.C., 1970).
HMPEC	*Historical Magazine of the Protestant Episcopal Church.*
Johnston	*Carolina Chronicle: The Papers of Commissary Gideon Johnston, 1707-1716,* ed. Frank J. Klingberg, (Berkeley, 1946).
Le Jau	*The Carolina Chronicle of Dr. Francis Le Jau, 1706-1717,* ed. Frank J. Klingberg (Berkeley, 1956).
RBPRO	*Records in the British Public Record Office Relating to South Carolina, 1663-1710,* 5 vols (Columbia, S.C., 1928-1947).
RBPRO	Records in the British Public Record Office Relating to South Carolina, 1663-1782, 36 vols., South Carolina Department of Archives and History, Columbia, S.C.
RSPG	Records of the Society for the Propagation of the Gospel in Foreign Parts, London, Eng.
SCG	*South Carolina Gazette* (Charleston, 1732-1776).
SCHGM	*South Carolina Historical and Genealogical Magazine.*
SCHM	*South Carolina Historical Magazine.*
Statutes	*The Statutes at Large of South Carolina,* ed. Thomas Cooper and David J. McCord. 10 vols. (Columbia, S.C., 1836-1841).

Whitefield *George Whitefield's Journals (1737-1741) To Which Is Prefixed His "Short Account" (1746) and "Further Account" (1747)* (1905; reprint ed., Gainesville, Fla., 1969).

WMQ *William and Mary Quarterly.*

NOTES

CHAPTER 1

1. John Calam, *Parsons and Pedagogues: The S.P.G. Adventure in American Education* (New York, 1971), pp. 168-69; Leonard Woods Labaree, *Conservatism in Early American History* (Ithaca, N.Y., 1959), pp. 70-75; Richard Hofstadter, *America at 1750: A Social Portrait* (New York, 1971), pp. 204-8; Carl Bridenbaugh, *Myths and Realities: Societies of the Colonial South* (New York, 1966), pp 30-32, 75; Clement Eaton, *A History of the Old South: The Emergence of a Reluctant Nation*, 3d ed. (New York, 1975), pp. 79-82.

2. Borden W. Painter, Jr., "The Anglican Vestry in Colonial America" (Ph.D. diss., Yale University, 1965), pp. 71, 155-56, 185, 189.

3. Daniel J. Boorstin, *The Americans: The Colonial Experience* (New York, 1958), p. 127; Jack P. Green, *The Quest for Power: The Lower Houses of Assembly in the Southern Royal Colonies, 1689-1776* (New York, 1972), p. 344.

4. H. Richard Niebuhr, *The Social Sources of Denominationalism* (1929; reprint ed., Cleveland, Ohio, 1964), pp. 122-32. Hofstadter, *America at 1750*, p. 205.

5. J. Sears McGee, *The Godly Man in Stuart England: Anglicans, Puritans and the Two Tables, 1620-1670* (New Haven, 1976), pp. 44-45; Lawrence A. Cremin, *American Education: The Colonial Experience, 1607-1783* (New York, 1970), pp. 147-48; Christopher Hill, *The Century of Revolution, 1603-1714* (New York, 1966), p. 292.

6. Frederick V. Mills, *Bishops by Ballot: An Eighteenth Century Ecclesiastical Revolution* (New York, 1978), pp. 100-106, 128-37; Carl Bridenbaugh, *Mitre and Sceptre: Transatlantic Faiths, Ideas, Personalities and Politics, 1689-1775*, (New York, 1962), 314-23; Mary Elizabeth Quinlivan, "Ideologi-

cal Controversy Over Religious Establishment in Revolutionary Virginia," (Ph.D. diss., University of Wisconsin, 1971), pp. 25-26.

7. Niebuhr, *Social Sources of Denominationalism*, pp. 111-12.

8. Quinlivan, "Ideological Controversy," pp. 22-28, 46-57.

9. Mills, *Bishops by Ballot*, pp. 86-92, 98-100.

10. Paul Conkin, "The Church Establishment in North Carolina, 1765-1776," *North Carolina Historical Review* 32 (1955): 1-30; Gary Freeze, "Like a House Built upon Sand: The Anglican Church and Establishment in North Carolina, 1765-1776," *HMPEC* 48 (1979): 405-32; Harold E. Davis, *The Fledgling Province: Social and Cultural Life in Colonial Georgia, 1733-1776* (Chapel Hill, N.C., 1976), pp. 205-30.

11. Quinlivan, "Ideological Controversy," pp. 10-12, 21, 28-38, 94-105.

12. John Calam, *Parsons and Pedagogues*, pp. 93-98; Mills, *Bishops by Ballot*, p. 93.

13. Rhys Isaac, "Religion and Authority: Problems of the Anglican Establishment in the Era of the Great Awakening and the Parsons' Cause," *WMQ*, 3d ser., 30 (1973): 3-36.

14. Rhys Isaac, "Evangelical Revolt: The Nature of the Baptists' Challenge to the Traditional Order in Virginia, 1765-1775," *WMQ*, 3d ser., 31 (1974): 345-68; idem, "Preachers and Patriots: Popular Culture and the Revolution in Virginia," in *The American Revolution: Explorations in the History of American Radicalism*, ed. Alfred Young, (De Kalb, Ill.: 1976), 127-56.

15. William H. Seiler, "The Anglican Parish Vestry in Colonial Virginia," *Journal of Southern History* 22 (1956): 310-37; Gerald E. Hartdagen, "The Anglican Vestry in Colonial Maryland: A Study in Corporate Responsibility," *HMPEC* 40 (1971): 315-35, 461-79; Alan D. Watson, "The Anglican Parish in Royal North Carolina, 1729-1775," *HMPEC* 48 (1979): 303-19.

16. Cremin, *American Education*, 333-47, 493-99; Calam, *Parsons and Pedagogues*, chap. 4.

17. Winthrop D. Jordan, *White over Black: American Attitudes toward the Negro, 1550-1812* (Baltimore, Md., 1968), pp. 206-12; Joan Rezner Gundersen, "The Anglican Ministry in Virginia, 1723-1776: A Study of Social Class," (Ph.D. diss., University of Notre Dame, 1972), 113-29; Thad W. Tate, Jr., *The Negro in Eighteenth Century Williamsburg* (Charlottesville, Va., 1965), pp. 134-58.

18. David C. Skaggs and Gerald E. Hartdagen, "Saints and Sinners: Anglican Clerical Conduct in Colonial Maryland," *HMPEC*, 47 (1978): 185; Joan Rezner Gundersen, "The Anglican Ministry in Virginia, 1723-1776," pp. 160-61; Richard Beale Davis, *Intellectual Life in the Colonial South*, 2 vols. (Knoxville, Tenn., 1978), 2: 708-9, 721-58.

19. Eaton, *History of the Old South*, pp. 81-82; George N. Clark, *The Later Stuarts, 1660-1714* (Oxford, 1955), p. 17.

20. Henry F. May, *The Enlightenment in America* (New York, 1976), 66-75.
21. Bridenbaugh, *Myths and Realities*, pp. 120-28, 180-85.
22. Lester Cappon, ed., *Atlas of Early American History: The Revolutionary Era, 1760-1790* (Princeton, N.J., 1976), p. 36; Elisha P. Douglas, *Rebels and Democrats: The Struggle for Equal Political Rights and Majority Rule during the American Revolution* (Chicago, 1965), pp. 47-49; Robert McClure Calhoun, *The Loyalists in Revolutionary America, 1760-1781* (New York, 1973), pp. 439-47.
23. William G. McLoughlin, "The Role of Religion in the Revolution: Liberty of Conscience and Cultural Cohesion in the New Nation," in *Essays on the American Revolution*, ed. Stephen G. Kurtz and James H. Hutson (New York, 1973), pp. 205-26, discusses disestablishment within the context of creating political unity. On the influence of western dissenters in Virginia, see Thomas E. Buckley, *Church and State in Revolutionary Virginia, 1777-1787* (Charlottesville, Va., 1977), pp. 12-14, 175.

CHAPTER 2

1. David S. Lovejoy, *The Glorious Revolution in America* (New York, 1972), pp. 368-70.
2. The charter is given in Mattie Erma Edwards Parker, ed., *North Carolina Charters and Constitutions, 1578-1698* (Raleigh, N.C., 1963), pp. 76-89. See also *CSC*, pp. 3-5.
3. The Fundamental Constitutions are reprinted in Parker, *North Carolina Charters*, pp. 128-240. See also *CSC*, pp. 6-15, 35-37.
4. *CSC*, pp. 3-6, 27-29, 36-37, 41-42; Richard S. Dunn, "The English Sugar Islands and the Founding of South Carolina," *SCHM* 72 (1971): 81-93; Babette M. Levy, *Early Puritanism in the Southern and Island Colonies* (Worcester, Mass., 1960), pp. 256-74; Arthur Henry Hirsch, *The Huguenots of Colonial South Carolina* (Durham, N.C., 1928), chap. 1.
5. These figures are based on Thomas Nairne's estimate of religious percentages in 1710, given in David Duncan Wallace, *The History of South Carolina*, 4 vols. (New York, 1934-35), 1: 146; Peter Girard's enumeration of French Protestants, March 14, 1699, *RBPRO*, 4: 75; and Governor and Council to Proprietors, March 17, 1708, *RBPRO*, 5: 203-4.
6. *HAPEC*, pp. 26-27.
7. "Blake of South Carolina," *SCHGM* 1 (1900): 153-57.
8. Gerald R. Cragg, *From Puritanism to the Age of Reason: A Study of Changes in Religious Thought within the Church of England, 1660-1700* (Cambridge, Eng., 1950), pp. 114-18; Basil Willey, *The Seventeenth Century Back-*

ground: Studies in the Thought of the Age in Relation to Religion and Poetry (New York, 1953), pp. 263-64.

9. Norman Sykes, "The Theology of Divine Benevolence," *HMPEC* 16 (1947): 280.

10. Cragg, *From Puritanism to the Age of Reason*, p. 86, also chap. 4.

11. H. P. Thompson, *Thomas Bray* (London, 1954), p. 38, also chaps. 3 and 5; Samuel Clyde McCullogh, "Dr. Thomas Bray's Commissary Work in London, 1696-1699," *WMQ*, 3d ser., 2 (1945): 333-48.

12. The "Memorial" is reprinted in Bernard C. Steiner, *The Reverend Thomas Bray: His Life and Selected Works Relating to Maryland* (Baltimore, 1901), pp. 157-73. The charter is given in C.F. Pascoe, *Classified Digest of the Records of the Society for the Propagation of the Gospel in Foreign Parts, 1701-1892* (London, 1895), pp. 925-28. See also Samuel Clyde McCullogh, "The Foundation and Early Work of the S.P.G.," *Huntington Library Quarterly* 8 (1945): 242-58; and Thompson, *Thomas Bray*, chap. 8.

13. George Every, *The High Church Party, 1688-1718* (London, 1956).

14. Proprietors to Governor Smith, April 24, 1694, *RBPRO*, 3: 122; Memorandum to Board of Trade, April 12, 1697, *RBPRO*, 3: 193; *Dictionary of National Biography* (London, 1937-1938), s.v. Grenville, John, Earl of Bath, 1628-1701.

15. Geoffrey Holmes, *British Politics in the Age of Anne* (New York, 1967), pp. 276, 395, 472 n.22.

16. Proprietors to Marshall, March 8, 1698, *RBPRO*, 4: 20-21; Proprietors to Governor Blake, April 11, 1698, *RBPRO*, 4: 44; Thompson, *Thomas Bray*, p. 22.

17. The law, dated October 8, 1698, exists only in mutilated form. William Sumner Jenkins, comp., Records of the States of the United States, a microfilm compilation (Library of Congress in association with the University of North Carolina, 1949), S.C., B. 2, 1a.

18. Stevens to SPG, February 3, 1708, RSPG, A, 3: 49.

19. Alexander S. Salley, ed., *Journals of the Commons House of Assembly, 1692-1735*, 21 vols. (Columbia, S.C., 1907-46), *1698*, pp. 28, 33.

20. January 17, 1700, cited in *HAPEC*, pp. 36-37.

21. *CSC*, pp. 75-86; Verner W. Crane, *The Southern Frontier, 1670-1732* (Philadelphia, Pa., 1929), pp. 22-70.

22. *DAB*, s.v. Johnson, Sir Nathaniel; Minutes of the Board of Trade, June 29, 1701, *RBPRO*, 5: 96; Richard S. Dunn, *Sugar and Slaves: The Rise of the Planter Class in the English West Indies* (Baltimore, 1974), pp. 133-34.

23. Proprietors to James Moore, June 18, 1702, *RBPRO*, 5: 77; Proprietors to Job Howes [*sic*], June 18, 1702, *RBPRO*, 5: 82; Granville to Broughton, June 18, 1702, *RBPRO*, 5: 89-90; *DAB*, s.v. Trott, Nicholas.

24. Commons House Journals, 1702-1706, "Green Transcripts" (South Carolina Department of Archives and History); *Statutes*, 2: 232, 233-35; William James Rivers, *A Sketch of the History of South Carolina to the Close of the Proprietary Government by the Revolution of 1719* (Charleston, 1856), pp. 218-19; *CSC*, pp. 86-88.

25. "The Case of the Reverend Mr. Edward Marston," in Daniel Defoe, *The Case of the Protestant Dissenters in Carolina* (London, 1706), p. 65; in Jenkins, Records of the States, North Carolina Miscellany; *HAPEC*, gives the proceedings against Marston, pp. 54-58.

26. *Statutes*, 2: 236-48.

27. Ibid., 2: 251-53.

28. *Party-Tyranny; or, An Occasional Bill in Miniature . . .* (London, 1705), in *Narratives of Early Carolina, 1650-1708*, ed. Alexander S. Salley (New York, 1911), pp. 224-64; Defoe, *The Case of the Protestant Dissenters*.

29. Defoe, *The Case of the Protestant Dissenters*.

30. George N. Clark, *The Later Stuarts, 1660-1714* (Oxford, Eng., 1955), p. 224; Leo F. Stock, ed., *Proceedings and Debates of the British Parliaments Respecting North America*, 5 vols. (Washington, D.C., 1924-41), 3: 120-21, also 115-25; Board of Trade to Queen, May 24, 1706, *RBPRO*, 5: 157-59; Proprietors to Governor and Council, *RBPRO*, 5: 141.

31. *Statutes*, 2: 260; *CSC*, p. 89.

32. *Statutes*, 2: 282-94.

33. Hirsch, *Huguenots*, 92-93, 126-27; Jerome W. Jones, "The Anglican Church in Colonial Virginia" (Ph.D. diss., Harvard University, 1960), pp. 236-37; and Edward F. Carpenter, *The Protestant Bishop, Being the Life of Henry Compton, 1632-1713, Bishop of London* (London, 1956), chap. 17. See also Amy Ellen Friedlander, "Carolina Huguenots; A Study in Cultural Pluralism in the Low Country, 1679-1768" (Ph.D. diss., Emory University, 1979).

34. See the chart in the Appendix.

35. Arthur Lyon Cross, *The Anglican Episcopate and the American Colonies* (New York, 1902), pp. 25-34.

36. Gideon Johnston to the bishop of Sarum, September 20, 1708, *Johnston*, pp. 19, 21-22; Johnston to SPG, July 5, 1710, *Johnston*, pp. 47-48.

37. Johnston to SPG, July 5, 1710, *Johnston*, pp. 49-51; Johnston to SPG, January 27, 1711, *Johnston*, pp. 80-81.

38. Johnston to SPG, July 5, 1710, *Johnston*, pp. 51-52; Johnston to SPG, January 27, 1711, *Johnston*, p. 77.

39. Gideon Johnston, "Present State of the Clergy . . . with respect to . . . Church Discipline," in Hirsch, *Huguenots*, p. 298.

40. Johnston to SPG, July 5, 1710, *Johnston*, pp. 55-57; Le Jau to SPG, August 5, 1709, *Le Jau*, pp. 56-57.

41. Johnston, "Present State," pp. 298-305.

42. Johnston to SPG, January 27, 1711, *Johnston*, p. 85.

43. Marston's quarrel with the governor can be followed in Salley, *Journals of the Commons House, 1706-1707*, pp. 4-5, and *June-July, 1707*, pp. 9-10, 12, 96, 99-100. For political developments between 1706 and 1712, see *CSC*, pp. 89-96.

44. Trott to SPG, September 13, 1707, RSPG, A, 3, no. 152; Governor and Council to SPG, September 19, 1707, RSPG, A, 3, no. 153; *Statutes*, 2: 330.

45. *Statutes*, 2: 338-42.

46. Edward McCrady, *The History of South Carolina under the Proprietary Government, 1670-1719* (New York, 1897), 506-7.

47. RSPG, Journal, May 30, 1707; Johnston to SPG, January 27, 1711, *Johnston*, pp. 81-84; Johnston to SPG, April 20, 1711, *Johnston*, p. 93; Trott to SPG, September 19, 1711, RSPG, A, 7: 380-82.

48. Le Jau to SPG, June 13, 1710, *Le Jau*, p. 79; Johnston to SPG, July 5, 1710, *Johnston*, pp. 39-40, 59-60; Johnston to SPG, January 27, 1711, *Johnston*, pp. 78-82, 85; and Johnston to SPG, June 17, 1712, *Johnston*, p. 113.

49. *Statutes*, 2: 366-76.

50. "Mr. Johnston's Memoriall," *Johnston*, pp. 132-33; Clergy to SPG, March 4, 1713, RSPG, B, 8: 339-40; Instructions from clergy to Commissary Johnston, March 4, 1713, RSPG, B, 8: 374-76; "Instructions...Enlarged and Explained by...Johnston," n.d., *Johnston*, pp. 119-31..

51. Gideon Johnston, "State of Mr. Jones' Case," n.d., RSPG, B, 8: 378-79; "Commissary Johnston concerning Mr. Jones and Mr. Osborn [*sic*]," RSPG, B, 8: 382-83; SPG to Osborne, November 30, 1713, RSPG, B, 8: 457-58; SPG to Jones, November 30, 1713, RSPG, B, 8: 458-59; SPG to inhabitants of Christ Church, RSPG, B, 8:459-60.

52. Johnston, "Present State," pp. 297-309.

53. Cross, *Anglican Episcopate*, pp. 88-101, 277-78; "Report of the S.P.G. Committee on American Bishops as Agreed upon," January 16, 1712, RSPG, A, 7: 105-9.

54. Every, *High Church Party*, chap. 8; William A. and Phyllis W. Bultmann, "The Roots of Anglican Humanitarianism; A Study of the Membership of the S.P.C.K. and the S.P.G., 1699-1720," *HMPEC* 33 (1964): 26-27; RSPG, Journal, March 6, 1716.

55. See the various notes and documents in *Johnston*, pp. 132-46.

56. Johnston to SPG, December 9, 1715, *Johnston*, pp. 148-49; Charles Burnham to Johnston, April 3, 1716, in Johnston to SPG, April 4, 1716, *Johnston*, pp. 163-64; Clergy to Bishop Robinson, May 31 and June 7, 1716, *Johnston*, pp. 167-69.

CHAPTER 3

1. SPG to Johnston, September 16, 1715, RSPG, A, 10: 132; Thomas Hasel to SPG, December 27, 1716, RSPG, B, 12: 160; *Le Jau*, p. 204.

2. Hasel to SPG, September 20, 1717, RSPG, B, 12: 83-84; *Statutes*, 3: 9-14.

3. RSPG, Journal, August 2, 1717; RSPG, Journal, November 15, 1717; RSPG, Journal, December 20, 1717; RSPG, Journal, July 18, 1718; Gilbert Jones to SPG, May 18, 1719, RSPG, A, 13: 230-31; Bull to SPG, January 27, 1720, RSPG, A, 14: 61-63; Bull to SPG, May 12, 1720, RSPG, A, 14: 75.

4. *CSC*, chap. 6.

5. Bull to SPG, January 27, 1720, RSPG, A, 14: 61-63.

6. Bull to SPG, May 12, 1720, RSPG, A, 14: 74-75; Bull to SPG, August 12, 1720, RSPG, A, 15: 56-57; Francis Yonge, *Narrative of the Proceedings of the People of South Carolina in the Year 1719* (London, 1721), in *Historical Collections of South Carolina...*, ed. Bartholomew Rivers Carroll, 2 vols. (New York, 1836), 2: 192.

7. Guy to SPG, October 17, 1720, RSPG, A, 14: 78-79.

8. Bull to SPG, December 19, 1720, RSPG, A, 15: 56; Steven Saunders Webb, "The Strange Career of Francis Nicholson," *WMQ*, 3d ser., 24 (1966): 513-48; Ruth M. Winton, "Governor Francis Nicholson's Relations with the Society for the Propagation of the Gospel in Foreign Parts, 1701-1727," *HMPEC* 17 (1948): 274-86; RSPG, Journal, August 19, 1720.

9. RSPG, Journal, November 17, 1721.

10. *Statutes*, 3: 171-72, 174-76; Bull to SPG, June 27, 1722, RSPG, A, 16: 69; Clergy to SPG, July 12, 1722, RSPG, A, 16: 76-78.

11. Middleton and Moore to SPG, RSPG, A, 16: 72-73.

12. "Instructions...Enlarged and Explained by...Johnston," n.d., *Johnston*, p. 127; Clergy of South Carolina to SPG, October 10, 1721, RSPG, A, 15: 58-59; Address of Clergy to Governor and Assembly, January 10, 1722, RSPG, A, 16: 121-23. The clergy seem to have been misinformed about the practice in England if not the law. See David Ogg, *England in the Reigns of James II and William III* (London, 1955), p. 97.

13. Copy of Stobo's Petition [1722], RSPG, A, 16: 107-10. The copy states that a "Mr Kinlock" convinced Stobo not to present his petition. This was probably James Kinlock, an Anglican merchant and member of Nicholson's Council. See *CSC*, p. 138 n.20, and for the outcome of the dispute, p. 141.

14. *Statutes*, 2: 137, no. 9; *Commons House*, June 11, 15, 16, 1724.

15. "Papers relating to the Presbyterian Minister at Charles Town, South Carolina," RSPG, A, 18: 110-12; George Howe, *History of the Presbyterian*

Church in South Carolina (Columbia, S.C., 1870), 1: 183; Guy to SPG, October 28, 1724, RSPG, A, 18: 95-96; Nicholson to the bishop of London, FP, 9: 156-57.

16. Clergy of South Carolina to SPG, May 16, 1723, RSPG, A, 18: 81-83.

17. Bull to Gibson, May 13, 1728, FP, 9: 216-17; Varnod to SPG, March 21, 1725, RSPG, A, 19: 60: Clergy to SPG, n.d., RSPG, A, 16: 76-78.

18. Garden to La Pierre, April 8, 1725, enclosed in La Pierre to the bishop of London, January 1, 1726, FP, 9: 178-79; Garden to Bishop Gibson, May 24, 1725, FP, 9: 176-77.

19. Vestry of Christ Church to SPG, October 21, 1728, RSPG, A, 21: 131-35; Winteley to SPG, October 22, 1728, RSPG, A, 21: 137-40; Winteley to Gibson, June 14, 1729, RSPG, A, 22: 246-59; RSPG, Journal, February 21, 1729; RSPG, Journal, October 17, 1729.

20. Arthur Lyon Cross, *The Anglican Episcopate and the American Colonies* (New York, 1902), pp. 54-58, 294-309; Garden to Gibson, June 28, 1729, FP, 9: 233-36.

21. Garden to Gibson, June 28, 1729, FP, 9: 239-40.

22. Vestry of Christ Church to SPG, May 10, 1734, RSPG, A, 25: 93-94; Garden to Gibson, December 28, 1733, FP, 9: 278-79.

23. Garden to Gibson, April 30, 1734, FP, 9: 298-99; Garden to Gibson, May 15, 1735, FP, 10: 7-10.

24. Garden to Gibson, May 15, 1735, FP, 10: 7-10; Garden to Gibson, March 8, 1737, FP, 10: 40-43.

25. Garden to Gibson, April 20, 1731, FP, 9: 254-55; Vestry to SPG, April 7, 1734, RSPG, A, 25: 83-84.

26. "Some Inhabitants of St. Paul's Parish...to the Rev. Mr. Garden," March 16, 1734, RSPG, A, 25: 122-24; Vestry of Saint Paul's to SPG, April 15, 1734, RSPG, A, 25: 86-87.

27. Garden to SPG, April 18, 1734, RSPG, A, 25: 90-91; Garden to the bishop of London, April 30, 1734, FP, 9: 298-99; Garden to SPG, November 6, 1734, RSPG, A, 25; 105-7.

28. RSPG, Journal, February 21, 1735; RSPG, Journal, May 16, 1735; Leslie to SPG, December 3, 1735, RSPG, A, 26: 149; Leslie to SPG, December 29, 1736, RSPG, A, 26: 371-72.

29. Garden to Gibson, November 8, 1732, FP, 9: 266-67.

30. Garden to Gibson, June 12, 1739, FP, 10: 56-57; Garden to Gibson, May 4, 1739, FP, 10: 54-55.

31. Garden to Gibson, December 28, 1733, FP, 9: 278-79.

32. Garden to Gibson, May 15, 1735, FP, 10: 7-10.

33. Garden to Gibson, June 4, 1736, FP, 10: 28-31.

34. *Whitefield*, pp. 381-83.

35. *Three Letters from the Reverend Mr. G. Whitefield*...(Philadelphia, 1740); *A Letter from the Reverend Mr. Whitefield from Georgia to a Friend in London, Shewing the Fundamental Error of a Book, Entitled, "The Whole Duty of Man"* (Charles Town, 1740).

36. *Three Letters*, pp. 13-16.

37. *Whitefield*, pp. 397-98; Alexander Garden, *Take Heed How Ye Hear* (Charles Town, 1741), pp. 17-20.

38. *Whitefield*, pp. 399-400; *SCG*, March 22, 1740.

39. Joseph Tracy, *The Great Awakening* (Boston, 1841), pp. 77-81; Garden, *Take Heed How Ye Hear*, pp. 7-10; Garden to Bishop Sherlock, February 1, 1750, FP, 10: 134-35; Whitefield to Gibson, September 8, 1740, FP, 10: 62-63.

40. *Six Letters from the Rev. Mr. Garden to the Rev. Mr. George Whitfield* [*sic*], 2d ed. (Boston, 1740), pp. 5-9, 36,39.

41. *SCG*, July 25, 1740; *Whitefield*, pp. 438-44.

42. *Whitefield*, pp. 437-38, 445-46. Several letters from Jones to Garden are given in Frank J. Klingberg, *An Appraisal of the Negro in Colonial South Carolina: A Study in Americanization* (Washington, D.C., 1941), pp. 70-71.

43. For example, see the pieces signed "J.S.," written by Josiah Smith, rector of the independent meetinghouse, in *SCG*, January 12, February 9, February 16, March 1, March 15, and March 22, 1740; and the answers by "Arminius," *SCG*, January 26, February 2, and February 9, 1740.

44. Alexander Garden, *Regeneration and the Testimony of the Spirit* (Charles Town, 1740) preface. See also the poetic attack on Whitefield and his followers in *SCG*, May 24, 1740; and the piece signed "Misanaides," *SCG*, , June 28, 1740.

45. *SCG*, July 12, 1740.

46. Ibid., August 8, 1740.

47. Ibid., August 30, 1740 and September 6, 1740; *Whitefield*, pp. 450-52.

48. William Guy to SPG, February 22, 1741, RSPG, B, 9, no. 132; J. H. Easterby and Ruth S. Green, eds., *The Colonial Records of South Carolina, Series I: The Journal of the Commons House of Assembly, 1736-1750*, 9 vols. (Columbia, S.C., 1951-62), 2: 408-9; Minutes of the Vestry of St. Philip's Parish, 1732-1755, typescript (South Caroliniana Library, Columbia, S.C.), pp. 58-72.

49. "A Letter from Mr. Hugh Bryan to a Friend." On Bryan, see Edward McCrady, *The History of South Carolina under the Royal Government, 1719-1776* (New York, 1901), p. 238; *Whitefield*, pp. 505-9; *SCG*, January 15, 1741.

50. Garden to Bishop Gibson, January 23, 1741, FP, 10: 67-68; *SCG*, January 15, 1741.

51. Garden to the bishop of London, January 28, 1742, FP, 10: 95-96; Garden to SPG, April 9, 1742, RSPG, B, 10, no. 138; *SCG*, February 13, 1742.

52. Garden to SPG, n.d., RSPG, A, 12, no. 122a.

53. Garden to Bishop Gibson, April 24, 1740, FP, 10: 58-59; Garden to Bishop Gibson, January 28, 1741, FP, 10: 67-68.

54. Roe to SPG, February 20, 1742, RSPG, B, 10, no. 175; Garden to SPG, October 10, 1743, RSPG, B, 11: 205.

55. Bearcroft to Roe, n.d., RSPG, B, 13, no. 23; Price to Garden, May 5, 1744, RSPG, A, 12, no. 79; RSPG, Journal, December 21, 1744; Garden to SPG, November 8, 1744, RSPG, A, 12, no. 119.

56. Thompson to SPG, April 23, 1743, RSPG, B, 10, no. 166; Vestry of St. Bartholomew's to SPG, January 6, 1744, RSPG, B, 11: 208; Thompson to SPG, June 11, 1743, RSPG, B, 1: 211; Thompson to SPG, June 30, 1744, RSPG, B, 11: 214-15.

57. Garden to SPG, January 31, 1744, RSPG, B, 11: 206-7; Thompson to SPG, August 16, 1743, RSPG, B, 11: 218; Thompson to SPG, January 30, 1744, RSPG, B, 11: 214-15.

58. Thompson to SPG, April 23, 1743, RSPG, B, 10, no. 166.

59. Bearcroft to Garden, December 15, 1744, RSPG, B, 13: 57; Boschi to SPG, October 30, 1745, RSPG, A, 12, no. 112; Boschi to SPG, June 20, 1747, RSPG, B, 15: 175.

60. Garden to SPG, April 23, 1745, RSPG, A, 12, no. 80; Garden to SPG, January 24, 1748, RSPG, B, 16: 133; Garden to SPG, May 4, 1748, RSPG, B, 16: 137; Boschi to SPG, February 20, 1749, RSPG, B, 16: 149.

61. Boschi to SPG, August 22, 1747, RSPG, B, 15: 178-80; Boschi to SPG, August 3, 1749, RSPG, B, 17: 177-78; Helena Boschi to SPG, November 3, 1749, RSPG, B, 17: 180; Garden to SPG, February 4, 1751, RSPG, B, 17: 183a.

62. RSPG, Journal, June 15, 1739; RSPG, Journal, June 17, 1741.

63. Cross, *Anglican Episcopate*, chap. 5; Garden to SPG, February 4, 1751, RSPG, B, 18: 183.

64. *HAPEC*, pp. 162-64; Garden to Gibson, September 16, 1748, FP, 10: 116-17; "Minutes of the Vestry of St. John's Parish, Berkeley County, March 22, 1731-April 14, 1813," microfilm (South Carolina Department of Archives and History), July 14, 1748.

65. *HAPEC*, pp. 165-75.

66. Parke Rouse, *James Blair of Virginia* (Chapel Hill, 1971); Alison Gilbert Olson, "The Commissaries of the Bishop of London in Colonial Politics," in *Anglo-American Political Relations, 1675-1775*, ed. Alison Gilbert Olson and Richard Maxwell Brown (New Brunswick, N.J., 1970), p. 111.

CHAPTER 4

1. Robert L. Meriwether, *The Expansion of South Carolina, 1729-1765* (Kingsport, Tenn., 1940), pp. 17-30, 38-40, 47-51, 64, 72, 97-98.

2. Garden to Gibson, May 4, 1739, FP, 10: 54-55

3. *HAPEC*, p. 347; Varnod to SPG, January 15, 1724, RSPG, A, 17: 120-21.

4. Varnod to SPG, July 21, 1724, RSPG, A, 18: 85-87; Varnod to SPG, June 21, 1726, RSPG, A, 19: 83; Varnod to SPG, September 4, 1729, RSPG, A, 22: 265; Varnod to SPG, February 13, 1731, RSPG, A, 23: 230; Varnod to SPG, August 9, 1731, RSPG, A, 23: 297.

5. Varnod to SPG, January 12, 1733, RSPG, A, 24: 342; Varnod to SPG, June 29, 1736, RSPG, A, 26: 362; Vestry of Saint George's to SPG, September 27, 1736, RSPG, A, 26: 368-69.

6. Dwight to SPG, June 1, 1731, RSPG, A, 23: 289-90; Bell to Morritt, July 12, 1727, RSPG, A, 21: 94; Garden to SPG, July 18, 1735, RSPG, A, 26: 138-39; Fordyce to SPG, February 1, 1739, RSPG, B, 7: 229-30.

7. Fordyce to SPG, December 1, 1742, RSPG, B, 10, no. 149; Fordyce to SPG, October 24, 1743, RSPG, B, 11: 233; Fordyce to SPG, November 4, 1745, RSPG, A, 12, no. 92; Roe to SPG, January 6, 1741, RSPG, B, 9, no. 134; Stone to SPG, March 6, 1750, RSPG, B, 17: 182.

8. Fordyce to SPG, 16—— 1742, RSPG, A, 10, no. 146; Fordyce to SPG, October 30, 1744, RSPG, A, 12, no. 90; Fordyce to SPG, March 29, 1745, RSPG, A, 12, no. 91; Fordyce to SPG, October 6, 1747, RSPG, B, 15: 181; Fordyce to SPG, April 18, 1748, RSPG, B, 16: 134; Vestry of Prince Frederick to SPG, October 23, 751, RSPG, B, 19: 147.

9. The population estimate is from Jackson Turner Main, *Political Parties before the Constitution* (New York, 1974), p. 268; the data on ministers is derived from Frederick Lewis Weis, *The Colonial Clergy of Virginia, North Carolina, and South Carolina* (Boston, 1955); and that on Presbyterians from Robert D. Mitchell, "The Presbyterian Church as an Indicator of Westward Expansion in the 18th Century America," *The Professional Geographer*, 18 (1966): 293-99.

10. Charles Woodmason's writings have been published as *The Carolina Backcountry on the Eve of the Revolution. The Journal and Other Writings of Charles Woodmason, Anglican Itinerant*, ed. Richard J. Hooker (Chapel Hill, N.C., 1953). For the details of his career, see the introduction by Richard J. Hooker.

11. Ibid., pp. 6-7, 42, 52, 56, 60.

12. Ibid., pp. 26, 48.

13. Ibid., pp. 12, 16, 18-19, 31, 33-34, 36-37, 39, 48, 58-59.

14. Ibid., pp. 101, 105.

15. Ibid., pp. 20, 47, 51.

16. For Woodmason's role in the Regulator Movement, see the account by Hooker and the documents, ibid., especially pp. 172-73, 183, 223, 225, and

231-32; also Richard M. Brown, *The South Carolina Regulators* (Cambridge, Mass., 1963), pp. 41-43, 113-23, 188-89.

17. *Statutes*, 4: 298-302; *HAPEC*, p. 327.

18. Orr to SPG, February 9, 1741, RSPG, B, 9, no. 123; Orr to SPG, March 31, 1742, RSPG, B, 10, no. 164; Orr to Churchwardens and Vestry of Saint Paul's, July 5, 1743, RSPG, B, 10: 223; Bearcroft to Orr, July 7, 1744, RSPG, B, 13, no. 54; RSPG, Journal, October 19, 1750.

19. Durand to SPG, December 29, 1741, RSPG, B, 10, no. 157; Durand to SPG, February 3, 1742, RSPG, B, 10, no. 159; Durand to SPG, April 19, 1744, RSPG, A, 12, no. 106; Durand to SPG, October 15, 1744, RSPG, A, 12, no. 107; Durand to SPG, May 10, 1749, RSPG, B, 17: 174-75; Durand to SPG, December 10, 1751, RSPG, B, 19: 143-43.

20. "Minutes of the Vestry of Saint John's Parish, Berkeley County" (Columbia, South Carolina Department of Archives and History), August 25, August 28, November 4, 1751; October 23, November 9, 1752; and March 14, 1753.

21. Fordyce to SPG, 16——1742, RSPG, A, 10, no. 146; Garden to SPG, May 20, 1741, RSPG, A, 9, no. 124; Boschi to SPG, April 7, 1746, RSPG, A, 9, no. 111; Boschi to SPG, n.d., RSPG, B, 14: 235-37.

22. "Minutes of the Vestry of St. John's, Colleton, 1738-1817," typescript (South Carolina Department of Archives and History), April 16, 1770; George W. Williams, *St. Michael's Charleston, 1751-1951* (Columbia, S.C., 1951), pp. 24-28; Bull to Earl of Dartmouth, February 22, 1775, RBPRO, 25: 22-23.

23. Petition of Charles Martyn, n.d., RSPG, B, 19: 148; Martyn to SPG, December 28, 1752, RSPG, B, 20: 138; Martyn to SPG, June 25, 1753, RSPG, B, 20: 137.

24. List of parishes with comments, March 30, 1762, FP, 10: 147-48; further notes attributed to Martyn, April 11, 1762, FP, 10: 153-54; Governor James Glen to a brother of Bishop Osbaldeston, April 10, 1762, FP, 10: 151-52; Martyn to Bishop Terrick, October 20, 1765, FP, 10: 160-61.

25. Martyn to the bishop of London, February 1, 1772, Fulham Papers, Library of Congress Transcripts, Washington, D.C., N.C., S.C., Ga., no. 16; Garden, Jr., to SPG, February 20, 1764, RSPG, B, 5, no. 218; Durand to SPG, RSPG, B, 5, no. 249; Garden, Jr., to SPG, March 31, 1767, RSPG, B, 5, no. 222.

26. *HAPEC* discusses the meetings of the clergy, pp. 162-63ff; its brief accounts of each parish are the source for the statements about tenure. Woodmason, writing in 1765, claimed that the church in Prince William's was second only to Saint Philip's, see Hooker, *Carolina Backcountry*, p. 72.

27. *Statutes*, 3: 650-51.

28. "South Carolina Material in *The Gentleman's Magazine*," typescript (South Caroliniana Library, Columbia, S.C.), pp. 64-65; Vestry to the bishop of

London, "Minutes of the Vestry of St. Philip's Parish, 1732-1755" (South Caroliniana Library, Columbia, S.C.), p. 110; *HAPEC*, pp. 157-58, 163; *SCG*, June 8, 15, 25, 1747; Langhorne to SPG, March 18, 1751, RSPG, B, 18: 190.

29. *Statutes*, 3: 753; *SCG*, April 29, 1751; Stone to SPG, March 22, 1751, RSPG, B, 18: 186.

30. *SCG*, February 22, 1752.

31. *HAPEC*, pp. 184-88; Williams, *St. Michael's Charleston*, pp. 9-25; *SCG*, April 13, 23, and May 11, 1767; George W. Williams, "Eighteenth-Century Organists at St. Michael's, Charleston," *SCHM* 53 (1952): 212-16.

32. *Statutes*, 4: 181; on the pews, see *SCG*, August 22, 1771, for example; and William Tennent's estimate of their value, in Newton B. Jones, ed., "Writings of the Reverend William B. Tennent, 1740-1777," *SCHM* 61 (1960): 201.

33. For the number of churches, see George C. Rogers, Jr., *Charleston in the Age of the Pinckneys* (Norman, Okla., 1969), p. 94; addresses by the Presbyterians are given in *SCG*, February 6, 1762, and July 7, 1766; announcements of Anglican sermons to the Masons, *SCG*, January 9, 1755; *South Carolina and American General Gazette* (Charles Town), December 29, 1766; *South Carolina Gazette and Country Journal* (Charles Town), January 3, 1769, and January 2, 1770; *SCG*, December 31, 1772; for the fellowship society, see *SCG*, April 4, 1771, and *SCG* Supplement, February 20, 1755; for Clarke's sermons, see *SCG*, December 8, 1759; and Wilton's elegies, *S.C. Gazette and Country Journal*, October 13, 20, and November 17, 1767.

34. Society for the Relief of the Widows and Orphans of the Clergy of the Protestant Episcopal Church in South Carolina (South Carolina Historical Society, Charleston), I; *S.C. Gazette and Country Journal*, October 18, 1774.

35. Williams, *St. Michael's Charleston*, pp. 29-36; "Letters from Hon. Henry Laurens to his Son John, 1773-1776," *SCHGM* 4 (1903): 271.

36. Williams, *St. Michael's Charleston*, pp. 36-38; Henry D. Bull, ed., "A Note on James Stuart, Loyalist Clergyman in South Carolina," *Journal of Southern History* 30 (1946): 570-75; Mabel L. Webber, ed., "South Carolina Loyalists," *SCHM*, 14 (1913): 36-43.

37. William Bull to Earl of Dartmouth, February 22, 1775, RBPRO, 35: 20-21; *HAPEC*, pp. 206, 214-20, 237-38, 300-301, 357-58; "Josiah Smith's Diary," *SCHM* 33 (1936): 6, 83-86. The remaining ministers were Edward Ellington of Saint James, Goose Creek; Alexander Finlay of Saint Stephen's; James Foulis of Saint David's and Saint Helena's; Alexander Garden, Jr., of Saint Thomas; James Harrison of Saint Bartholomew's; Samuel Hart of Saint John's, Berkeley; Samuel Frederick Lucius, Cuffee Town; Charles Moreau of Saint Helena's and Saint Philip's; and Offspring Pearce of Saint George's, Dorchester.

38. The revolutionary movement in South Carolina may be followed in Merrill Jensen, *The Founding of a Nation: A History of the American Revolu-*

tion, 1763-1776 (New York, 1968), pp. 28-29, 117-21, 137-38, 142-43, 189, 206, 259-61, 306-12, 354-55, 370-71, 377-80, 443-44, 478-79, 517-18, 540-41, 598-600, 644, 677-78, 700. See also Robert M. Weir, "'The Harmony We Were Famous For': An Interpretation of Pre-Revolutionary South Carolina Politics," *WMG*, 3d ser., 26 (1969): 473-501; and George C. Rogers, Jr., *Evolution of a Federalist: William Loughton Smith of Charleston (1758-1812)* (Columbia, S.C., 1962), chap. 4.

39. Brown, *South Carolina Regulators*, stresses the vigilante quality of the movement, but he admits that sectionalism was a factor, see especially pp. 137-42. Hooker, *Carolina Backcountry*, places more emphasis on sectionalism, pp. 165-89. On the continuation of regional separation, see Bull to Dartmouth, May 15, 1773, RBPRO, 33: 263-64.

40. An account of the Drayton-Tennent-Hart mission by Gordon DenBoer includes the quotation from Middleton; see "The Early Revolutionary Movement in South Carolina, 1773-1776," (Master's thesis, University of Wisconsin, 1968), chap. 3. See also Gary D. Olson, "Loyalists and the American Revolution: Thomas Brown and the South Carolina Backcountry, 1775-1776," *SCHM* 67 (1967): 201-19 and 69 (1968): 45-56.

41. The figures on representation are from DenBoer, "The Early Revolutionary Movement," pp. 40, 128, On the South Carolina constitution of 1776, see Jerome Joshua Nadelhoft, "The Revolutionary Era in South Carolina, 1775-1788," (Ph.D. diss., University of Wisconsin, 1965), pp. 17-21, 32; and Elisha P. Douglass, *Rebels and Democrats: The Struggle for Equal Political Rights and Majority Rule during the American Revolution* (New York, 1955), pp. 34, 41-42.

42. *SCG*, April 3, 1762; [Wood Furman], *A Biography of Richard Furman*, ed. Harvey T. Cook (Greenville, S.C., 1913), pp. 53-54; Jones, "Writings of the Reverend William B. Tennent, 1740-1777," pp. 194-95.

43. Jones, "Writings of Tennent," pp. 196-209. On the continuing importance of sectionalism in the Confederation, see Main, *Political Parties before the Constitution*, pp. 268-95.

44. Jones, "Writings of Tennent," p. 195; Edward McCrady, *The History of South Carolina in the Revolution, 1775-1780* (New York, 1901), pp. 212-13; Marvin R. Zahniser, *Charles Cotesworth Pinckney: Founding Father* (Chapel Hill, N.C., 1967), pp. 50-51.

45. Nadelhoft, "Revolutionary Era," pp. 32-44; Douglass, *Rebels and Democrats*, pp. 42-44; Anson Phelps Stokes, *Church and State in the United States*, 3 vols. (New York, 1950), 1: 432-34. William G. McLoughlin, "The Role of Religion in the Revolution: Liberty of Conscience and Cultural Cohesion in the New Nation," in *Essays on the American Revolution*, ed. Stephen Kurtz and James H. Hutson (Chapel Hill, N.C., and New York, 1973), pp. 215-17.

46. *Statutes*, 1: 191; McLoughlin, "Role of Religion in the Revolution," p. 255.

CHAPTER 5

1. *SCG*, June 8, 1747; Vestry of Saint Helena's Parish to Charles Martyn, April 1761, *The Minutes of the Vestry of St. Helena's Parish, South Carolina, 1726-1812*, ed. A. S. Salley (Columbia, S.C., 1919), p. 115.

2. See, for example, Richard Hofstadter, *America at 1750: A Social Portrait* (New York, 1971), pp. 198-99, 204-8.

3. The bear story is confirmed in Thomas Smith to Robert Stevens, January 16, 1708, RSPG, A, 4, no. 20, and John Wright to Stevens, December 10, 1707, RSPG, A, 4, no. 21, and denied in Le Jau to SPG, February 19, 1710, *Le Jau*, pp. 72-73. Gideon Johnston was suspicious of Williamson, but the government of South Carolina gave him a pension in 1711. See Johnston to SPG, July 5, 1710, *Johnston*, p. 57; and "An Act for erecting a brick church in Charles Town," in *The Laws of the British Plantations in America Relating to the Church and the Clergy, Religion and Learning*, ed. Nicholas Trott (London, 1721), p. 37.

4. Vestry of Christ Church to SPG, October 21, 1728, RSPG, A, 21: 131-35.

5. See Appendix.

6. *Le Jau*, p. 204; S. C. Bolton, "South Carolina and the Reverend Doctor Francis Le Jau: Southern Society and the Conscience of an Anglican Missionary," *HMPEC* 40 (1971): 63-79.

7. RSPG, Journal, January 25, 1712; Guy to SPG, August 20, 1712, RSPG, A, 7: 434-35; Inhabitants of St. Helena to SPG, March 16, 1713, RSPG, B, 8: 351-52.

8. Le Jau to SPG, July 4, 1714, *Le Jau*, p. 142; Guy to SPG, May 25, 1715, RSPG, A, 10: 101; SPG to Guy, April 23, 1716, RSPG, A, 11: 220; Guy to SPG, March 27, 1717, RSPG, B, 12: 79-80; Guy to SPG, May 10, 1717, RSPG, B, 12: 77-78; Guy to SPG, April 18, 1718, RSPG, A, 13: 500-503; Guy to SPG, October 1, 1718, RSPG, A, 13: 520-21; Guy to SPG, November 20, 1718, RSPG, A, 13: 185-86; RSPG, Journal, September 20, 1717.

9. Guy to SPG, May 19, 1719, RSPG, A, 13: 231-33; Guy to SPG, September 28, 1719, RSPG, A, 13: 241; Guy to SPG, March 26, 1724, RSPG, A, 18: 69; Guy to SPG, March 29, 1725, RSPG, A, 19: 64; Guy to SPG, July 12, 1731, RSPG, A, 23: 293-96; Guy to SPG, March 26, 1746, RSPG, B, 14: 116; Guy to SPG, September 30, 1746, RSPG, B, 14: 222.

10. Gideon Johnston, "Present State of the Clergy...with respect to...Church

Discipline," in Arthur H. Hirsch, *The Huguenots of Colonial South Carolina* (Durham, N.C., 1928), pp. 297-309.

11. "Some Reasons Humbly Offered... by the Parishioners of St. Andre[w]'s, Why Mr. Ebenezer Taylor Should Be No Longer Suffered to Officiate in the Said Parish," n.d., RSPG, A, 13: 144-45.

12. *HAPEC*, pp. 54-58.

13. Gideon Johnston to SPG, July 5, 1710, *Johnston*, pp. 45-51.

14. Dunn to SPG, April 21, 1707, RSPG, A, 3: 99.

15. Fleming H. James, "Richard Marsden, Wayward Clergyman," *WMQ*, 3d ser., 11 (1954): 578-91.

16. Le Jau to SPG, January 10, 1712, *Le Jau*, pp. 106-7; Johnston to John Chamberlaine, May 28, 1712, *Johnston*, p. 110.

17. Vestry of Saint John's, Berkeley, to SPG, June 1, 1719, RSPG, A, 13: 235-36; RSPG, Journal, October 2, 1719.

18. RSPG, Journal, November 15, 1717; RSPG, Journal, December 20, 1717; RSPG, Journal, July 18, 1718; Gilbert Jones to SPG, RSPG, A, 13: 230-31.

19. *HAPEC*, pp. 171, 177-78.

20. A correspondent of Bishop Gibson's rated Jones as good a clergyman as Garden, H. Herbert to Gibson, April 20, 1733, FP, 9: 270-71. On Jones' career, see Jones to SPG, February 19, 1726, RSPG, A, 19: 84; Jones to SPG, June 2, 1730, RSPG, A, 23: 210-12; Jones to SPG, June 10, 1734, RSPG, A, 25: 96; Jones to SPG, February 3, 1742, RSPG, B, 10, no. 153; Jones to SPG, August 4, 1742, RSPG, B, 10, no. 154; St. Helena Parish to SPG, March 25, 1745, RSPG, A, 12, no. 118.

21. Richard Beale Davis, *Intellectual Life in the Colonial South*, 2 vols. (Knoxville, Tenn., 1978), 2: 756-58.

22. On Bugnion, see Garden to Gibson, May 15, 1735, FP, 10: 7-10; for Boschi, see Garden to SPG, April 23, 1745, RSPG, A, 12, no. 80, and February 4, 1751, RSPG, B, 18: 183a; and for Morritt, Garden to SPG, July 18, 1735, RSPG, A, 26: 138-39. Other competent ministers were Betham, Durand, Dwight, Fordyce, Fullerton, Garden, Jr., Keith, Leslie, Ludlam, Millechamp, Orr, Pouderous, Quincy, St. John, Standish, Thompson, and Varnod. Those for whom there is insufficient information are Chiffelle, Clark, Collodon, Cotes, Coulet, Cuming, De Plessis, Gowie, Lambert, McGilchrist, Pownal, Small, Stone, Tissot, Tustian, and Warden.

23. Bull to SPG, October 29, 1722, RSPG, A, 16: 87; Vestry of Goose Creek Parish to SPG, April 22, 1723, RSPG, A, 17: 100-101.

24. Clergy of South Carolina to SPG, May 9, 1727, RSPG, A, 20: 79-80, and January 2, 1728, RSPG, A, 20: 104-6.

25. Vestry of Christ Church to SPG, October 21, 1728, RSPG, A, 21: 131-35; Winteley to the bishop of London, June 14, 1729, RSPG, A, 22: 246-59.

26. FP, 9: 287-93.

27. Garden to Gibson, May 15, 1735, FP, 10: 7-10.

28. Garden to Gibson, June 8, 1734, FP, 9: 304-6; Garden to Gibson, May 15, 1735, FP, 10: 7-10; Fullerton to SPG, May 5, 1735, RSPG, A, 26: 128-29; *SCG*, June 8, 1734, and May 17, 1735.

29. Garden to SPG, October 10, 1743, RSPG, B, 11: 205; Garden to SPG, November 8, 1744, RSPG, A, 12, postscript to no. 119.

30. David Ramsay, *The History of South Carolina from Its First Settlement in 1670 to the Year 1808*, 2 vols. (1809), 2: 251; George C. Rogers, Jr., *Evolution of a Federalist: William Loughton Smith of Charleston (1758-1812)* (Columbia, S.C., 1962), pp. 61-71; *HAPEC*, pp. 181-83.

31. Hooker, *Carolina Backcountry*, intro.

32. Albert Sidney Thomas, "Robert Smith—First Bishop of South Carolina," *HMPEC* 15 (1946): 15-29.

33. See the various documents in RSPG, B, 5 nos. 49-66.

34. *Minutes of the Vestry of St. Helena's Parish*, pp. 73-86. St. Helena also fired Edward Ellington in 1772 for "Conduct...extremely Offensive to the Generality of the Inhabitants of Beaufort," but the minister went on to serve Saint James, Goose Creek, from 1775 until 1793 and therefore does not seem to have been scandalous. Ibid., pp. 151-56; *HAPEC*, pp. 262-63, 380.

35. Hooker, *Carolina Backcountry*, pp. 74-75. The clergymen are Baron, Bullman, Cooper, Copp, Crallan, Green, Harrison, Langhorne, Lewis, Martyn, Pearce, Henry Purcell, Turquand, Warren, and Wilton.

36. Jones, "Writings of Tennent," pp. 194-209.

37. *Minutes of the Vestry of St. Helena's Parish*, p. 116.

38. For the attitude of the SPG, see SPG to Saint Bartholomew's, December 15, 1744, RSPG, B, 13: 58; on the prevailing practice, see Bull to Earl of Dartmouth, RBPRO, 35: 22.

39. John Kendall Nelson, "Anglican Missions in America, 1701-1725: A Study of the Society for the Propagation of the Gospel in Foreign Parts," (Ph.D. diss., Northwestern University, 1962), pp. 31-32.

40. Vestry of St. James, Goose Creek, to SPG, October 29, 1717, RSPG, B, 12: 153-54; H. Herbert to Bishop Gibson, April 20, 1733, FP, 9: 270-271.

41. *Statutes*, 2: 174-75, 286-87; Ludlam to SPG, December 12, 1727, RSPG, A, 20: 99; *HAPEC*, p. 175; Hooker, *Carolina Backcountry*, pp. 70-73.

42. Maule to SPG, July 21, 1708, RSPG, A, 4, no. 141; Vestry of Saint John's to SPG, February 6, 1721, RSPG, A, 16: 56-57; further notes attributed to Charles Martyn, FP, 10: 153-54.

43. Hooker, *Carolina Backcountry*, pp. 70, 75; Henry D. Bull, "A Note on James Stuart, Loyalist Clergyman in South Carolina," *Journal of Southern History* 30 (1946), 570-75.

CHAPTER 6

1. Gary B. Nash discusses colonial society as the interaction of three cultures in *Red, White, and Black: The People of Early America* (Englewood Cliffs, N.J., 1974); Verner W. Crane details the relations between the Carolinians and the Indians in *The Southern Frontier, 1670-1732* (Ann Arbor, 1956); and Peter H. Wood provides a brilliant study of his subject in *Black Majority: Negroes in Colonial South Carolina from 1670 through the Stono Rebellion* (New York, 1975).

2. Robert Stevens to SPG, November 1705, RSPG, A, 2, no. 156; Thomas Nairne to Doctor Marston, August 20, 1705, RSPG, A, 2, no. 156; Robert Stevens to SPG, February 21, 1706, RSPG, A, 2, no. 158.

3. "Documents Concerning Rev. Samuel Thomas, 1702-1707," *SCHGM* 5 (1904): 21-55, especially pp. 24, 39-47; see also "Letters of Rev. Samuel Thomas, 1702-1710," *SCHGM* 4 (1903): 221-30; and "Letters of Rev. Samuel Thomas, 1702-1706," *SCHGM* 4 (1903): 278-85.

4. *A Sermon Preached before the . . .* [S.P.G.] *. . .February the 20th, 1701/2* (London, 1702), p. 17; *A Sermon Preached before the . . .* [S.P.G] *. . .February 15, 1705/6* (London, 1706).

5. Le Jau to Philip Stubs, April 15, 1707, *Le Jau*, p. 24; Le Jau to SPG, April 22, 1708, *Le Jau*, pp. 38-39; Le Jau to SPG, October 20, 1709, *Le Jau*, p. 61; Dennis to SPG, July 3, 1711, RSPG, A, 6, no. 143; Maule to SPG, August 2, 1711, RSPG, A, 7: 363-64.

6. Maule to SPG, August 2, 1711, RSPG, A, 7: 363-64; Le Jau to SPG, February 1, 1710, *Le Jau*, p. 68; Le Jau to SPG, January 4, 1712, *Le Jau*, pp. 105-6; Le Jau to SPG, September 18, 1708, *Le Jau*, p. 45; Varnod to SPG, January 15, 1723, RSPG, A, 17: 121-22. On the idea of natural religion, see Basil Willey, *The Eighteenth Century Background, Studies on the Idea of Nature in the Thought of the Period* (Boston, 1961), pp. 3-14; and Frank E. Manuel, *The Eighteenth Century Confronts the Gods* (Cambridge, Mass., 1959), pp. 57-64.

7. Le Jau to SPG, October 20, 1709, *Le Jau*, p. 61; Le Jau to SPG, September 15, 1708, *Le Jau*, p. 41; Dennis to SPG, July 3, 1711, RSPG, A, 6, no. 143; Dennis to SPG, March 21, 1714, RSPG, A, 10: 23-24.

8. Maule to SPG, n.d., RSPG, A, 5, no. 133.

9. Frank J. Klingberg, "The Mystery of the Lost Yamassee [*sic*] Prince," *SCHM* 63 (1962): 18-32. On the Iroquois chiefs, see Richmond P. Bond, *Queen Anne's American Kings* (Oxford, 1952), chap. 1.

10. *CSC*, pp. 111-15; Nash, *Red, White, and Black*, pp. 145-55; Crane, *Southern Frontier*, chap. 7.

11. Le Jau to SPG, February 18, 1709, *Le Jau*, p. 50; Le Jau to SPG, February 18, 1709, *Le Jau*, p. 52; Le Jau to SPG, March 22, 1709, *Le Jau*, p. 55; Le Jau to SPG, June 13, 1710, *Le Jau*, p. 78.

12. Le Jau to SPG, August 10, 1713, *Le Jau*, p. 134; Bull to SPG, August 10, 1715, in Klingberg, "Yamassee Prince," p. 25; Clergy of South Carolina to Bishop Robinson, October 13, 1715, *Johnston*, p. 147.

13. Hasel to SPG, October 20, 1722, RSPG, A, 16: 80-82; Orr to SPG, March 30, 1743, RSPG, B, 11: 219-20; Fordyce to SPG, October 6, 1746, RSPG, B, 14: 239-40.

14. Under Nairne's plan, the Queen and the proprietors would have contributed substantial sums for the missionaries. He hoped that the SPG would use its influence in England to see that political pressure would be brought to bear on the government of South Carolina. Nairne to Dr. Marston, August 20, 1705, RSPG, A, 2: 156.

15. Bishop of London to SPG, January 18, 1713, RSPG, A, 7, no. 49. Consideration was postponed until a financial report was received. RSPG, Journal, February 6, 1713. Varnod to SPG, July 21, 1724, RSPG, A, 18: 85-87; Varnod to SPG, April 1, 1724, RSPG, A, 18: 72-74; see also a description of the Creeks obtained by Varnod, RSPG, A, 19: 92-94; Ludlam to SPG, March 22, 1725, RSPG, A, 19: 62-63.

16. Le Jau to SPG, February 18, 1709, *Le Jau*, p. 50; Le Jau to SPG, February 18, 1709, *Le Jau*, p. 54; Le Jau to SPG, August 5, 1709, *Le Jau*, p. 57; Le Jau to SPG, March 22, 1709, *Le Jau*, p. 55; Le Jau to SPG, October 20, 1709, *Le Jau*, pp. 60-61; Le Jau to SPG, September 15, 1708, *Le Jau*, pp. 41-42.

17. Le Jau to SPG, April 15, 1707, *Le Jau*, p. 24; Le Jau to SPG, February 1, 1710, *Le Jau*, p. 70; Le Jau to SPG, June 13, 1710, *Le Jau*, p. 77.

18. Le Jau to SPG, June 13, 1710, *Le Jau*, pp. 76-77; *Le Jau* to SPG, July 14, 1710, *Le Jau*, p. 81; Le Jau to SPG, August 30, 1712, *Le Jau*, pp. 120-21; Le Jau to SPG, January 22, 1714, *Le Jau*, pp. 136-37.

19. Le Jau to SPG, June 13, 1710, *Le Jau*, p. 76; Le Jau to SPG, February 9, 1711, *Le Jau*, p. 86; Le Jau to SPG, January 4, 1712, *Le Jau*, p. 105; Le Jau to SPG, August 30, 1712, *Le Jau*, p. 120; Le Jau to SPG, February 23, 1713, *Le Jau*, p. 129; Le Jau to SPG, August 10, 1713, *Le Jau*, p. 133; Le Jau to SPG, January 22, 1714, *Le Jau*, p. 136; Le Jau to SPG, July 4, 1714, *Le Jau*, p. 141; Le Jau to SPG, July 4, 1714, *Le Jau*, p. 140; Le Jau to SPG, January 26, 1715, *Le Jau*, p. 145. On the number of slaves in Goose Creek, see Wood, *Black Majority*, p. 146.

20. Taylor to SPG, July 28, 1713, RSPG, B, 8: 354-58; Taylor to SPG,

[1714], RSPG, A, 10: 85-87; Taylor to SPG, April 18, 1716, RSPG, A, 11: 171; Varnod to SPG, August 26, 1728, RSPG, A, 21: 123-24.

21. Hasel to SPG, September 4, 1711, RSPG, A, 6, no. 148; Hasel to SPG, March 12, 1712, RSPG, A, 7: 400-402; Hasel to SPG, August 18, 1712, RSPG, A, 7: 435; Hasel to SPG, July 12, 1718, RSPG, A, 13: 180-82; Whitehead to SPG, September 26, 1715, RSPG, A, 11: 70-71; Bull to SPG, January 20, 1715, RSPG, A, 10: 90.

22. Johnston is quoted in Frank J. Klingberg, *An Appraisal of the Negro in Colonial South Carolina: A Study in Americanization* (Washington, D.C., 1941), p. 7; see also "Extract of a Letter from Mr. Haig," RSPG, A, 10: 81-83; and Le Jau to SPG, September 18, 1711, *Le Jau*, p. 102.

23. Dunn to SPG, April 21, 1707, RSPG, A, 3: 99; Maule to SPG, n.d., RSPG, A, 5, no. 133; Gignilliat to SPG, May 28, 1710, RSPG, A, 5, no. 119; Bull to SPG, January 20, 1715, RSPG, A, 10: 90; Jones to SPG, November 6, 1716, RSPG, B, 12: 143; La Pierre to SPG, April 5, 1719, RSPG, A, 13: 208-10. For a full account of the problem as perceived by Commissary Johnston in 1713, see Klingberg, *An Appraisal*, pp. 6-7.

24. On the growing tensions between whites and blacks in South Carolina, see Wood, *Black Majority*, part 3. On the fear of insurrection and its effect on missionary work, see Varnod to SPG, January 15, 1723, RSPG, A, 17: 121.

25. Maule to SPG, n.d., RSPG, A, 5, no. 133.

26. "A Sermon Preached before the...S.P.G....," in Frank J. Klingberg, *Anglican Humanitarianism in Colonial New York* (Philadelphia, 1940), p. 206.

27. "To the Masters and Mistresses of Families in the English Plantations abroad...," in *HAPEC*, pp. 104-12.

28. Ludlam to SPG, July 2, 1724, RSPG, A, 18: 83; *SCG*, April 23 and July 30, 1737.

29. *SCG*, April 12, 1739.

30. Dennis to SPG, July 3, 1711, RSPG, A, 6, no. 143; Le Jau to SPG, March 22, 1709, *Le Jau*, p. 55; Le Jau to SPG, June 13, 1710, *Le Jau*, p. 78; Le Jau to SPG, February 20, 1712, *Le Jau*, p. 109; Thompson to SPG, January 30, 1744, RSPG, B, 11: 215.

31. *Statutes*, 2: 239; Le Jau to SPG, April 12, 1711, *Le Jau*, p. 89; Vestry of St. John's, Berkeley, to General Nicholson, February 6, 1721, RSPG, A, 16: 55; Hunt to SPG, May 12, 1725, RSPG, A, 19: 73-74; Fulton to SPG, December 4, 1740, RSPG, A, 22: 221-22.

32. Winthrop D. Jordan, *White over Black: American Attitudes toward the Negro, 1550-1812* (Baltimore, Md., 1968), pp. 206-8.

33. Hasel to SPG, December 2, 1731, RSPG, A, 23: 308-9; Fulton to SPG, December 4, 1730, RSPG, A, 23: 221-22; SPG to All Missionaries, July 30,

1725, RSPG, A, 19: 113; Hasel to SPG, February 12, 1731, RSPG, A, 22: 229-30; Hunt to SPG, November 5, 1725, RSPG, A, 19: 80.

34. Roe to SPG, December 22, 1741, RSPG, B, 10, no. 171; Guy to SPG, January 10, 1739, RSPG, B, 7: 221-22; Guy to SPG, March 26, 1742, RSPG, B, 10, no. 163; for other examples, see Klingberg, *An Appraisal.*

35. *Three Letters from the Reverend Mr. G. Whitefield . . .* (Philadelphia, 1740), pp. 13-15.

36. *Six Letters from the Rev. Mr. Garden to the Rev. Mr. George Whitfield* [*sic*], 2d ed. (Boston, 1740), pp. 50-54.

37. Klingberg, *An Appraisal*, pp. 104-7; Stuart C. Henry, *George Whitefield: Wayfaring Witness* (Nashville, Tenn., 1957), pp. 147-48. *SCG* for February 2, 1740, refers to the letter. The exact date of its Philadelphia publication is unknown to this author.

38. Klingberg, *An Appraisal*, pp. 104-17. The advertisement for donations is in *SCG*, March 14, 1742.

39. J.H. Easterby and Ruth S. Green, eds., *The Colonial Records of South Carolina, Series I: The Journal of the Commons House of Assembly, 1736-1750*, 9 vols. (Columbia, S.C., 1951-62), 3: 380-82, 405-8, 461-62, and 4: 72; *The Letterbook of Eliza Lucas Pinckney, 1739-1762*, ed. Elise Pinckney (Chapel Hill, N.C., 1972), pp. 27-28, 30; Joseph Tracy, *The Great Awakening* (Boston, 1841), pp. 240-41 n.

40. *SCG*, April 17, 24, 1742.

41. The debate may be followed in *SCG*, July 4, 1743, and April 2, August 27, October 15, and November 19, 1744. The orphanage was a favorite target of Whitefield's opponents, see Henry, *Wayfaring Witness*, pp. 149-50.

42. Klingberg, *An Appraisal*, pp. 118-21. Klingberg follows *HAPEC* in asserting that the school closed in 1764, but according to the vestry minutes Harry stopped teaching in 1768; see "Minutes of the Vestry of St. Philip's Parish."

43. Klingberg, *An Appraisal*, pp. 93-98.

44. Martyn to SPG, June 25, 1753, RSPG, B, 20: 137. Armory's story is in *HAPEC*, pp. 361-62. Klingberg gives a rather cursory survey of parish activity in the period after the Great Awakening. He is optimistic about the work being done, but the evidence indicates that few blacks were baptized, *An Appraisal*, pp. 77-92.

CHAPTER 7

1. H. Roy Merrens, ed., "A View of Coastal South Carolina in 1778: The Journal of Ebenezer Hazard," *SCHM* 73 (1972): 193; Penuel Bowen to General Lincoln, July 9, 1786, Bowen-Cooke Papers, South Carolina Historical Society, Charleston; Boschi to SPG, April 7, 1746, RSPG, A, 12, no. 111.

2. "Broughton Letters," *SCHGM* 15 (1914): 175-76; Vestry of Saint Helena, to SPG, June 8, 1730, RSPG, A, 23: 212-14.

3. *The Letterbook of Eliza Lucas Pinckney, 1739-1762*, ed. Elise Pinckney (Chapel Hill, N.C., 1972), pp. 51-54, 71-72; Marvin R. Zahniser, *Charles Cotesworth Pinckney: Founding Father* (Chapel Hill, N.C., 1967), pp. 4-5, 8-9, 11, 271-75.

4. Robert Pringle is one example. See "Entries in the Old Bible of Robert Pringle," *SCHGM* 22 (1921): 30; and "Journal of Robert Pringle, 1746-1747," *SCHGM* 26 (1925): 22, 24, 26.

5. "Peter Manigault's Letters," *SCHGM* 31 (1930): 271-72; *HAPEC*, p. 383.

6. Maule to SPG, April 4, 1711, RSPG, A, 6, no. 127; Maule to SPG, August 2, 1712, RSPG, A, 7: 431-32.

7. Le Jau to SPG, September 5, 1722, *Le Jau*, p. 98; Maule to SPG, January 23, 1715, RSPG, A, 10: 77-79.

8. "Instructions of the Clergy of South Carolina. . .Enlarged and Explained," *Johnston*, pp. 130-31.

9. Peter Manigault to Mrs. Manigault, London, June 24, 1753, "Peter Manigault's Letters," *SCHGM* 32 (1931): 179.

10. Wilbur K. Jordan, *Philanthropy in England, 1480-1660: A Study of the Changing Pattern of English Social Aspirations* (London, 1959), chap. 7.

11. Hasel to SPG, September 6, 1707, RSPG, A, 3, no. 145; Johnston to SPG, July 5, 1710, *Johnston*, p. 39; Johnston to SPG, January 27, 1716, *Johnston*, p. 159; Le Jau to SPG, November 16, 1716, *Le Jau*, p. 182.

12. "Papers relating to Mr. Morritt & the School at Charles Town," RSPG, A, 17: 131-39; Morritt to SPG, June 27, 1723, RSPG, A, 17: 90-92; Morritt to SPG, December 11, 1723, RSPG, A, 17: 114-18; Morritt to SPG, October 22, 1724, RSPG, A, 18: 92-94; Morritt to SPG, March 22, 1725, RSPG, A, 19: 61-62; Morritt to SPG, October 27, 1725, RSPG, A, 19: 78-79.

13. Hasel to SPG, March 20, 1722, RSPG, A, 16: 60-62; Vestry of St. Thomas to SPG, n.d., RSPG, A, 16: 65-67; "Mr. Aylosses Opinion upon the Will of Rich Berresford," RSPG, A, 16: 119-21; Hasel to SPG, August 16, 1727, RSPG, A, 20: 96-97.

14. Hasel to SPG, August 16, 1727, RSPG, A, 20: 96-97; Hasel to SPG, February 16, 1730, RSPG, A, 22: 272-73; Hasel to SPG, January 15, 1736, RSPG, A, 26: 154; RSPG, Journal, January 21, 1727; Hasel to SPG, January 15, 1739, RSPG, B, 7: 219; Garden, Jr., to SPG, April 7, 1749, RSPG, B, 17: 176; Garden, Jr., to SPG, May 10, 1763, RSPG, B, 17, no. 217.

15. Stevens to SPG, May 7, 1718, RSPG, A, 13: 150-51; "A Copy of the Last Will of Mr. George Boyle," RSPG, A, 13: 199; SPG to Nicholson, March 2, 1724, RSPG, A, 17: 169-70; "Petition of ye vestry of St. Johns to Genl

Nicholson," n.d., RSPG, A, 17: 154-55; SPG to Saint John's vestry, March 23, 1724, RSPG, A, 17: 168-69; Nicholson to SPG, August 6, 1724, RSPG, A, 18: 88.

16. Bull to SPG, January 14, 1724, RSPG, A, 17: 17-18; Whitmarsh bequest, RSPG, A, 18: 116-17.

17. SPG to Guy, October 2, 1725, RSPG, A, 19: 114; Guy to SPG, November 7, 1726, RSPG, A, 19: 338-39; Guy to SPG, April 24, 1729, RSPG, A, 22; 235-37; Guy to SPG, November 16, 1731, RSPG, A, 23: 305-06; papers relating to the arbitration of the Boyle-Brassier dispute, RSPG, A, 19: 360-68.

18. Guy's correspondence with the vestry of Saint Paul's, RSPG, A, 19: 356-59; Guy to SPG, March 30, 1730, RSPG, A, 23: 199-201; Guy to SPG, January 5, 1732, RSPG, A, 24: 340.

19. Guy to SPG, October 16, 1728, RSPG, A, 21: 130-31; "A Journal of the Proceedings of Mr. Dry as Administrator of the Estate of the Revd. Mr. Ludlam," RSPG, A, 21: 161-209; Garden and Guy to SPG, April 16, 1735, RSPG, 26: 120-22; Millechamp to SPG, August 24, 1742, RSPG, B, 10, no. 168; Millechamp to SPG, November 15, 1744, RSPG, B, 4, no. 278; Bearcroft to Stone, July 21, 1750, RSPG, B, 18: 224; Garden to SPG, September 9, 1750, RSPG, B, 18: 182; Stone to SPG, March 22, 1751, RSPG, B, 18: 186.

20. Vestry of St. James, Goose Creek, to S.P.G., RSPG, A, 25: 97-98; *SCG*, August 26, 1732.

21. Penuel Bowen to General Lincoln, July 9, 1786, Bowen-Cooke Papers.

22. Le Jau to SPG, April 15, 1707, *Le Jau*, p. 22; Maule to SPG, n.d. [1710], RSPG, A, 5, no. 133; Le Jau to SPG, March 12, 1715, *Le Jau*, p. 149.

23. Le Jau to SPG, August 10, 1713, *Le Jau*, pp. 133-34; Le Jau to SPG, August 30, 1712, *Le Jau*, pp. 121-22.

24. Nicholson to the bishop of London, October 31, 1724, FP, 9: 156-57; Clergy to SPG, October 1, 1724, RSPG, A, 18: 90-92; Edward McCrady, *The History of South Carolina under the Royal Government*, 1719-1776 (New York, 1901), pp. 57-60.

25. Eliza Lucas to George Lucas, *The Letterbook of Eliza Lucas Pinckney*, pp. 51-52.

26. Ibid., p. 53.

27. *SCG*, May 20, 1732.

28. Ibid., August 12, 1732.

29. Ibid., May 27, October 14, and November 23, 1732.

30. Ibid., September 23, 1732.

31. Ibid., September 30, 1732.

32. Ibid., October 28, November 4, and November 11, 1732.

33. Garden to Gibson, April 20, 1731, FP, 9: 254-55.

34. *SCG*, November 18, 1732.

35. Durand to SPG, December 10, 1751, RSPG, B, 19: 142-43.
36. Durand to SPG, April 23, 1747, RSPG, B, 15: 171-72.
37. "Minutes of the Vestry of St. John's Parish, Berkeley County, March 22, 1731-April 14, 1813," microfilm (Columbia, S.C.: Department of Archives and History), September 25, 1754.
38. Clergy to SPG, May 9, 1727, RSPG, A, 20: 79-80; Allen and Hill to SPG, June 24, 1727, RSPG, A, 20: 87-90; Garden to the bishop of London, May 26, 1727, FP, 9: 198-99.
39. Hunt to SPG, November 5, 1725, RSPG, A, 19: 80-82; Hunt to SPG, November 24, 1726, RSPG, A, 19: 339-41; Hunt to SPG, February 9, 1727, RSPG, A, 19: 348-57.
40. Garden to Bishop Gibson, May 26, 1727, FP, 9: 198-99.
41. Allen and Hill to SPG, June 24, 1727, RSPG, A, 20: 87-90; Clergy to SPG, May 9, 1727, RSPG, A, 20: 79-80; Guy to SPG, June 19, 1727, RSPG, A, 20: 84-85; Varnod to SPG, May 4, 1727, RSPG, A, 20: 81.
42. RSPG, Journal, September 15, 1727; Vestry of Saint John's to SPG, July 3, 1727, RSPG, A, 20: 90-93; Clergy to SPG, January 2, 1728, RSPG, A, 20: 104-6.
43. Brian Hunt's Defense, February 1728, RSPG, A, 20: 119-36; Hunt to SPG, May 6, 1728, RSPG, A, 21: 102-3.
44. RSPG, Journal, August 20, 1725; RSPG, Journal, October 15, 1725; Allen and Hill to SPG, June 24, 1727, RSPG, A, 20: 87-90.

CHAPTER 8

1. Borden W. Painter, Jr., "The Anglican Vestry in Colonial America" (Ph.D. diss., Yale University, 1965), pp. 7-18.
2. Ibid., pp. 155-56, 177.
3. Ibid., pp. 86, 185, 189.
4. William H. Seiler, "The Anglican Parish Vestry in Colonial Virginia," *Journal of Southern History* 22 (1956): 320-25; Joan Rezner Gundersen, "The Myth of the Independent Virginia Vestry," *HMPEC* 44 (1975): 133-41; Paul Conkin, "The Church Establishment in North Carolina 1765-1776," *North Carolina Historical Review* 32 (1955): 2-5.
5. Seiler, "Anglican Parish Vestry in Virginia," pp. 325-26; Alan D. Watson, "The Anglican Parish in Royal North Carolina 1729-1755," *HMPEC* 48 (1979): 312-19; Gerald E. Hartdagen, "The Anglican Vestry in Colonial Maryland: A Study in Corporate Responsibility," *HMPEC* 40 (1979).
6. James Kimbrough Owen, "The Virginia Vestry, A Study in the Decline of a Ruling Class" (Ph.D. diss., Princeton University, 1947), pp. 144-207; Watson, "Anglican Parish in North Carolina," pp. 312-19.

7. Here and below, material on Saint Philip's vestry is from "Minutes of the Vestry of St. Philip's Parish, 1732-1755" and "Minutes of the Vestry of St. Philips Parish, 1761-1795," typescript copies at the South Caroliniana Library, Columbia, S.C. Biographical data is from Walter B. Edgar, ed., *Biographical Directory of the South Carolina House of Representatives*, vol. 2, *The Commons House of Assembly, 1692-1775* (Columbia, S.C., 1977).

8. *Statutes*, 3: 175.

9. *Minutes of St. Michael's Church Charleston, S.C., 1758-1812* (S.C. Colonial Dames, n.d., n.p.), pp. 13-14.

10. In addition to those of Saint Philip's and Saint Michael's, the following vestry records are extant and have been consulted: "Minutes of the Vestry of Christ Church, 1708-1759," "Minutes of the Vestry of St. David's, 1768-1832," "Minutes of the Vestry of Prince Frederick's, 1729-1763," "Minutes of the Vestry of St. John's Parish, Berkeley County, 1731-1783," and "Minutes of the Vestry of St. John's, Colleton, 1738-1817," all of which are on microfilm at the South Caroliniana Library; "Minutes of the Vestry of St. Stephen's Parish, 1754-1873," ed. Anne Alston Porcher, *SCHGM* 45 (1944): 65-70, 157-71, 217-21; *SCHGM* 46 (1945): 40-48; and *Minutes of the Vestry of St. Helena's Parish, South Carolina, 1726-1812*, ed. A. S. Salley (Columbia, S.C. 1919).

11. Painter, "Anglican Vestry," pp. 21-22, 78-80, 111, 178-79.

12. If duties and clerical salaries for 1765 are doubled and added to average figures for general expenses and parochial expenses, the total of religious expenses is 2.8 percent of total estimated revenues. "Accounts of Receipts and Payments of the General Tax, 1761-1769," Journal C. -1765, Records of the Public Treasurer of South Carolina, 1725-1776, South Carolina Department of Archives and History, Columbia, S.C.

13. Edgar, *Biographical Directory*, 2: 3; *Statutes*, 3: 135-36.

14. Owen, "The Virginia Vestry," p. 2; Painter, "Anglican Vestry," p. 45; Seiler, "Anglican Parish Vestry in Virginia," pp. 313-15; Gundersen, "Myth of the Independent Virginia Vestry."

15. Gerald E. Hartdagen, "The Anglican Vestry in Colonial Maryland: Organizational Structure and Problems," *HMPEC* 38 (1969): 349-60; Watson, "Anglican Parish in North Carolina," pp. 304-5.

16. Data on length of service has been compiled from parish records. Biographical material is from Edgar, *Biographical Directory*, 2, which omits the vestry service of Nathaniel Barnwell, who appears to have been the Colonel Nathaniel Barnwell who served for many years.

17. The five rural parishes are Saint David's, Prince Frederick's, Saint Stephen's, Saint John's, Colleton, and Saint Helena's. Election to the assembly was derived from Edgar, *Biographical Directory*, 2.

18. Election records from 1772 are in Edgar, *Biographical Directory*, 1, *Session Lists 1692-1973*.

19. George Maclaren Brydon, *Virginia's Mother Church and the Political Conditions under Which It Grew*. 2 vols. (Philadelphia, 1952), 2: 127-28.

CONCLUSION

1. Avery Craven, *The Coming of the Civil War* (Chicago, 1966), p. 33.

BIBLIOGRAPHICAL NOTE

There is a fairly extensive literature dealing with the Church of England in the southern colonies, but very little has been done to understand Anglicanism as a regional institution. H. Richard Niebuhr, *The Social Sources of Denomination- alism* (Cleveland, Ohio, 1964), has been helpful in formulating the concept of Southern Anglicanism. Richard Beale Davis, *Intellectual Life in the Colonial South*, 2 vols. (Knoxville, Tenn., 1978), and Henry F. May, *The Enlightenment in America* (New York, 1976), have sympathetic accounts of Southern Angli- cans and Anglicanism. Frederick V. Mills, *Bishops by Ballot, An Eighteenth Century Ecclesiastical Revolution* (New York, 1978), provides a good review of colonial Anglicanism as well as an account of its particular subject.

Among the studies of Anglicanism in particular colonies, none are more stimulating than three articles by Rhys Isaac, which have helped historians to understand the social importance of the Church of England and the nature of the threat posed to it and the Anglican gentry by the Great Awakening: "Religion and Authority: Problems of the Anglican Establishment in Virginia in the Era of the Great Awakening and the Parsons' Cause," *William and Mary Quarterly*, 3d ser., 30 (1973): 3-36; "Evangelical Revolt: The Nature of the Baptists' Chal- lenge to the Traditional Order in Virginia, 1765-1775," *WMQ*, 3d ser., 31 (1974): 345-68; and "Preachers and Patriots: Popular Culture and the Revolu- tion in Virginia," in *The American Revolution: Explorations in the History of American Radicalism*, ed. Alfred Young (De Kalb, Ill., 1976), pp. 127-56.

Among other studies of the colonial establishments, George Maclaren Brydon, *Virginia's Mother Church and the Political Conditions under Which It Grew*, 2 vols. (Philadelphia, 1952), is a basic work. Nelson W. Rightmyer, *Maryland's Established Church* (Baltimore, 1956), is less comprehensive and less reliable. On the church in North Carolina, I have used Paul Conkin, "The Church Establishment in North Carolina," *North Carolina Historical Review* 42 (1955):

11-30; on the church in Georgia, I have used Harold E. Davis, *The Fledgling Province: Social and Cultural Life in Colonial Georgia, 1733-1766.* Three articles are particularly helpful on the vestry system in the southern colonies: William H. Seiler, "The Anglican Parish Vestry in Colonial Virginia," *Journal of Southern History* 22 (1956); 310-37; Gerald E. Hartdagen, "The Anglican Vestry in Colonial Maryland: A Study in Corporate Responsibility," *Historical Magazine of the Protestant Episcopal Church* 40 (1971); 315-35; and Alan D. Watson, "The Anglican Parish in Royal North Carolina, 1729-1775," *HMPEC* 48: (1979), 303-19.

The serious scholar of Southern Anglicanism will want to consult unpublished dissertations as well as material in print. My analysis of the vestry system outside the South rests heavily on Borden W. Painter, Jr., "The Anglican Vestry in Colonial America" (Ph.D. diss., Yale University, 1965). I have also benefited greatly from Mary Elizabeth Quinlivan, "Ideological Controversy Over Religious Establishment in Revolutionary Virginia" (Ph.D. diss., University of Wisconsin, 1971); Joan Rezner Gundersen, "The Anglican Ministry in Virginia, 1725-1776: A Study in Social Class" (Ph.D. diss., University of Notre Dame, 1972); and James Kimbrough Owen, "The Virginia Vestry, A Study in the Decline of a Ruling Class," (Ph.D. diss., Princeton University, 1947).

The Society for the Propagation of the Gospel in Foreign Parts did a great deal for the established church of South Carolina and even more for its historians. Because the SPG required its missionaries to send periodic reports of their activities, we have a full account of the Church of England until about 1750 and a great amount of information about the environment in which it functioned. The records of the SPG are available on microfilm and they include a useful introduction by Belle Pridemore. Series A consists of contemporary copies of letters received between 1702 and 1737. Series B includes the originals of some of the copied letters and also copies and original letters received after 1737. I cited the copies where possible since they are much more legible than the originals. There are also letters from the SPG, but the selection is much less complete. In the same collection is the SPG Journal, which includes records of SPG meetings and also some abstracts of incoming letters. There are indexes for both the letter volumes and the SPG Journals.

A second major source is the Fulham Papers, which contain the correspondence of the bishop of London. There are a good number of letters from South Carolina, particularly from the commissaries. For the most part, I used the transcripts made for the Library of Congress and available there, but I have cited the letters as they appear in the original collection as described by William W. Manross, *The Fulham Papers in the Lambeth Palace Library; American Colonial Section Calendar and Indexes* (Oxford, Eng. 1964). Only a sample of vestry records are available. Particularly important are those for Saint Philip's, which may be used in typescript copies, "Minutes of the Vestry of St. Philip's Parish, 1732-1755" and "Minutes of the Vestry of St. Philip's Parish, 1761-1795," at the South Caroliniana Library in Columbia. At the same place are typescripts of "Minutes of the Vestry of St. John's Colleton, 1738-1817" and "Minutes of the Vestry of St. Matthew's Parish, 1767-1838." Microfilm copies of the "Minutes of the Vestry of St. John's Parish, Berkeley County, March 22, 1731-April 14, 1813," and "Minutes of the Vestry of Christ Church, 1708-1759" are available at the South Carolina Department of Archives and History in Columbia. *The Minutes of the Vestry of St. Helena's Parish, South Carolina, 1726-1812*, ed. A. S. Salley (Columbia, S.C., 1919) have been published. Also available are the *Minutes of St. Michael's Church Charleston, S.C., 1758-1812* (S.C. Colonial Dames, n.d. n.p.), and "Minutes of the Vestry of St. Stephen's Parish, 1754-1783," ed. Anne Alston Porcher, *South Carolina Historical and Genealogical Magazine* 45 (1944); 56-70, 157-71, 217-21; and 46 (1945); 40-48.

A number of small manuscript collections are also important to the history of the established church. The "Church Commissioners Book, 1717-42" is located at the South Carolina Department of Archives and History and so also is "Green Transcripts, 1702-1706," the only extant version of he fall assembly of 1704. Alexander Keith's "Commonplace Book," which gives an insight into the mind of that clergyman, is located at the South Caroliniana Library. The Bowen-Cooke Papers, containing the letters of the Reverend Penuel Bowen, a former Congregationalist clergyman from Massachusetts who came to South Carolina after the revolutionary war looking for a position in the disestablished church, are at the South Carolina Historical Society in Charleston. Also at the Historical Society are the two-volume records of the Society for the Relief of the Widows and Orphans of the Clergy of the Protestant Episcopal Church in South Carolina, which give the proceedings of that organization and also list the members.

A large amount of primary materials related to church history has been printed. Of particular importance are the two volumes edited by Frank J. Klingberg, *Carolina Chronicle: The Papers of Commissary Gideon Johnston, 1707-1716* (Berkeley, 1946), and *The Carolina Chronicle of Dr. Francis Le Jau, 1706-1717* (Berkeley, 1956), which make readily available the letters of two of the most important and prolific of the missionaries. Klingberg's *An Appraisal of the Negro in Colonial South Carolina: A Study in Americanization* (Washington, 1941) contains an overly optimistic view of race relations, but also prints many valuable letters. SPG records concerning the SPG's first missionary in South Carolina are available as "Letters of the Rev. Samuel Thomas. . ." *South Carolina Historical and Genealogical Magazine* 4 (1903): 221-30, 278-85, and "Documents Concerning Rev. Samuel Thomas, 1702-1707," *SCHGM* 5 (1904): 21-55. Richard J. Hooker, ed., *The Carolina Backcountry on the Eve of the Revolution: The Journal and Other Writings of Charles Woodmason, Anglican Itiner-*

ant (Chapel Hill, N.C. 1953), is an excellent edition of writings of an important clergyman who is less idiosyncratic than he often seems. *The Letterbook of Eliza Lucas Pinckney, 1739-1762*, ed. by Elise Pinckney (Chapel Hill, N.C., 1972), provides some insight into the thought of the Anglican gentry. *George Whitefield's Journals (1737-1741) To Which Is Prefixed His "Short Account" (1746) and "Further Account" (1747)* (Gainesville, Fla., 1969), is an excellent vehicle for understanding the author and the phenomenon he helped to create.

Alexander S. Salley, *Narratives of Early Carolina, 1650-1708* (New York, 1911), and Bartholomew Rivers Carroll, ed., *Historical Collections of South Carolina* 2 vols., (New York, 1836), reprint contemporary published material relating to the establishment of the Church of England and the general history of South Carolina. Daniel Defoe, *The Case of the Protestant Dissenters in Carolina* (London, 1706) and *An Account of the Fair and Impartial Proceedings of the Lords Proprietors, Governor and Council of South Carolina*, along with other materials, are available in William Sumner Jenkins, comp., Records of the States of the United States, (Library of Congress in association with the University of North Carolina, 1949). The pamphlet warfare associated with the Great Awakening may be read in Clifford K. Shipton, ed., *Early American Imprints, 1639-1800* (Worcester, Mass., 1956-64). SPG anniversary sermons in their original state are now rare; I used the collection at the Wisconsin State Historican Society in Madison. Finally the *South Carolina Gazette* (1732-1776) is an indispensable source for historians of colonial South Carolina.

Among secondary accounts none has been more useful for this study than Frederick Dalcho's *An Historical Account of the Protestant Episcopal Church in South Carolina from the First Settlement of the Province to the War of the Revolution* (Charleston, 1820), which was reprinted in Charleston in 1970. Dalcho provides little overview or analysis, but he gives a wealth of information about a church he knew almost at first hand. Equally important is Frederick Lewis Weis, *The Colonial Clergy of Virginia, North Carolina, and South Carolina* (Boston, 1955). There are some errors in Weis's data and a few omissions, but his volume remains an extremely valuable tool. With respect to other denominations, both George Howe, *History of the Presbyterian Church in South Carolina* 2 vols. (Columbia, S.C., 1870), and Arthur Henry Hirsch, *The Huguenots of Colonial South Carolina* (Durham, N.C. 1928), are very useful. Robert D. Mitchell, "The Presbyterian Church as an Indicator of Westward Expansion in 18th Century America," *The Professional Geographer* 18 (1966): 293-99, shows in a clear manner the rapid growth of that church in South Carolina.

My views on the Great Awakening have been much influenced by the perspective of Alan Heimert, *Religion and the American Mind: From the Great Awakening to the Revolution* (Cambridge, Mass., 1966). Two other important volumes are Joseph Tracy, *The Great Awakening: A History of the Revival of Religion in the Time of Edwards and Whitefield* (Boston, 1941), which contains documents and details available nowhere else, and Stuart C. Henry, *George Whitefield: Wayfaring Witness* (Nashville, Tenn., 1957), which gives a convincing portrait of its subject. I believe that William Howland Kenny, III, "Alexander Garden and George Whitefield: The Significance of Revivalism in South Carolina, 1738-1741," *South Carolina Historical Magazine* 71 (1970): 1-16, overplays Whitefield's success and discounts the response of the establishment, and the same is true of David T. Morgan, "The Great Awakening in South Carolina, 1740-1755," *South Atlantic Quarterly* 70 (1971): 595-606, but each of these articles gives an important interpretation.

The secular history of South Carolina has benefited in recent years from the efforts of several gifted historians. Eugene Sirmans, *Colonial South Carolina: A Political History, 1663-1763* (Chapel Hill, N.C., 1966), functioned almost as a handbook for me, both for its masterful account of political development and its rich, annotated bibliography. Among the books discussed in Sirmans, I found Edward McCrady, *The History of South Carolina under the Proprietary Government, 1670-1719* (New York, 1897), and *The History of South Carolina under the Royal Government, 1719-1776* (New York, 1901), to be most helpful for background material. Verner W. Crane, *The Southern Frontier, 1670-1732* (Philadelphia, 1929), describes the interaction of the colonists with the Indians and with European imperial rivals; while Robert L. Meriwether, *The Expansion of South Carolina, 1729-1765* (Kingsport, Tenn., 1940), traces the settlement of western areas and shows the changes it brought. George C. Rogers, Jr., *Charleston in the Age of the Pinckneys* (Norman, Okla., 1969), makes a convincing case for the significance of the city and its lively nature. Last here, but hardly least, is the superb study by Peter H. Wood, *Black Majority: Negroes in Colonial South Carolina from 1670 through the Stono Rebellion* (New York, 1975).

There is no full-scale, modern narrative of the American Revolution in South Carolina. I found the relevant passages in Merrill Jensen, *The Founding of a Nation: A History of the American Revolution, 1763-1776* (New York, 1968) to be very helpful. Also important is the material in David Ramsay, *The History of South Carolina from Its First Settlement in 1670 to the Year 1808*, 2 vols. (Charleston, S.C., 1809). Among more specialized studies Richard Maxwell Brown, *The South Carolina Regulators* (Cambridge, Mass., 1963), is excellent, and I benefited as well from George C. Rogers, Jr., *Evolution of a Federalist: William Loughton Smith of Charleston (1758-1812)*, (Columbia, S.C., 1962), and Marvin R. Zahniser, *Charles Cotesworth Pinckney: Founding Father* (Chapel Hill, N.C., 1967). Two articles that were influential well beyond their length are Robert M. Weir, " 'The Harmony We Were Famous For': An interpretation

of Pre-Revolutionary South Carolina Politics," *WMQ*, 3d ser., 26 (1969): 474-501,
and Gary D. Olson, "Loyalists and the American Revolution: Thomas Brown
and the South Carolina Backcountry, 1775-1776," *South Carolina Historial
Magazine* 68 (1967): 201-19 and *SCHM* 69 (1968): 45-56. Two unpublished
studies were also very useful: Gordon DenBoer, "The Early Revolutionary
Movement in South Carolina, 1773-1776" (master's thesis, University of Wisconsin, 1968), and Jerome Joshua Nadelhoft, "The Revolutionary Era in South
Carolina, 1775-1788" (Ph.D. diss., University of Wisconsin, 1965).

To understand the English side of Anglo-American ecclesiastical develop-
ment in the early eighteenth century, I found George N. Clark, *The Later
Stuarts, 1660-1714* (Oxford, Eng., 1955), particularly helpful. On the relation
between religion and government in England, Norman Sykes, *Church and State
in England in the Eighteenth Century* (Cambridge, Eng., 1934), is standard.
Also indispensable is Edward F. Carpenter, *The Protestant Bishop, Being the
Life of Henry Compton, 1632-1713, Bishop of London* (London, 1956), and
Arthur Lyon Cross, *The Anglican Episcopate and the American Colonies* (New
York, 1902). Useful too, are George Every, *The High Church Party, 1688-1718*
(London, 1956), and Norman Sykes, *Edmund Gibson, Bishop of London,
1669-1748: A Study in Politics and Religion in the Eighteenth Century* (London,
1926). Gerald R. Cragg, *From Puritanism to the Age of Reason: A Study of
Changes in Religious Thought within the Church of England,1600-1700* (Cam-
bridge, Eng., 1950), is an excellent study, which I supplemented with Norman
Sykes, "The Theology of Divine Benevolence," *Historical Magazine of the
Protestant Episcopal Church*, (1947): 278-91. Wilbur Kitchener Jordan, *Philanthropy in England, 1480-1660: A Study of the Changing Pattern of English
Social Aspirations* (London, 1959), helped me to understand the nature of
benevolence in South Carolina. Also useful in that respect is Mary G. Jones,
*The Charity School Movement: A Study of Eighteenth Century Puritanism in
Action* (London, 1964). William Addison, *The English Country Parson* (London, 1947), provides a nice account of the life that a South Carolina clergyman
might have expected if he had found a living at home.

The Society for the Propagation of the Gospel in Foreign Parts is the subject
of a recent study by John Calam, *Parsons and Pedagogues: The S.P.G. Adventure in American Education* (New York, 1971), which contains an excellent
bibliography. On the SPG itself, see C. F. Pascoe, *Classified Digest of the
Records of the Society for the Propagation of the Gospel in Foreign Parts,
1701-1892* (London, 1895); H. P. Thompson, *Into All Lands: The History of the
Society for the Propagation of the Gospel in Foreign Parts* (London, 1950); and
John Kendall Nelson, "Anglican Missions in America, 1701-1725: A Study of
the Society for the Propagation of the Gospel in Foreign Parts" (Ph.D. diss.,
Northwestern University, 1962). Samuel Clyde McCullogh, "The Foundation

and Early Work of the S.P.G.," *Huntington Library Quarterly* 8 (1945): 242-58 provides insight into the beginning of the SPG. The founder of the SPG is described in H. P. Thompson, *Thomas Bray* (London, 1954), and his memorial on religion in North America is reprinted in Bernard C. Steiner, *The Reverend Thomas Bray: His Life and Selected Works Relating to Maryland* (Baltimore, 1901).

As a postscript, I wish to add that I have read and cited many more articles from the *Historical Magazine of the Protestant Episcopal Church* and the *South Carolina Historical Magazine* than can be conveniently mentioned in an abbreviated bibliography such as this. Each journal is a treasure chest of information on the topics with which it deals.

INDEX

About the Author

S. Charles Bolton is an Associate Professor of History at the University of Arkansas at Little Rock. He is currently at work on a social history of the Arkansas Territory.